JEAN GERSON:
PRINCIPLES OF CHURCH
REFORM

STUDIES
IN MEDIEVAL AND
REFORMATION THOUGHT

EDITED BY

HEIKO A. OBERMAN, Tübingen

IN COOPERATION WITH

E. JANE DEMPSEY DOUGLASS, Claremont, California
LEIF GRANE, Copenhagen
GUILLAUME H. M. POSTHUMUS MEY JES, Leiden
ANTON G. WEILER, Nijmegen

VOLUME VII

LOUIS B. PASCOE, S.J.

JEAN GERSON:
PRINCIPLES OF CHURCH
REFORM

LEIDEN
E. J. BRILL
1973

JEAN GERSON: PRINCIPLES OF CHURCH REFORM

BY

LOUIS B. PASCOE, S.J.

LEIDEN
E. J. BRILL
1973

ISBN   90 04 03645 8

TO MY MOTHER
AND
IN MEMORY OF MY FATHER

TABLE OF CONTENTS

PREFACE

My interest in the history of medieval church reform owes much to the influence and work of Gerhart B. Ladner. His scholarship and personal interest inspired and guided me during my doctoral studies at the University of California at Los Angeles. That inspiration and guidance continued in the subsequent years which witnessed the maturation of my thought and culminated in the production of the present work. To him, therefore, I extend my sincerest gratitude. I am also most grateful to my Jesuit colleagues who over the past few years have read the manuscript and offered their criticisms and suggestions, especially, Robert E. McNally, Fordham University, and Walter J. Burghardt and Avery R. Dulles, Woodstock College. To Robert S. Curry I express my sincerest thanks for his invaluable aid in preparing the complete manuscript for publication. A debt of gratitude is also owed to Gerald J. Fitzpatrick, George F. Mahoney, and Harry R. Untereiner, students at Woodstock College, who assisted me in the preparation of individual chapters, and to Robin Ann Colquhoun, Columbia University, who compiled the indices.

Gratitude must also be expressed to my Jesuit superiors who not only provided me with the time necessary to bring the manuscript to completion but also with the subvention which aided in its publication. For these reasons, I am especially grateful to James L. Connor, Francis M. O'Connor, and Joseph P. Whelan. Among the many libraries and librarians to whom I am indebted, personal mention must be made of John J. Alhadef, librarian at the Jesuit School of Theology at Berkeley, who so graciously provided me with prolonged use of the early editions of Gerson's works. Sincere thanks, finally, are due to Heiko A. Oberman of the University of Tübingen who showed considerable interest in my research from its earliest stages. That interest continued over the years and was again shown in his acceptance of my book in the present series.

Louis B. Pascoe, S. J.

New York City
May 2, 1972

ABBREVIATIONS

AHDL	Archives d'Histoire Doctrinale et Littéraire du Moyen Âge.
AHP	Archivum Historiae Pontificiae
AHR	American Historical Review.
AKG	Archiv für Kulturgeschichte.
AKK	Archiv für katholische Kirchenrecht.
BEC	Bibliothèque de l'École des Chartes.
BLE	Bulletin de Littérature Ecclésiastique.
CBQ	Catholic Biblical Quarterly.
CCSL	Corpus Christianorum. Series Latina.
CHR	The Catholic Historical Review.
CSEL	Corpus Scriptorum Ecclesiasticorum Latinorum.
DA	Deutsches Archiv für Erforschung des Mittelalters.
DB	Dictionnaire de la Bible.
DDC	Dictionnaire de Droit Canonique.
DSAM	Dictionnaire de Spiritualité Ascetique et Mystique.
DTC	Dictionnaire de Théologie Catholique.
DVLG	Deutsche Vierteljahrsschrift für Literaturwissenschaft und Geistesgeschichte.
EJ	Eranos Jahrbuch.
EL	Ephemerides Liturgicae.
ETL	Ephemerides Theologicae Lovanienses.
FS	Franciscan Studies.
HJ	Historisches Jahrbuch.
JHI	Journal of the History of Ideas.
JTS	Journal of Theological Studies.
LTK	Lexikon für Theologie und Kirche.
MGH	Monumenta Germaniae Historica.
MH	Medievalia et Humanistica.
MHE	Miscellanea Historiae Ecclesiasticae.
MIÖG	Mitteilungen des Instituts für österreichische Geschichtsforschung.
MPG	Migne, Patrologia Graeca.
MPL	Migne, Patrologia Latina.
MS	Medieval Studies.
MSR	Mélanges de Science Religieuse.
NCE	The New Catholic Encyclopedia.
RAC	Reallexikon für Antike und Christentum.
RBS	Rerum Britannicarum Medii Aevi Scriptores.
RHDFE	Revue Historique de Droit Français et Étranger.
RHE	Revue d'Histoire Ecclésiastique.
RMAL	Revue du Moyen Âge Latin.
RSPT	Revue des Sciences Philosophiques et Théologiques.
RSR	Revue des Sciences Religieuses.
RTAM	Recherches de Théologie Ancienne et Médiévale.

TS   Theological Studies.
TTQ   Tübinger Theologische Quartalschrift.
TWNT   Theologisches Wörterbuch zum Neuen Testament.
TZ   Theologische Zeitschrift.
ZKT   Zeitschrift für katholische Theologie.
ZSSRk   Zeitschrift der Savigny-Stiftung für Rechtsgeschichte, Kanonistische
                Abteilung.
ZTK   Zeitschrift für Theologie und Kirche.

INTRODUCTION

1. METHODOLOGY AND RESEARCH

This study of reform in Jean Gerson follows in the tradition of recent works which are concerned more with the idea of reform than with its concrete and practical manifestations. Emphasis, therefore, is placed not so much on detailed programs of reform as on the ideological presuppositions upon which such programs are constructed. Concrete programs of reform are studied primarily in order to understand the manner in which they embody and express those presuppositions. This approach to the study of reform has been characteristic of the writings of Gerhart B. Ladner.[1] Our study, moreover, will be restricted to the domain of church reform both in its institutional and personal aspects and will attempt to ascertain the principles which guided and inspired Gerson's thinking. The major areas of ecclesiastical reform that attracted his attention will be analyzed in an effort to determine the ideological principles operative in those areas. Through such a study we hope to demonstrate the ideological pattern of reform at work in his writings.

Gerson's writings have never been extensively studied according to this methodology. The only major study of Gerson as a reformer is that of J. L. Connolly.[2] While broadly investigating the various areas

---

[1] Gerhart B. Ladner, *The Idea of Reform: Its Impact on Christian Thought and Action in the Age of the Fathers* (Cambridge, Mass., 1959), pp. 9-35; "Erneuerung," *RAC*, 6, 240-275; "Die mittelalterliche Reform-Idee und ihr Verhältnis zur Idee der Renaissance," *MIÖG*, 60 (1952), 31-59; "Two Gregorian Letters: On the Sources and Nature of Gregory VII's Reform Ideology," *Studi Gregoriani*, 5 (1956), 221-242; "Vegetation Symbolism and the Concept of Renaissance," *De artibus opuscula XL: Essays in Honor of Erwin Panofsky*, ed. Millard Meiss, 1 (New York, 1961), 303-322; "Reformatio," *Ecumenical Dialogue at Harvard*, ed. S. Miller and G. E. Wright (Cambridge, Mass., 1964), pp. 172-190; "Religious Renewal and Ethnic-Social Pressures as Forms of Life in Christian History," *Theology of Renewal*, ed. L.K. Shook, 2 (New York, 1968), 328-357. The most recent works on reform following Ladner's methodology have been those of John W. O'Malley, "Historical Thought and the Reform Crisis of the Early Sixteenth Century," *TS*, 28 (1967), 531-548, and *Giles of Viterbo on Church and Reform*, Studies in Medieval and Reformation Thought, 5 (Leiden, 1968); Nelson H. Minnich, "Concepts of Reform Proposed at the Fifth Lateran Council," *AHP*, 7 (1969), 163-251, and Robert E. McNally, "Pope Adrian VI (1522-23) and Church Reform," *AHP*, 7 (1969), 253-285. See also Y. M.-J. Congar, *Vraie et fausse réforme dans l'Église* (2nd ed.; Paris, 1968).

[2] J. L. Connolly, *John Gerson, Reformer and Mystic* (Louvain, 1928).

of church reform treated by Gerson, Connolly was primarily interested in the more concrete aspects of reform and did not make any serious attempt to understand the ideological basis of Gerson's program. A similar approach characterizes the research of Palémon Glorieux and André Combes. Glorieux's work is primarily an exposition of Gerson's program of theological reform at the University of Paris and does not study the ideology behind that program.[3] André Combes has presented perhaps the most detailed study of Gerson's program for theological reform but has not attempted to place that program in the total context of Gerson's ideas on reform. Combes's interest in Gerson's concept of theological reform has been centered primarily upon its relationship to the development of his mystical theology.[4]

Steven Ozment has recently addressed himself to the relationship between university and church reform in Gerson's writings. Ozment seeks to determine the unifying principles that characterize Gerson's reform thought in these areas. He successfully shows the Spirit-directed orientation of Gerson's program for theological as well as church reform, thereby establishing the fact that the Holy Spirit was operative as a principle of reform in Gerson's writings at an earlier date than that designated by Combes.[5] In the area of episcopal reform there is the article of E. Vansteenberghe, but, like Connolly, he has confined himself to the analysis of concrete proposals for the reform of the episcopacy. Vansteenberghe, therefore, has studied neither the ideological basis of episcopal reform nor the relationship between the ideological and concrete aspects of that reform.[6]

Although not primarily concerned with the question of reform, the recent works of John B. Morrall and G. H. M. Posthumus Meyjes also deserve some mention. Morrall was the first to treat in detail the historical development of Gerson's attitude towards the schism[7]. He traces the events and circumstances which conditioned Gerson's thought and resulted in his adoption of conciliarism. Morrall's approach to the evolution of Gerson's thought on the schism has

---

[3] Palémon Glorieux, "Le chancelier Gerson et la réforme de l'enseignement," *Mélanges offerts à Étienne Gilson* (Paris, 1959), pp. 285-298.

[4] André Combes, *La théologie mystique de Gerson*, 1 (Rome, 1963), 37-64.

[5] Steven Ozment, "The University and the Church. Patterns of Reform in John Gerson," *MH*, New Series, 1 (1970), 111-126.

[6] E. Vansteenberghe, "Un programme d'action épiscopal au début du xvᵉ siècle," *RSR*, 19 (1939), 24-47. Cf. Connolly, *John Gerson*, pp. 71-138.

[7] John B. Morrall, *Gerson and the Great Schism* (Manchester, 1960).

been taken up in greater detail by G. H. M. Posthumus Meyjes who shows that Gerson's conciliarism is not in the laicizing tradition of Marsilius of Padua († 1342), William of Ockham († 1349), Conrad of Gelnhausen († 1390), Henry of Langenstein († 1397), or even Pierre d'Ailly († 1420). Gerson emerges from Meyjes' study as a firm proponent of a hierarchical ecclesiology. His ecclesiology, however, avoids the extremes of the hierarchical school characteristic of Giles of Rome († 1316) and Alvaro Pelayo († c. 1349). Gerson thus remains free of the absolutistic, laicizing, and spiritualistic tendencies characteristic of much of the ecclesiology of his day.[8]

Given the new orientation in reform studies introduced by Ladner's research and the incomplete state of contemporary scholarship on Gerson's reform thought, there is need for a comprehensive study of church reform in Gerson's writings. With the exception of Connolly's work all existing scholarship on reform in Gerson has investigated but partial aspects of his program for church reform. No recent work has attempted to present a comprehensive study of the various areas of ecclesiastical reform that attracted his attention. Practically all existing scholarship, moreover, has been restricted to an elaboration of the various concrete aspects of his reform program. The article of Ozment is perhaps the one exception to this tendency. The present work, therefore, promises to be comprehensive in its investigation of Gerson's program for church reform and will strive primarily to establish the ideological principles that motivated and directed that program.

At the present time there is no complete critical edition of the works of Gerson. This need is being filled, however, by the scholarly endeavors of Palémon Glorieux, who has projected a modern twelve-volume edition of his writings. Seven volumes of this new edition have thus far been published.[9] For works not yet edited by Glorieux recourse must be had to the older edition of L. Ellies du Pin, which incorporates many works of Gerson discovered since the seventeenth-century edition of Edmond Richer.[10]

---

[8] G. H. M. Posthumus Meyjes, *Jean Gerson. Zijn Kerkpolitiek en Ecclesiologie* (s'Gravenhage, 1963). For an excellent analysis of Meyjes' work see the review article by Heiko A. Oberman, "From Occam to Luther," *Concilium*, 17 (1966), 126-130.

[9] Jean Gerson, *Oeuvres complètes*, ed. Palémon Glorieux, 7 vols. (Paris, 1960-1968). This edition will contain all of Gerson's writings whether in Latin or in French. Doubtful works will be printed in a separate volume. Future references to this edition will be cited by the abbreviation G and will be followed by volume and page numbers.

[10] Joannes Gerson, *Opera omnia*, ed. L. Ellies du Pin, 5 vols. (Antwerp, 1706);

2 THE CAREER OF JEAN GERSON

For the sake of chronological orientation, it will be helpful to trace briefly the main events in Gerson's life. Jean Gerson was born in the town from which he took his name on December 14, 1363. Gerson-lès-Barbey was located near Rethel in the diocese of Rheims. Unfortunately nothing remains of the town today. Gerson's father was Arnulph Charlier, who supported his family by farming as did most of the inhabitants of the town. His mother was Elizabeth Chardenière; she brought into the world twelve children, seven girls and five boys. With the exception of Peter, who died while still a child, and Nicholas, all the remaining boys of the Charlier family were named Jean, and all, including Nicholas, studied for the priesthood. Jean Gerson was the eldest son of the family and became a member of the secular clergy. Nicholas and the youngest Jean entered the Celestines, the latter becoming prior of the order's monastery at Lyons where Gerson spent the last years of his life. Another Jean became a member of the Benedictine monastery at Rheims. With one exception, all of Gerson's sisters remained unmarried. They lived a fervent life of Christian piety at home under the guidance of Gerson, who frequently wrote treatises for their spiritual welfare.[11]

The times in which Gerson lived were certainly not the most propitious for the church. It had suffered considerable loss of prestige during the prolonged period of the Avignon papacy. The spiritual life of the church, moreover, both in its clerical and lay elements was certainly not at its highest. Many, including Gerson, felt that the church of that period was too frequently preoccupied with temporal matters, especially as they related to ecclesiastical taxation and benefices. The prestige and vitality of the church suffered additional

---

Opera omnia, ed. Edmond Richer, 4 vols. (Paris, 1606). Future references to du Pin's edition will be cited by the abbreviation P and will be followed by volume and column numbers.

[11] Connolly, *John Gerson*, pp. 16-18. For a more comprehensive study of Gerson's life see J. B. Schwab, *Johann Gerson, Professor der Theologie und Kanzler der Universität Paris* (Würzburg, 1858). The biographical essay of P. Glorieux in *Œuvres complètes*, 1, 105-139, is especially helpful in establishing the chronology of Gerson's writings. An earlier and somewhat more expanded version of this essay appeared in "La vie et les œuvres de Gerson," *AHDL*, 18 (1950-51), 149-192. Glorieux also wrote the article on Gerson in *NCE*, 6, 449-450. There is an excellent chapter on Gerson in E. Delaruelle et al., *L'Église au temps du Grand Schisme et de la crise conciliaire*, 2 (Paris, 1964), 837-860. Delaruelle's treatment is more topological than chronological. A brief biographical sketch can also be found in Morrall, *Gerson*, pp. 1-16.

diminution as a result of the Great Schism. The attempt to settle the schism and restore the church to peace and unity occupied a considerable portion of Gerson's reforming activities. France itself was politically torn by the internal conflicts that raged between Armagnacs and Burgundians during the reign of Charles VI (1380-1422) and Charles VII (1422-1461). Much of her land, moreover, lay devastated by the Hundred Years War.[12]

Gerson received his elementary education either at the priory of Rethel or with the Benedictines of St. Rémy in Rheims. At the age of fourteen he journeyed to Paris to begin his university education and was inscribed as a member of the College of Navarre. At Paris Gerson numbered among his teachers and fellow students several who were also destined to be prominent in the life of the church. His contemporaries among the students included Nicholas of Clémanges († 1437) and Jean Courtecuisse († 1423). Noteworthy among his teachers were Henry Totting of Oyta († 1396), Gilles Deschamps († 1413), and Pierre d'Ailly, who became rector of the College of Navarre in 1384, chancellor of the University of Paris in 1389, Bishop of Cambrai in 1397 and later cardinal. The early association of Gerson and d'Ailly eventually developed into the close friendship that characterized their later lives.[13]

Gerson received his arts degree in 1381 and immediately matriculated in the theological faculty while remaining a resident of the College of Navarre. He spent the traditional six years as *auditor*, attending lectures on the Bible for the first four years. In his fifth and sixth years he studied the *Sentences* of Peter Lombard. Gerson then passed through the various bachelor's grades that led to the doctorate, becoming a *baccalarius biblicus* in 1387 and a *sententiarius* in 1389. The *biblicus* usually lectured on one book of the Bible during each of the two years he held that title. The work of the *sententiarius* was concerned with lecturing on the four books of Lombard's *Sentences* and lasted about nine months. During the academic years 1390-1392, Gerson enjoyed the title of *baccalarius formatus* and in December, 1392, under the sponsorship of d'Ailly, received the licentiate in theology. By the academic year 1394-1395, he had acquired the honors of the doctorate as well.[14]

---

[12] The entire background for the period spanned by Gerson's life is masterfully treated by Delaruelle, *L'Église au temps du Grand Schisme*.

[13] Connolly, *John Gerson*, pp. 41-42; Morrall, *Gerson*, p. 2.

[14] Morrall, *Gerson*, pp. 4-5; Meyjes, *Jean Gerson*, p. 9. A description of the course

While still a student of theology, Gerson served as procurator of the French nation at Paris during the academic year 1383-1384. In 1388 he accompanied d'Ailly as a member of the university's commission to the papal court at Avignon to argue in favor of the condemnation of the Dominican John of Monzón (✝ c. 1412) who had denied the doctrine of the Immaculate Conception. The university's delegation was successful and the Dominicans were excluded from Paris until 1403. During his years of study, Gerson also became renowned as a preacher and in 1391 delivered his first sermon to the royal court.[15] In 1393 he served as almoner to Philip the Bold, Duke of Burgundy (✝ 1404), and with his support was appointed dean of the collegiate church of St. Donatien at Bruges. With this appointment he entered the political circles of the house of Burgundy and was to remain close to its leaders until his condemnation of John the Fearless (✝ 1419) for the assassination of the Duke of Orleans in 1407. One of the highest university honors came to Gerson in 1395 when he was selected to succeed his close friend, Pierre d'Ailly, as chancellor of the University of Paris.[16]

In 1394 the University of Paris, never a strong advocate of the Avignon cause, voted to endorse the *via cessionis* as its official policy regarding the schism.[17] The king, however, reacted strongly to this move and imposed silence upon the university. Hopes for a solution to the schism increased with the death of the Avignon pope, Clement VII (1378-1394), but it soon became evident to all that his successor, Benedict XIII (1394-1424), would prove no less intransigent. The new pope avoided any firm commitment to the *via cessionis* and, depending upon circumstances, varied between the *via facti* and the *via conventionis*. The momentum for a solution to the schism attained added intensity in 1395 when the assembly of the clergy meeting in Paris advocated the double abdication of the Roman

---

of studies in the faculty of theology at Paris is given by H. Rashdall in *The Universities of Europe in the Middle Ages*, ed. F. M. Powicke and A. B. Emden, 1 (Oxford, 1936), 474-479. See also the recent study of Palémon Glorieux, "L'enseignement au moyen âge. Techniques et méthodes en usage à la faculté de théologie de Paris, au xiiie siécle," *AHDL*, 35 (1968), 94-100.

[15] Connolly, *John Gerson*, pp. 48-49.
[16] Morrall, *Gerson*, pp. 5-6.
[17] The *via cessionis* called for the abdication of both popes in order to end the schism. Other means proposed at varying times throughout the schism were the *via facti*, which would settle the controversy by military force, the *via conventionis*, which urged negotiation between the contenders, and the *via concilii*, which sought a solution through the convocation of a general council.

pope, Boniface IX (1389-1404), and Benedict XIII. Talk was
also growing about the possibility of withdrawing from the
Avignon obedience. Gerson opposed the movement for subtraction
because he feared that such action would constitute a new schism;
he urged, rather, new negotiations with the Roman and Avignon
lines. Despite his efforts the movement grew in strength and in 1398
the synod of bishops, clergy, and university officials meeting in
Paris voted to withdraw their obedience from Benedict. This state of
affairs was to last until 1403, when France again recognized Benedict
as pope.[18]

Gerson took little part in the controversy over the withdrawal of
obedience and many of his predictions on such a course of action
proved true. France's move was not followed by the other countries
which supported Benedict XIII; nor did the countries adhering to the
Roman line withdraw their obedience from Boniface IX. Little
progress, consequently, was made in the quest for peace and unity
within the church. In June, 1399, Gerson made a prolonged visit to
Bruges, where he administered his benefice at St. Donatien. While at
Bruges he seriously contemplated resigning the chancellorship but
changed his mind upon the insistence of Philip the Bold of
Burgundy. Gerson was of the opinion that his natural temperament
and retiring disposition made him unsuited for such an important
position. He always desired, moreover, to return to a life of quiet
contemplation and work. His stay at Bruges, lengthened by a period
of illness, lasted until September of 1400 and provided him with
sufficient time to reflect upon the condition of theological studies at
Paris and to draw up the first outlines of his program for theological
reform.[19] Upon his return to Paris he continued his efforts for
theological renewal, especially through his writings on mystical
theology. He intensified, moreover, his work among the young and
in 1403 with his appointment as curate of the parish church of St.
Jean-en-Grève began to labor for the cause of reform among the
laity. In that same year, he was named a canon of the cathedral
chapter of Notre Dame.[20] During this period of his life he also

---

[18] Delaruelle, *L'Église au temps du Grand Schisme*, 1, 82-111.

[19] For Gerson's stay at Bruges see Connolly, *John Gerson*, pp. 71-81, as well as E. Vansteenberghe, "Gerson à Bruges," *RHE*, 31 (1935), 5-52.

[20] Morrall, *Gerson*, pp. 11-12. During the reign of Benedict XIII, the chancellor of the university became automatically pastor of St. Jean-en-Grève. Cf. N. Valois, *La France et le Grand Schisme d'Occident*, 3 (Paris, 1901), 349, and 4 (Paris, 1902), 382.

became immersed in the controversy over the *Romance of the Rose*.[21]

As Gerson had predicted, the withdrawal of obedience failed to make Benedict XIII any more tractable. The Synod of Paris, nevertheless, on January 4, 1407 again voted to withdraw French obedience from Benedict. This time, however, the subtraction was to be partial; France would continue to recognize the spiritual authority of the Avignon pope but control over more temporal matters such as nomination to benefices and taxation would remain with the Gallican Church.[22] There appeared no hope, therefore, for a settlement of the schism until the election of Gregory XII (1406-1415). Early in his pontificate Gregory had indicated that he would be willing to meet with Benedict to discuss the possibility of a bilateral abdication. Gerson saw some promise in these developments. On an earlier visit to the papal court at Avignon as a representative of the university during the winter of 1403-1404, he had merited the displeasure of Benedict by his outspokenness on the need to settle the schism. In March 1407, however, Gerson left Paris with renewed hope as part of a royal commission to advance the cause of church unity and to ascertain whether the new expectations raised by Gregory's offer could be brought to fulfillment.

Early in April of 1407, before the arrival of the French delegation, Benedict XIII met with representatives of Gregory XII at Marseilles. As a result of these negotiations both popes agreed to meet at Savona in September in order to seek a settlement of the schism. In May the French commission also met with Benedict in Marseilles but failed to win him over to the *via cessionis*. The members of the commission then proceeded to Rome for negotiations with Gregory XII but upon

---

[21] One of the most popular medieval romances, the *Roman de la Rose* was written in the first half of the thirteenth century by Guillaume de Lorris and completed by Jean de Meung about 1275-80. The controversy over the *Roman de la Rose* centered around Jean de Meung's portion of the work with its attacks on woman and marriage and its glorification of nature as the primary norm of morality. In 1399, Christine de Pisan publically championed the cause of women by an attack on Jean de Meung. Gerson, in 1402, condemned the *Roman de la Rose* as destructive of private and public morality. Jean de Montreuil, and Gontier and Pierre Col, leading humanists of the time, showed themselves more favorable towards Meung's work without, however, fully espousing its naturalistic principles. For a brief history of the controversy see Charles Frederick Ward, *The Epistles on the Roman of the Rose and Other Documents in the Debate* (Chicago, 1911), pp. 3-10. Gerson's position in the controversy is revealed in his *Contre le Roman de la Rose*, G, 7, 301-316 and his *De innocentia puerili*, P, 3, 293 A-296 D.

[22] Meyjes, *Jean Gerson*, pp. 112-118.

their arrival in July they found the attitude of the Roman pope most ambiguous. Plagued by financial difficulties, political pressure, and personal uncertainty, Gregory entertained serious reservations about his earlier offers to negotiate. Unable therefore to exert any influence upon the Roman pope, the commission departed in August. Although Benedict had arrived in Savona by September, Gregory had only advanced as far as Siena. He continued to procrastinate by demanding that the meeting be held in a more favorable location. Pisa was ultimately agreed upon but the proposed encounter never took place, although both popes at one time were no more than a day's journey apart, Benedict at Portovenere and Gregory at Lucca. After several months stay in Genoa, Gerson returned to Paris in February, 1408.[23]

During Gerson's absence from Paris, the prolonged quarrel between the Houses of Orleans and Burgundy was intensified by the murder of the Duke of Orleans on November 23, 1407 at the hands of assassins in the employment of the Duke of Burgundy. The talents of Jean Petit († 1411), a theologian at the University of Paris, were enlisted by the Duke to justify the Burgundian course of action. Petit developed his theoretical justification of the murder on the basis of tyrannicide. Despite his traditional devotion to the House of Burgundy, Gerson attacked Petit's position in 1408 and again in 1409, even though the power of Burgundy was on the increase in Paris. These attacks resulted in the loss of his benefice at Bruges in 1411. With the expulsion of the Burgundians from Paris in 1413, Gerson renewed his attacks against Jean Petit and was instrumental in securing his condemnation by the Synod of Paris in 1414. The controversy was renewed the following year at the Council of Constance.[24]

Although initially an advocate of the *via cessionis*, Gerson, as early as 1403, had given consideration to the *via concilii* as a means of settling the schism. He hesitated, however, to follow this course of action because he did not feel that a council enjoyed infallibility in cases where questions of fact were at issue. The vain attempt of the

---

[23] A detailed analysis of the proposed meeting at Savona can be found in Delaruelle, *L'Église au temps de Grand Schisme*, 1, 125-138. For the negotiations of the French commission at Marseilles and Rome see Meyjes, *Jean Gerson*, pp. 122-126.

[24] Connolly, *John Gerson*, pp. 164-167; Morrall, *Gerson*, pp. 13-14. For a detailed treatment of the controversy see A. Coville, *Jean Petit, La question du tyrannicide au commencement du xvᵉ siècle* (Paris, 1932).

French commission of 1407-1408 to secure the abdication of both popes as well as the failure of the Savona meeting, nevertheless, turned Gerson into a committed advocate of the *via concilii*. The Council of Pisa, convoked in March 1409 by the dissident cardinals of both the Avignon and Roman popes, therefore found in him a strong supporter.[25] Early in 1409 he published several treatises defending the convocation of the council. Prominent among these was his address to the English delegation on its way to Pisa. Gerson himself did not attend the council, being detained in France by his duties as chancellor, professor, and pastor. At Pisa both Gregory XII and Benedict XIII were declared deposed and Alexander V (1409-1410) elected as the new pope.[26]

Despite the successful conclusion of the Council of Pisa, the unity of the church was still not a realized fact. The council indeed only served to deepen the schism by adding a third claimant for the papal dignity. Yielding to pressure exerted by the Emperor Sigismund (1410-1437), John XXIII (1410-1415), successor of Alexander V, agreed to seek the resolution of the schism again through conciliar means. On December 9, 1413, John issued an official decree convoking the Council of Constance. The actual opening of the council, however, did not take place until November 16, 1414. Early in February, 1415, Gerson left Paris for Constance as the representative of the king, the University of Paris, and the ecclesiastical province of Sens. Although Gerson did not know it, he would never again return to Paris. By February 21 he had arrived in Constance.

John XXIII came to the council with the full expectation that the Pisan decrees against Gregory and Benedict would be renewed, thereby confirming his title as legitimate pope. As the council progressed, however, the Emperor and many delegates became increasingly convinced that the schism could only be resolved by the resignation or deposition of all three contenders. Fearing such a course of action, John at first offered to abdicate but then decided to flee Constance early on the morning of March 21, 1415. His action considerably compromised the legitimacy of the council. Amid the confusion and anxiety engendered by the pope's departure, Gerson delivered his famous sermon to the council urging the members to

---

[25] Meyjes, *Jean Gerson*, p. 131.

[26] For the events leading up to the Council of Pisa as well as the proceedings of the council see Delaruelle, *L'Église au temps du Grand Schisme*, 1, 139-166.

remain in session and providing them with the theological arguments which would justify their continued existence as a council despite the absence of the pope. The deposition of John XXIII occurred on May 29, 1415, to be followed shortly afterward on July 4 by the abdication of Gregory XII. In a sermon given on July 21, 1415, Gerson prayed for the successful outcome of Sigismund's mission to Perpignan where the emperor hoped to secure the abdication of Benedict XIII. The mission, however, proved a failure and after much deliberation Benedict was deposed on July 26, 1417. On November 11, 1417, the council brought the schism to a close with the election of Martin V (1417-1431) as the new pope.[27]

Gerson meanwhile was also intensely engaged in other activities of the council. The question of heresy attracted his attention and he played an important role in the condemnation of Wyclif († 1384) and Hus. Shortly before the convocation of the council, Gerson had written to the archbishop of Prague urging him to take action against the spread of Wyclif's writings. He even recommended to the archbishop that Hus be handed over to the secular power. In his capacity as chancellor, Gerson also forwarded to the archbishop twenty propositions from Hus' *De Ecclesia* which had been condemned by the theological faculty of the University of Paris. While at Constance, Gerson continued his attacks against Hus. Throughout the judicial process that led to Hus' condemnation, Gerson served as close advisor to Pierre d'Ailly, who was president of the preliminary commission which interrogated Hus and a member and leading protagonist of the commission which led to his condemnation. Both Wyclif and Hus were condemned on July 6, 1415. Hus was burned at the stake in Constance on that same day. Earlier, Wyclif's remains were ordered removed from consecrated ground.[28]

The same decree that condemned Wyclif and Hus also branded as heretical Jean Petit's theory of tyrannicide. Much of Gerson's time at the council was spent in denouncing Petit's justification of the murder of the Duke of Orleans. The council, however, condemned Petit's theory in general without mentioning him by name. Despite

---

[27] Delaruelle, *L'Église au temps du Grand Schisme*, 1, 167-188; Meyjes, *Jean Gerson*, pp. 156-176; Connolly, *John Gerson*, pp. 175-184.

[28] Joseph Alberigo et al., eds., *Conciliorum oecumenicorum decreta* (Rome, 1962), 397-407. For a detailed treatment of Hus' condemnation at Constance see Paul de Vooght, *L'hérésie de Jean Huss* (Louvain, 1960), pp. 298-460.

Gerson's continued efforts, the council never personally censured Petit.[29] In 1418 another case of tyrannicide attracted Gerson's attention. The Dominican John of Falkenberg, representing the interests of the Knights of the Teutonic Order, sanctioned the future murder of the King of Poland as a form of tyrannicide. Gerson naturally joined with the Poles on this issue but the council did not take any decision on the matter since the newly elected pope, Martin V, imposed a moratorium on the entire issue. In the final days of the council Gerson also became involved in the case of Matthew Grabow, O.P., who had attacked the Brethren of the Common Life because they claimed to lead a life of Christian perfection without professing the traditional vows of the religious life. Grabow would have restricted the practice of Christian perfection to the members of the monastic and mendicant orders because of their vows of poverty, chastity, and obedience. Gerson argued strongly against Grabow's position and advocated that the practice of Christian perfection was open to all Christians. Christian perfection and the life of the vows were not exclusively related.[30]

Although the council had successfully achieved two of its major objectives, the settlement of the schism and the condemnation of heresy, its third goal, that of reform, proved elusive. Personal and national interests blocked the road to true ecclesiastical reform. The various reform commissions concerned themselves primarily with papal taxation and appointment to benefices, both of which had become extensively developed during the Avignon papacy. Closely associated with these issues was that of simony. The first reform commission in 1415 achieved little results but in 1417 a second commission succeeded in having five of its proposals approved by the council on October 9th. Among these was the famous decree *Frequens* which provided for the convocation of general councils at regular intervals. Papal reservation of benefices was prohibited as well as papal acquisition of the property of deceased prelates.[31] On March 21, 1418 seven more decrees were passed by the council. The merging of benefices was censured; the pope renounced income from vacant benefices and simony was strongly denounced.[32] More controversial issues were to be settled by the pope through means of

---

[29] Alberigo, *Decreta*, pp. 397-408.
[30] Connolly, *John Gerson*, pp. 185-188.
[31] Alberigo, *Decreta*, pp. 414-419.
[32] Alberigo, *Decreta*, pp. 423-426.

concordats with the respective nations. Like much of Constance's reform legislation, the various concordats were rather inadequate.[33]

While Gerson contributed considerably to the resolution of the schism by means of sermons and ecclesiological treatises, he did not play a major role in the formulation of the various reform decrees. It has been argued that his preoccupation in securing the condemnation of Petit's theory of tyrannicide prevented him and his French associates from exercising their full weight in the area of reform.[34] While this may be the case, it can also be said that with the exception of simony and the frequent convocation of councils, Gerson showed little interest in the aspects of reform under consideration at Constance, especially the areas of papal taxation and control of benefices. While he did object to excessive papal control of benefices, Gerson's concept of reform had a decidedly spiritual orientation. He was primarily concerned with the spiritual nature of ecclesiastical office and not with its temporalities. Furthermore, while not completely neglecting the papacy and curia as agents for reform, he made the episcopacy and clergy the major instruments for renewal. Institutional renewal, finally, was useless unless accompanied by a genuine personal conversion on the part of both clergy and laity.

On April 22, 1418, the Council of Constance came to an end. In France the Duke of Burgundy became the controlling power at Paris as Charles VI lived out the last few years of his life in madness. Under these circumstances the time was not opportune for Gerson to return to Paris, for his continued attack against Petit's doctrine of tyrannicide at the council had only increased the Duke's wrath against him. Instead of returning home, Gerson traveled through Bavaria and lived for a brief time at the Abbey of Melk in Austria, whose abbot he had befriended while at Constance. In the fall of 1418 Gerson received an invitation from Archduke Albrecht V of Austria, later Albrecht II of Germany (1438-1439), to teach at the University of Vienna. Gerson's teaching career at Vienna was shortlived, for circumstances in France changed suddenly in September, 1419, when the Duke of Burgundy was assassinated at the instigation of the Dauphin. The path to his homeland now lay open.[35]

---

[33] Delaruelle, L'Église au temps du Grand Schisme, 1, 214-215.
[34] Morrall, Gerson, p. 95.
[35] Connolly, John Gerson, pp. 189-191.

Gerson, however, was intelligent enough to realize that despite the duke's death the power of the Burgundians in Paris still remained strong; he directed his journey, therefore, towards Lyons which was under the protection of the Dauphin. Gerson, moreover, had a close friend in the archbishop of that city, Amédée de Talaru († 1444). An additional reason for his going to Lyons was that his brother Jean was then prior of the Celestine monastery located in that city and he could easily take up lodging there. Gerson arrived in Lyons in November, 1419. Technically he still remained chancellor of the University of Paris but his duties were performed in his absence by his close friends, Gerard Machet († 1448) and John Courtecuisse.[36]

Although removed from the center of university life, Gerson made his stay in Lyons one of the most productive literary periods of his life and carried on the cause of church reform through sermons, spiritual treatises and correspondence with members of the various religious orders, who from time to time sought his prudent advice.[37] He demonstrated his continued interest in diocesan reform when, upon the invitation of the archbishop, he addressed the Synod of Lyons in 1421. He had spoken before a similar archdiocesan synod at Rheims in 1408. On both occasions Gerson took the opportunity to advance the cause of church reform within dioceses. In 1425, at the request of the archbishop, Gerson moved from the Celestine monastery to lodgings in the collegiate church of St. Paul. Here he took charge of the training and education of the church's choir and was thereby able to resume one of his favorite apostolates, that of working with the young.[38]

While in Lyons Gerson composed several treatises on the education of princes. The first treatise was written for Charles VII's eldest son. When this son died, Gerson turned his attention to the education of Louis XI (1461-1483), who was now destined to succeed his father. In the final year of his life, upon the request of Louis' tutor, Gerson composed a second treatise on the education proper to a royal prince. Among Gerson's last writings was a defense of Joan of Arc († 1431) against the Burgundians and those of the University of Paris who were plotting her downfall, despite her victory at the head of the French forces at Orleans. Gerson died on July 12, 1429, and was buried in the chapel of St. Lawrence adjacent to the church of St.

---

[36] Morrall, *Gerson*, pp. 15-16.

[37] P. Glorieux, "L'activité littéraire de Gerson à Lyon," *RTAM*, 18 (1951), 238-307.

[38] Morrall, *Gerson*, p. 16.

Paul in Lyons. His tomb, however, was destroyed in 1793 when the forces of the Revolution burnt and destroyed the chapel.[39]

The events of Gerson's life clearly show that he was at the center of the political, intellectual and ecclesiastical movements of the late fourteenth and early fifteenth century in northern Europe. His position as chancellor of the University of Paris immersed him in the intellectual and ecclesiastical activity of his day. His role as court preacher and his association with both the Burgundian and French rulers elevated him to a position of political prominence. His driving concern to secure the peace and unity of the church gave him an importance exceeded by relatively few personalities of his day. At the Council of Constance, Gerson was at the height of his influence and to him is due in no little degree the ultimate success of that council. His numerous writings on the spiritual life as well as his vast correspondence with members of the various religious orders, especially after his retirement at Lyons, made him one of the most important figures in the religious thought of the period. In all these activities, his role was always that of a reformer. He knew well how much the church of his day was in need of reform and he expended his every effort in that endeavor. Because of his prominent position in the ecclesiastical reform movements of the fourteenth and fifteenth centuries, Gerson's writings well deserve our attention. From the study of his works there will emerge a deeper understanding of the ideological principles that so strongly motivated and guided his reform activity.

---

[39] Connolly, *John Gerson*, pp. 193-199.

CHAPTER ONE

THE CHURCH: ORDER, HIERARCHY, AND REFORM

All study of ecclesiastical reform in Gerson must begin with his concept of the church, for every genuine reformer must have some understanding of what the church should be before he can address himself to the question of its reform. Without such an understanding, his program of reform will be aimless and necessarily end in confusion. That understanding, moreover, may be consciously and explicitly formulated or it may remain in the realm of the implicit and subconscious. In any case, all reform is directed toward a more comprehensive realization of the church's nature. Church reform, finally, may be restorative in so far as it looks to the past or it may be ameliorative and evolutionary to the extent that it is orientated towards the future. Very frequently it represents a combination of various orientations. A study of Gerson's conception of the church, therefore, is a necessary presupposition to any understanding of the ideological principles operative in his reforming activities.

1. Celestial Archetypes

Central to Gerson's thought is the notion of the church as made to the image of a celestial archetype. He describes that archetype in several different ways. At times he sees the church as an image of the angelic hierarchies. In this respect he patterns his thought closely upon the angelic triads so prominent in the writings of Pseudo-Dionysius, especially the *De coelesti hierarchia*.[1] In Dionysius the

---

[1] The body of writings ascribed to Dionysius belong to an unknown author of the late fifth century. Throughout the Middle Ages he was generally identified with Dionysius the Areopagite whose conversion by St. Paul is recorded in Acts 17 : 34. Gerson believed furthermore that this same Dionysius brought Christianity to France and established the monastery of St. Denis at Paris. The Dionysian corpus was a synthesis of Christian and Neo-Platonist teaching and exercised a major influence upon medieval thought, especially in the area of mysticism. As of Gerson's time, the works of Dionysius had undergone four translations. Abbot Hilduin of St. Denis prepared the first translation around 832; he was followed about 867 by John Scotus Erigena. Around 1167 and 1235 translations were made by John Sarrazin and Robert

first angelic triad is composed of Seraphim, Cherubim and Thrones.[2] For Gerson the pope and cardinals correspond to the first celestial triad.[3] The second celestial triad in the Dionysian schema comprises Dominations, Virtues, and Powers.[4] To this celestial triad, Gerson compares the offices of patriarchs, archbishops, bishops and priests.[5] Finally, paralleling the third celestial tread of Principalities, Archangels and Angels are the laity and religious.[6]

The ecclesiastical hierarchy as envisioned by Gerson differs considerably from that described by Dionysius. Dionysius conceived the church's structure as essentially twofold: clergy and faithful. The first contained bishops, priests, and ministers such as porters, lectors, acolytes, and exorcists. The second comprised monks, the saints, i.e. members of the laity leading holy lives, and finally those orders undergoing purification, namely catechumens, energumens, and penitents.[7] Because of its threefold division, Gerson's vision of the church reflects more faithfully the triadic nature of the angelic hierarchies than does that of Dionysius. This difference is explained primarily by the fact that Dionysius and Gerson attempt to represent the church of their time. The church of Dionysius' day did not lend itself to an overall triadic division. For Dionysius the bishop of Rome was merely first among equals whereas the growth of the papacy and the creation of the college of cardinals in the Middle Ages enabled

---

Grosseteste respectively. Hugh of St. Victor, Albert the Great, and Thomas Gallus wrote commentaries on the Dionysian writings. The textual tradition of Dionysius' writings through the thirteenth century is treated by H. F. Dondaine, *Le Corpus Dionysien de l'Université de Paris au xiii⁰ siècle* (Rome, 1953). For a survey of the writings, doctrine, and influence of Dionysius see René Roques *et al.*, "Denys L'Aréopagite," in *DSAM*, 3, 244-429. The most recent comprehensive study of Dionysian thought is that of René Roques, *L'univers Dionysien* (Paris, 1954). J. G. Bougerol has studied the influence of Dionysius' concept of hierarchy upon Bonaventure's thought in his "Saint Bonaventure et la hiérarchie Dionysienne," *AHDL*, 36 (1969), 131-167.

[2] *De coelesti hierarchia*, 7, 1, *MPG*, 3, 206 B-D.

[3] *De potestate ecclesiastica*, G, 6, 227. "Exemplum aliud est in angelica triplici hierarchia.... Papalis auctoritas suo modo cum suis cardinalibus imitatur triplicitatem primam...."

[4] *De coelesti hierarchia*, 8, 1, *MPG*, 3, 238 B-D, 239 A-B.

[5] *De potestate ecclesiastica*, G, 6, 227. "... alteram vero mediam imitatur patriarchalis, archiepiscopalis, episcopalis, et sacerdotalis auctoritas in habentibus subjectos sibi...."

[6] *De coelesti hierarchia*, 9, 1-2, *MPG*, 3, 258 B-D, 259 A-B, *De potestate ecclesiastica*, G, 6, 227. "Ultimi sunt instar tertiae hierarchiae qui hierarchizantur in Ecclesia sed non alios auctoritative hierarchizant, quemadmodum sunt populi et simplices religiosi secundum Dionysium."

[7] For a detailed description of the ecclesiastical hierarchy according to Dionysius see Roques, *L'univers Dionysien*, pp. 171-199.

Gerson to consider them as a separate division in the church's hierarchy. Interestingly, Gerson never accorded the monks the privileged position given them by Dionysius.

Gerson also refers to the church's celestial archetype as the *ecclesia coelestis*[8] or the *ecclesia triumphans*.[9] The church on earth is frequently labeled the *ecclesia terrena* or *militans*. The *ecclesia terrena* is the visible image of the *ecclesia coelestis* and reflects the life of the heavenly kingdom.[10] He sees the church on earth and its celestial archetype as a twofold manifestation of the kingdom of Israel. The Ascension of Christ is a particularly unique moment in the history of the *ecclesia coelestis* and the *ecclesia terrena* because it represents the moment when both aspects of the kingdom of Israel, on earth and in heaven, are raised up from their sinful condition and brought to full restoration. The Ascension constitutes the period in time when the Pauline words of "*instaurare omnia in Christo*" attain their fullest realization, for it is then that the *ecclesia coelestis* and the *ecclesia terrena* are again united in Christ.[11]

Another celestial archetype upon which the church is patterned is that of the heavenly Jerusalem. The key scriptural source which Gerson relies upon for this conception of the church is Ap 21:2 where the author professes, in one of his visions, to have seen the holy city, the new Jerusalem, descending from heaven. For Gerson, therefore, the church is an image of the new Jerusalem.[12] The life and government of the church on earth, moreover, is to be patterned upon the exemplar of the heavenly Jerusalem.[13] The theme of a new Jerusalem was already prominent in the Old Testament, especially in the writings of the prophets Isaiah, Jeremiah, and Ezekiel, but remained primarily associated with a renewal of the historical Jerusalem. With the writers of the New Testament, the idea of a new Jerusalem became more eschatological and identified with the city of

---

[8] *De auferibilitate sponsi ab Ecclesia*, G, 3, 294. "Nam ad exemplar coelestis Ecclesia terrena formata est."

[9] *De potestate ecclesiastica*, G, 6, 228. "... et optimo regimine gubernetur ad exemplar Ecclesiae triumphantis...."

[10] *Domine si in tempore hoc*, G, 5, 211. "Ecce rex et conditor meus me regni sanctorum coelestis expressam imaginem esse decreverat ut quantum fas esset terranarum rerum oblita coelo propinquarem et regnum illud supremum oculis mortalium presentarem."

[11] *Domine si in tempore hoc*, G, 5, 204. Cf. Eph 1 : 10.

[12] *De auferibilitate sponsi ab Ecclesia*, G, 3, 294. The theme of the heavenly Jerusalem can also be found in Gal 4 : 24-31 and Heb 12 : 22.

[13] *Domine si in tempore hoc*, G, 6, 211.

the living God. In the Apocalypse the idea of a new Jerusalem denotes more the idea of the church in its final perfection. The prophetic texts of Ezekiel and Isaiah are so reinterpreted that the earthly city is lost to view. What alone remains predominant is the heavenly model in whose image the church on earth has been made and in whose ultimate mystery it essentially shares.[14] Gerson adopts fully the vision of the Apocalypse which sees the heavenly Jerusalem as the supreme archetype of the church on earth.[15] He does not, however, see the new Jerusalem in the strict eschatological sense as does the author of the Apocalypse but as an actual realization within the church, more in the sense of what might be called a realized eschatology.

Gerson also uses Ex 25:40 to illustrate the fact that the church is built upon a celestial archetype. The scriptural locus, however, tells us very little about the nature of the archetype. When Moses appears before the Lord on Mount Sinai, he is given detailed instructions as to how he is to construct the ark of the Covenant, the table for the holy bread and sacred vessels as well as the lampstand of gold which is to illumine the interior of the holy place. At the conclusion of these instructions Moses receives a special admonition: "And see that you make them after the pattern for them, which is being shown you on the mountain." [16] Gerson sees the ark of the Covenant as a prefiguration of the church. Just as the ark was a model of the archetype shown Moses on the mountain, so is the church an image of a heavenly archetype.[17]

The final manner in which Gerson describes the celestial archetype of the church is similar to the Augustinian idea of the *civitas Dei*. He uses the same passage from Ps 86 which Augustine utilized as the

---

[14] For a brief but thorough study of the history of the term "Jerusalem" in biblical writings see Xavier Léon-Dufour, ed., *Vocabulaire de théologie biblique* (2nd ed.; Paris, 1970), pp. 585-592. See, however, the apocryphal 1 Enoch 90 : 28 for an eschatological interpretation of the Jerusalem theme during Old Testament times.

[15] *De auferibilitate sponsi ab Ecclesia*, G, 3, 294; cf. *Domine si in tempore hoc*, G, 6, 211; *Quomodo stabit regnum*, G, 7, 980; *De considerationibus quas debet habere princeps*, P, 3, 228 C-D.

[16] Ex 25 : 40. English translations from the Scriptures will be cited according to the Revised Standard Version. Biblical texts will be in Latin whenever the Latin text is necessary for a clearer understanding of Gerson's exegesis. The Latin text will be that utilized by Gerson. Enumeration of the Psalms will be according to the Vulgate.

[17] *De considerationibus quas debet habere princeps*, P, 3, 228 C-D. "...et Moyses arcam testamenti figurativam hujus Ecclesiae fabricavit, 'sicut in monte' sibi 'monstratum est.'"

theme for his famous *De civitate Dei*: "Glorious things are spoken of you, O city of God." [18] There is one notable divergence between Gerson and Augustine in their usage of the above passage. Unlike Augustine, Gerson does not employ the term city of God but uses the phrase, "city of paradise." [19] At times he substitutes *"église de paradis"* for *"cité de paradis,"* but his understanding of the two terms remains substantially the same.[20] The inhabitants of the city of paradise are the nine orders of angels, the patriarchs, the prophets, apostles, martyrs, confessors, and virgins; indeed, the city of paradise is the heavenly kingdom of all the saints.[21] The princes of this city are the angels, for to them is committed the care of humans. Theirs is the task to teach, exhort, defend, and aid men in their attempts to arrive at the heavenly city of paradise.[22] At times he imagines the city of paradise as laid out in seven different quarters or as possessing seven streets whereon reside the various inhabitants of the celestial city. Following in the medieval tradition, Gerson is rather fond of the number seven since it is the number which sums up the deadly sins, the beatitudes, and the petitions of the Our Father.[23]

The celestial archetypes utilized by Gerson reveal his indebtedness to and continuity with the patristic and medieval ecclesiological traditions. Similar descriptions of the church were used by Origen, Augustine, Gregory the Great, Isidore of Seville, and Bede, and continued throughout the Middle Ages.[24] The image of Jerusalem, moreover, was the most privileged example used to describe the fourfold nature of medieval biblical exegesis. Jerusalem, consequently, was regarded, literally, as the historical city in Palestine, allegorically, as the church on earth, morally, as the soul of the individual Christian, and, anagogically, as the celestial church. Of all the senses of Jerusalem used throughout the Middle Ages that of the heavenly Jerusalem remained predominant.[25] Gerson's concept of

---

[18] Ps. 86:3. Cf. Augustine, *De civitate Dei*, 11, 1, *CCSL*, 48, p. 321.
[19] *La mendicité spirituelle*, G, 7, 250. "... la noble cité de paradis de qui tant glorieuses choses sont dittes."
[20] *La mendicité spirituelle*, G, 7, 221, 227.
[21] *La mendicité spirituelle*, G, 7, 250.
[22] *La mendicité spirituelle*, G, 7, 249.
[23] *La mendicité spirituelle*, G, 7, 242, 278.
[24] Y. M.-J. Congar, *L'ecclésiologie du haut moyen âge* (Paris, 1968), pp. 98-113.
[25] Henri DeLubac, *Exégèse médiévale* 1, pt. 2 (Paris, 1959), 645-648. In this tradition, the early Middle Ages saw the appearance of the famous hymn: *Urbs beata Jerusalem.* Cf. H. Ashworth, " 'Urbs beata Jerusalem,' Scriptural and Patristic Sources," *EL*, 70 (1956), 238-241.

a celestial archetype upon which the church on earth was patterned also reveals the influence of patristic and medieval cosmological traditions which saw a close continuity between the celestial and terrestrial worlds.[26]

2. ORDER AND HIERARCHY

Whether conceived as the angelic hierarchies, the *ecclesia coelestis*, the heavenly Jerusalem, or the *cité de paradis*, the notion of a celestial archetype upon which the church is patterned and of which it is a visible image remains foremost in Gerson's thought. A closer study of the nature of that archetype is now in order, for the more clearly the archetype is known the better understood will be its image on earth, the church. Study of Gerson's writings reveals that in all his conceptions of the church the notion of hierarchical order emerges as a predominant theme.

The whole universe, in Gerson's thought, is ordered and reflects the order of the heavenly city. The heavens, the stars, indeed, all the elements of the earth, together with the laws that govern them, speak of God's order. This order was even recognized by the pagan world, for the Roman priesthood subordinated the *flamines* to the *archiflamines*. Geographically, moreover, the Roman empire was ordered and this order was manifested in its division into provinces and dioceses. Finally all power, whether political or spiritual, is characterized by hierarchy and order. Gerson finds support for this idea in Rom. 13:1: *"Non est potestas nisi a Deo; quae autem a Deo sunt, ordinata sunt."*[27]

While the entire universe reflects the order of the heavenly city, the church, nevertheless, is a more visible manifestation of that order.[28] If all the works of God are ordered, then the church as God's supreme handiwork is essentially a church of order. Gerson understands *ordo* in the traditional Augustinian sense and even

---

[26] Congar, *L'ecclésiologie*, pp. 101-102.

[27] *Domine si in tempore hoc*, G, 5, 212. "Omnia civitatis illius ordinem eloquuntur; coeli, sidera, elementa mixta cum ordinatissimis legibus Deo serviant. Unde et natura duce ante Christum meum natum gentilium sacerdotum potestates ita erant ordinatae ut archiflaminibus flamines subessent, a quibus adhuc provinciarum ac dioecesium discretionem partitionemque retineo. Potestates autem terrenas quis ordinatas ambigat? Non est potestas nisi a Deo; quae autem a Deo sunt, ordinata sunt."

[28] *Domine si in tempore hoc*, G, 5, 212. "Verum ordinis mei pulchritudo longe praestantior, expressior atque vicinior."

employs Augustine's classic definition: *"parium dispariumque rerum sua unicuique tribuens dispositio."* [29] This definition has been translated as "an arrangement of like and unlike things whereby each of them is disposed in its proper place."[30] So great is Gerson's stress on the concept of order in the church that he does not hesitate to call the church an *acies ordinata,* an image he borrows from the Book of Canticles.[31] Gerson also describes the church as an *acies ordinata* in his famous address to the English delegation on its way to the Council of Pisa.[32] Elsewhere he states that *Christianitas* can only be maintained by preserving the order characteristic of the heavenly kingdom.[33] The order which the church reflects, moreover, is essentially hierarchical, for God has established fixed gradations within his heavenly kingdom. Each major gradation within the celestial order is termed a *hierarchia* and can contain within itself further gradations.[34]

For Gerson, the Trinity emerges as the first of the heavenly hierarchies; it is indeed the *supercoelestis hierarchia.* The dignity and authority of the Trinity is rooted in the Father and proceeds from the Father as from a font because he is, as it were, the unbegotten member of the Trinity, a *principium de non principio.* The Son proceeds from the Father, and the Spirit from both Father and Son

---

[29] *Gratia vobis*, G, 2, 233. For Augustine's definitons on *ordo* see *De civitate Dei,* 19, 13, *CCSL*, 48, p. 679 and *De ordine, CSEL*, 63, p. 121. Cf. J. Rief, *Der Ordobegriff des jungen Augustinus* (Paderborn, 1962). For medieval notions on order see, Gerhart B. Ladner, "Homo Viator: Medieval Ideas on Order and Alienation," *Speculum*, 42 (1967), 233-259; Hermann Krings, *Ordo: Philosophisch-historische Grundlegung einer abendländischen Idee* (Halle-Saale, 1941) See also Krings' article, "Das Sein und die Ordnung," *DVLG*, 18 (1940), 233-249.

[30] Augustine, *The City of God,* 19, 13, trans. Gerald G. Walsh, and Daniel J. Honan, *The Fathers of the Church,* 24 (New York, 1954), 218.

[31] *Responsio ad errores de orationibus privatis fidelium,* P, 2, 653 D. "Ecclesia fundata est a Christo nedum stabilissime supra firmam petram, sed etiam sapientissime et ordinatissime; quoniam si omnia 'quae sunt a Deo ordinata sunt,' secundum Apostolum, Rom. xiii, 1, hoc maxime reperitur in Ecclesia, quae dicitur ideo 'terribilis, ut castrorum acies ordinata,' Cant. vi, 3."

[32] *Propositio facta coram Anglicis,* G, 6, 133. "... congregatio ecclesiastica instituta est ut castrorum acies ordinata...."

[33] *Quomodo stabit regnum,* G, 7, 980. "S'aucuns doncques demande comment aura stabilite le royaume de crestiente ca jus, response que ce sera par garder l'ordre et l'exemplaire du royaume des cieulx lassus."

[34] *Quomodo stabit regnum,* G, 7, 980. "Le royaume des cieux se institue en certaines ordres ou ordonnances essentielles et permanentes que nous appellons hierarchies. C'est la determination saint Denis en son livre que pour ce il appela de hierarchie celeste, par l'instruction saint Pol."

without thereby suffering any diminution in nobility and dignity. Without endangering the nature of the three persons of the Trinity or their essential unity, Gerson does see logical gradations among the members of the Trinity according to the varying manner in which the Son proceeds from the Father and the Spirit from both Father and Son.[35] He is most likely thinking of the manner in which Augustine distinguishes the persons in the Trinity by making the Father the *inprincipiatum principium*, the Son the *principiatum principium* and the Spirit *ex utroque principiatum*. He may also have in mind Gregory of Nyssa's distinction between *principium, immediate principiatum* and *mediate principiatum* as applied to the Father, Son, and Holy Spirit.[36]

The glorified Christ also holds a prominent position among the heavenly hierarchies. By virtue of his divinity, he is above the angelic hierarchies and purifies, illuminates and perfects those hierarchies. His supreme power over the material universe is clearly manifested in his miracles.[37] Surprisingly, Gerson has relatively little to say about the role of the glorified Christ among the celestial hierarchies. This deficiency may be explained by the fact that Gerson is normally reluctant to speculate in detail on matters of such a lofty nature. Another reason, perhaps more revealing, is the fact that Gerson's thinking on reform is considerably more Trinitarian than Christocentric in its orientation. This point will be gradually substantiated as our study of Gerson's thought proceeds.

The angels are also part of the heavenly kingdom and are

---

[35] *De nobilitate*, P, 3, 209 A. "Nobilitas in primis est supereminenter in Trinitate Beata, quae ad sanum intellectum dicitur supercoelestis hierarchia: est enim in Patre fontalis nobilitas seu dignitas vel autoritas, quae notificatur per duas notiones istas: innascibilitas, et principium de non principio. Similiter in Filio respectu Spriritus sancti, nec sequitur ignobilitas idcirco in Spiritu sancto. . . ."

[36] The operative Greek terminology in Gregory of Nyssa's thought is: αἴτιος, αἰτιατός, τὸ μὲν πρόσεχῶς ἐκ τοῦ πρώτου, τὸ δε διὰ τοῦ προσεχῶς ἐκ τοῦ πρώτου. For Gregory of Nyssa and Augustine's position cf. Bernard Lonergan, S. J., *De Deo Trino*, 1 (Rome, 1964), 203-204, 219-222. For a general survey of Augustinian and Cappadocian trinitarian thought see J. N. D. Kelly, *Early Christian Doctrines* (New York, 1960), pp. 263-279. The concept of the Trinity as a *hierarchia* is not Dionysian but reflects the influence of Hugh of St. Victor and Bonaventure. Cf. J. G. Bougerol, "Saint Bonaventure et la hiérarchie Dionysienne," p. 132.

[37] *Apparuit gratia*, G, 5, 67-68. "Nam et benigna humanitas Dei Salvatoris nostri universum mundum spiritualium aeternarumque creaturarum purgat, illuminat et perficit, superior eis in ordine hierarchico stabilita ut sol quidem aeternitatis. Imperium quoque possidet super universale materiale atque corporeum, ut ex miraculorum operatione monstratum est."

designated as the *coelestis hierarchia*. He divides the angelic orders into the traditional nine categories: seraphim, cherubim, thrones, dominations, principalities, powers, virtues, archangels, angels.[38] These nine orders are then divided into three groups of three, with each group constituting a distinct hierarchy and possessing within itself distinct gradations.[39]

The new Jerusalem, therefore, which the writer of the Apocalypse saw descending from heaven, was essentially a hierarchically ordered church which primarily reflected the angelic hierarchies.[40] As we have seen, the pope, his cardinals and the Roman curia correspond to the first angelic triad with the patriarchs, archbishops, bishops, and priests paralleling the second.[41] The third and lowest level in the church's order is composed of religious and the laity; these are compared to the third angelic triad of virtues, archangels, and angels.[42] Just as the angelic orders are subordinated to one head which is God, so too are patriarchs, archbishops, bishops, archpriests, and priests subordinated to the one visible head of the church, the pope. The church, then, in imitation of the angelic kingdom, is hierarchically ordered in all its members under the one head.[43] Gerson, indeed, does not hesitate to call the pope the *primus hierarcha*.[44] Through this hierarchical order and subordination, the church manifests itself as a visible image of the celestial kingdom.[45]

---

[38] *Quomodo stabit regnum*, G, 7, 980. Cf. *La mendicité spirituelle*, G, 7, 250-251.

[39] *De nobilitate*, P, 3, 209 A-B. "Nobilitas est in angelis, secundum triplicem hierarchiam, quae coelestis appelatur, primam, secundam, tertiam. Nobilitas rursus est in eisdem angelis in ista qualibet triplici hierarchia, secundum tres ordines contentos in qualibet, ut in prima Cherubin, Seraphin, et Throni."

[40] *Responsio ad errores de orationibus privatis fidelium*, P, 2, 654 A. "Ecclesia fundata est in suis ordinibus ad exemplar coelestis hierarchiae. Propterea dicit Joannes in Apoc. xxi, 10 quod vidit eam 'descendentem de caelo.' "

[41] *De potestate ecclesiastica*, G, 6, 227. "Papalis auctoritas suo modo cum suis cardinalibus imitatur triplicitatem primam; alteram vero mediam imitatur patriarchalis, archiepiscopalis, episcopalis et sacerdotalis auctoritas in habentibus subjectos sibi. . . ."

[42] *De potestate ecclesiastica*, G, 6, 227. "Ultimi sunt instar tertiae hierarchiae qui hierarchizantur in Ecclesia sed non alios auctoritative hierarchizant, quemadmodum sunt populi et simplices religiosi secundum Dionysium."

[43] *Quomodo stabit regnum*, G, 7, 981. "Le royaume de saincte eglise doit avoir ordre hierarchique en tous ses membres et ses estats quant a ung souverain pasteur ou gouverneur que nous pouons nommer roy pontifical ou evesque royal. C'est ung vray pere. Appert car ainsy est ou royaume des cielz." The designation of the pope as *roy pontifical* and *evesque royal* reflects the medieval notion of the pope as *rex-sacerdos* and is related to the principle: *papa est verus imperator*. Cf. Michael Wilks, *The Problem of Sovereignty in the Later Middle Ages* (Cambridge, 1963), pp. 254-287.

[44] *De potestate ecclesiastica*, G, 6, 215.

[45] *Domine si in tempore hoc*, G, 5, 211.

The order established within the church is both stable and permanent.[46] The striking parallel between the angelic and the ecclesiastical hierarchies is neither the product of accident nor of mere human design. If the church is hierarchically ordered, then it is so because this was the design of its most benevolent creator. Gerson takes Henry of Langenstein to task for asserting that the church could create for itself a sovereign pontiff even if one had not been directly constituted by Christ. For Gerson the office of the sovereign pontiff is so much an integral part of the ecclesiastical hierarchy as constituted by Christ that the possibility of its absence is inconceivable. He feels that Henry of Langenstein could only be referring to the possibilities open to the Holy Spirit and not to the actual reality.[47]

Gerson further insists that the hierarchical order of the church existed in its integrity and perfection from the very moment of its foundation. He frequently takes up this theme in many of his speculations on the church. If the church is to remain until the consummation of the world, it will remain as perfectly constituted as at the time of its establishment by Christ. He finds scriptural justification for his position in Dt 32:4: *Dei perfecta sunt opera.* God's work is perfect not only in its inception but even more so in its conservation and consummation. The church, consequently, will remain integrally the same and perfect in its members.[48] Church and hierarchy are thus synonymous for Gerson throughout history.[49] From its earliest beginnings, the church was constituted an *acies ordinata* and a *corpus integerrime perfectum*.[50]

When Gerson maintains that the hierarchical structure of the church was always integrally perfect, he does not claim that the multifold hierarchical structure of the fifteenth-century church was already visible and functioning at the time of the *ecclesia primitiva*.

---

[46] *Quomodo stabit regnum*, G, 7, 981

[47] *Propositio facta coram Anglicis*, G, 6, 132.

[48] *De auferibilitate sponsi ab Ecclesia*, G, 3, 296. "Si enim permanebit Ecclesia usque ad consummationem saeculi, permanebit ut perfecta; Dei enim perfecta sunt opera, non solum in inchoatione sed magis in conservatione et consummatione."

[49] *De auferibilitate sponsi ab Ecclesia*, G, 3, 296. "Auferibilis non est ab Ecclesia militante sponsus suus Christus homo quin semper influat in eamdem Ecclesiam sponsam suam per membra varia gradus hierarchicos officiorum et administrationum et dignitatum et statuum ab ipso constitutorum dum Ecclesiam fundavit primitus et aedificavit."

[50] *Propositio facta coram Anglicis*, G, 6, 133.

He is aware of the considerable development that occurred within the hierarchical structure of the church from the time of its foundation until the period in which he lived.[51] Conscious of the differences effected by centuries of church history, Gerson, nevertheless, maintains the essential identity of the church's hierarchical structure. He regards the entire hierarchical structure of the church as already inchoatively present in the *ecclesia primitiva*.

To express this inchoative presence as well as the developmental aspects of the ecclesiastical hierarchy, Gerson resorts to comparisons related to natural growth. He first compares the church to a nursery garden. As seeds which are planted in a nursery in time develop into fully grown plants, so too does the hierarchy, inchoatively present in the *ecclesia primitiva*, develop to its fullness in the succeeding periods of the church's history. The full hierarchical order of the church, therefore, is virtually contained in the *ecclesia primitiva* in a manner similar to the way in which a plant is essentially contained in its seed. To express this inchoative presence and growth of the church's hierarchy, Gerson also utilizes the analogy of a young vine which gradually spreads forth leaves, develops branches, and then blossoms.[52] Another favorite example is the young blade of wheat which contains essentially the same number of kernels as when fully grown. A final example is that of the acorn which contains the potentialities of a completely developed tree. Many of the same examples, Gerson acknowledges, have been used by philosophers to describe the inchoative presence of forms in matter. Whatever the manner of description utilized, Gerson's main point is that all hierarchical states of the church were present in the *ecclesia primitiva*, although not in the fully developed sense in which they were to be found in the church of his day.[53]

---

[51] *De potestate ecclesiastica*, G, 6, 224. "Sed dicamus hic aliter esse discernendum in ecclesiastica politia dum est ordinata complete sub quadam explicatione perfecta et numerosa membrorum suorum in ministris per status gradus et officia, aliter dum ab initio formata est Ecclesia in magna tam ecclesiasticorum quam fidelium paucitate velut in quodam seminario vel germine seu botro."

[52] *De auferibilitate sponsi ab Ecclesia,* G, 3, 297. "Fuerunt enim primitus velut in quodam seminario vivifico positi in Ecclesia per Christum et postmodum, crescente Ecclesia, discretio talium magis innotuit velut si botrus vineae se in folia et flores et ramos explicuerit." Cf. *De potestate ecclesiastica*, G, 6, 232-233.

[53] *Propositio facta coram Anglicis*, G, 6, 133. "... sunt enim gradus omnes seminati a Christo in Ecclesia primitiva quamquam parvula in qua nondum erant sic explicati gradus ecclesiasticae hierarchiae ut nunc inspicimus, quemadmodum spica totos numeros suos habet in grano, et nux arbor in nuce virtualiter continetur; has vocant philosophi inchoationes formarum in materia."

Since he considers the church as perfectly constituted in its hierarchical structure and as remaining such throughout its history, he reacts strongly against the assertion of Ockham and his followers that the church could continue to exist in a single member of the laity, even in a woman. Gerson asserts strongly that the church will always have faithful bishops and priests.[54] The church is so integrally and perfectly constituted in its essential hierarchy, that is, papacy, cardinalate, patriarchate, archiepiscopacy, episcopacy and priesthood, that if it lost one of these hierarchical orders it would cease to be the church that Christ established. If one were to separate the papacy from the hierarchical structure of the church what remains would not and could not truly be called the church.[55] To grant the opposite would be tantamount to admitting that the church could be deficient in its essential hierarchical structure.

Betraying, perhaps, some Ockhamistic influence, Gerson does concede that the hierarchical constitution of the church can be changed but never through human instrumentality. Divine intervention is absolutely necessary if there is to be any modification in the church's essential nature. The Holy Spirit alone is capable of creating new channels of authority and order within the church, thereby restructuring its essential framework. This possibility is implied by his use of the principle: "*lege stante et non facta nova institutione.*" The present hierarchical structure has been constituted by divine decree and can only be changed by subsequent divine intervention and the establishment of a new dispensation.[56]

The only reason given by Gerson for his arguments is simply the fact that God has the power to do so. In this respect his thought is reminiscent of the nominalistic concept of *potentia Dei absoluta*. He argues that before God created the present hierarchical order in the

---

[54] *Propositio facta coram Anglicis*, G, 6, 132. Ockham identified the church more with belief than with hierarchical structure. Relying upon a medieval tradition which saw in Mary the sole possessor of the faith when Christ had been abandoned by his disciples after the crucifixion, Ockham argued that the true faith and consequently the true church could well be restricted to a small number of the laity or even to a single individual. Cf. *Dialogus*, 2, 25 and 6, 12, ed. M. Goldast, *Monarchia*, 2 (Frankfurt, 1614), 429, 527. For Ockham's conception of the church see George de Lagarde, *La naissance de l'esprit laïque au déclin du moyen âge*, 5 (Paris, 1963), 30-52. The tradition concerning Mary and the faith has been studied by Y.M.-J. Congar, "Incidence ecclésiologique d'un thème de dévotion mariale," *MSR*, 7, (1950), 277-292.

[55] *De potestate ecclesiastica*, G, 6, 222.

[56] *De auferibilitate sponsi ab Ecclesia*, G, 3, 298.

church no one doubted his ability to do so and consequently no one should doubt his ability to create new structures in the future. For now, however, the present dispensation and structure of the church stand and no gathering or congregation of humans is able to change the established order. Gerson is reacting strongly against some conciliarists, presumably Henry of Langenstein, who would make the papacy merely an institution of the church gathered in council.[57]

Gerson's position on the essential immutability and integrity of the church's hierarchical structure is especially important in understanding his attitude toward the schism. In a treatise against Benedict XIII written in 1417, Gerson lists the times in which the church can congregate in a general council. These occasions are: when there is no pope, when the existing pope has fallen into heresy or when he is unable to consent to a general gathering of the church because he has become insane or imprisoned. Under such circumstances, when a council is necessary and of clear utility to the church, it may be summoned without the consent of the pope. Gerson would add an additional reason: when the existing pope has been sufficiently requested to call a council for the attainment of unity in faith or morals or to determine who is the legitimate pope and contumaciously refuses to do so.

Gerson bases his arguments primarily on the fact that the church has been perfectly instituted by Christ to provide for its own conservation and the unity of its members in faith and morals. The church, moreover, as constituted by Christ must have a single head if its hierarchical structure is to be perfectly maintained. To deny, therefore, the reasons advanced by Gerson as to when a general council can be called without the pope's consent, is tantamount to a denial that the hierarchical structure and order of the church has been perfectly instituted by Christ from its inception. If there is uncertainty as to who is the true head of the church or if the unity in faith and morals that should exist between members of the one body is not realized, then the church has within itself the power to gather in a general council in order to restore its hierarchical constitution and unity. Gerson thus returns in his argumentation to his basic exegesis of Dt 32:4: *Dei perfecta sunt opera.*[58]

---

[57] *De auferibilitate sponsi ab Ecclesia*, G, 3, 298. "Additum est: non facta divinitus institutione nova; quia Spiritu sancto dictante et operante, nova praestari posset auctoritas qualis nondum collata est. . . ."

[58] *Libellus articulorum contra Petrum de Luna*, G, 6, 266.

He finds additional scriptural support for his position both in Ephesians and Hosea. While he does not cite the exact passages in the fourth chapter of Ephesians to which he is referring, it is obvious that Gerson has in mind Eph 4:46 wherein is described the oneness of body and spirit that is to characterize the church. In the church there is to be one faith, one baptism, one God. Eph 4:11, moreover, enumerates the various divisions of offices that characterize the early church: apostles, prophets, evangelists, pastors and teachers. There can be no doubt that Gerson sees here the hierarchical structure of the early church as instituted by Christ. In the first chapter of Hosea, Gerson is clearly referring to the final verse, which was the main theme of his address to the English delegation on its way to the Council of Pisa. Hos 1:11 proclaims that the sons of Judah and Israel are to gather together and appoint for themselves one head. The Scriptural parallels with the Councils of Pisa and Constance are obvious.[59]

3. HIERARCHICAL ACTIVITY

Our study thus far has shown that hierarchy and order are central to Gerson's understanding of the church. He sees the universe as a complete hierarchical system. Within that system he singles out three major hierarchical orders: the supercelestial, the celestial and the subcelestial. The first or supercelestial hierarchy is that of the Blessed Trinity. The second or celestial hierarchy comprises the nine orders of angels which are further divided into three subhierarchies. The church constitutes the third or subcelestial hierarchy. The question now arises as to the type of activity characteristic of the various hierarchies. Following closely in the Dionysian tradition, Gerson identifies this activity with the threefold functions of *purgare, illuminare,* and *perficere*: purgation, illumination, and perfection. These activities are generically the same in all hierarchies.[60]

Gerson rarely speaks of the Trinity as purifying, illuminating, and perfecting the celestial hierarchies. When discussing hierarchical activity within the celestial hierarchies, he refers primarily to Christ.

---

[59] *Propositio facta coram Anglicis*, G, 6, 126.

[60] For Dionysius' use of the hierarchical activities of purgation, illumination, and perfection see *De coelesti hierarchia*, 3, 1, *MPG*, 3, 165 B-C. Practically every page of his *De coelesti hierarchia* and *De ecclesiastica hierarchia* contains some reference to the hierarchical activities.

Placed higher in the hierarchical order than the angels, Christ is able to purify, illuminate, and perfect the entire world of spiritual creatures.[61] The blessed in heaven are also illuminated and perfected by him.[62] Christ's hierarchical activities reach also into the realm of the subcelestial hierarchy. He especially purifies, illuminates and perfects his bishops in the church so that they might more effectively carry out their hierarchical functions with regard to those subject to them.[63] Christ, moreover, is portrayed by Gerson as purifying, illuminating and perfecting the activities of all Christians and thereby leading them to peace and truth.[64]

The angels also possess the hierarchical powers of purgation, illumination, and perfection within the celestial hierarchies according to their respective rank. The first angelic triad directs its hierarchical activity towards the lower angelic orders but because of its exalted hierarchical position it itself is not the recipient of hierarchical action from other angelic spirits. The intermediate triad of angels is both the agent and recipient of hierarchical action. This middle triad is purified, illuminated and perfected by the first triad of angles and in turn purifies, illuminates and perfects the lower angelic triad. The lowest angelic triad is only the recipient of hierarchical activity; it is purified, illuminated and perfected by the intermediate triad of angels, but does not exercise those activities on behalf of other angelic spirits.[65] In accordance with Dionysian principles, however, the lowest of the angelic hierarchies purifies, illuminates, and perfects the subcelestial hierarchy which is the church.[66]

---

[61] *Apparuit gratia*, G, 5, 67-68. "Nam et benigna humanitas Dei Salvatoris nostri universum mundum spiritualium aeternarumque creaturarum purgat, illuminat et perficit, superior eis in ordine hierarchico stabilita ut sol quidam aeternitatis."

[62] *Apparuit gratia*, G, 5, 68. ". . . beatos illuminat et perficit in coelo. . . ."

[63] *Domine si in tempore hoc*, G, 5, 212. ". . . vestrum est officium ut ceteros purgetis, illuminetis, perficiatis, quatenus coelestem portent imaginem; idcirco vos purgavi, illuminavi, perfici quia nec sordulentum mundificat, nec tenebrosum illuminat, nec diminuta perficiunt."

[64] *Reverendo in Christo . . . Poscenti reverendissimae*, G, 2, 335. "Suscipiatur obsequium istud servitutis meae et placeat in Domino cujus res agitur, qui purget, illuminet et perficiat actiones omnium christianorum fidelium suorum in viam veritatis et pacis, qui et reverendam paternitatem vestram conservet feliciter et longaeve."

[65] *De potestate ecclesiastica*, G, 6, 227. "Unde licet quoad naturam, gratiam et gloriam sit quilibet angelus immediate formatus a Deo, nihilominus quoad exercitium actuum hierarchorum qui sunt purgare, illuminare et perficere, tres primi ordines hierarchizant non hierarchizati ab aliis: tres medii hierarchizantur et hierarchizant, tres infirmi hierarchizantur et non alios angelos hierarchizant."

[66] *De potestate ecclesiastica*, G, 6, 214-215. ". . . prout inferior angelorum hierarchia purgat, illuminat et perficit subcoelestem vel humanam hierarchiam. . . ."

Just as the church mirrors the angelic orders in its hierarchical structure so too does it imitate those orders in its hierarchical activity. Papacy and cardinalate purify, illuminate, and perfect the lower segments of the ecclesiastical hierarchy without in turn being purified, illuminated, or perfected by any other division of the hierarchy. Bishops and priests are, as it were, the middle segments of the ecclesiastical hierarchy and as such purify, illuminate, and perfect the lower elements of the church, namely, laity and religious, and in turn are purified, illumined, and perfected by the upper division of the ecclesiastical hierarchy. The laity and religious, in imitation of the lowest angelic order, are purified, illumined, and perfected by the episcopacy and priesthood, but themselves possess no such hierarchical powers.[67]

With the concentration of hierarchical activity solely in the first and second divisions of the ecclesiastical hierarchy, Gerson concludes that those divisions essentially constitute the church. The laity, among whom Gerson especially mentions women, does not possess hierarchical power and is consequently less a part of the church than popes, cardinals, bishops, and priests. The church thus becomes essentially a church of prelates.[68] For Gerson, moreover, the whole of Christianity has its foundation in the order of prelates; God has so constituted his church that the prelates have been entrusted with the task of governing his people and leading them back to him. For this purpose prelates have been given the hierarchical powers of purification, illumination, and perfection. Only by respecting the order of prelates and its authority can the church be sure that it is properly imitating the hierarchical order of the celestial realm.[69]

---

[67] *De potestate ecclesiastica*, G, 6, 227. Cf. *Responsio ad errores de orationibus privatis fidelium*, P, 2, 654 A. "Ecclesia secundum tres actus hierarchicos, qui sunt purgare, et illuminare et perficere, continet tres ordines principales, scilicet supremum, infimum et medium. Supremus purgat, illuminat et perficit et non e contra. Infimus purgatur, illuminatur et perficitur et non e contra. Medius participat in utroque."

[68] *Responsio ad errores de orationibus privatis fidelium*, P, 2, 654 A. "Ecclesia consistit principalius in ordine primo et secundo, quam in tertio, qui est ordo laicorum, et maxime feminarum, quibus actus hierarchici nullo modo conveniunt, nec ordines sacri, nec praedicatio publica vel solemnis, juxta prohibitionem Apostoli."

[69] *Quomodo stabit regnum*, G, 7, 982. "Le royaume de crestiente est fonde et institue en ordre ou ordenance hierarchique de prelations, c'est a dire que Dieu ordena son eglise en ceste maniere qu'il veult ordre de prelature en sainte eglise pour gouverner les autres et les adrecier a Dieu, selon trois operacions qui appartiennent a prelature: purger, enluminer, et parfaire. Et en gardant cest ordre doit estre estable le royaume de sainte eglise ca jus car ainsi est ou royaume de cielz lassus."

The notion of hierarchical functions takes on added importance when seen in the context of a general council. If the episcopal and priestly office is defined primarily in terms of the hierarchical functions of purgation, illumination and perfection, then it is most logical that an ecumenical council would provide the highest opportunities for the exercise of those functions. As the assembly of bishops and clergy, the council can, therefore, be defined in terms of the hierarchical activities which it collectively exercises. The council, indeed, should be the place, par excellence, wherein the hierarchical activities find their fullest realization.

This in effect is what Gerson tells the bishops and clergy in his famous sermon, *Ambulate dum lucem habetis*, given at Constance on March 23, 1415, shortly after the withdrawal of John XXIII from the city. Gerson argues that if the episcopal office has been given to them primarily in order that they might purify, illumine and perfect those committed to their care, then the council provides the best opportunities for the exercise of those activities, for it is then that the entire hierarchical order of the church is gathered together to seek God's mercy and enlightenment as it determines what actions are to be taken for the church's benefit. The bishops are to purge, illumine and perfect a church torn by schism, threatened by heresy, and engulfed in a moral corruption that permeates the entire ecclesiastical body.[70]

Gerson's teaching on the hierarchical functions of purgation, illumination, and perfection becomes further defined as he specifies the concrete means by which those activities are realized by the clergy and the church. At times he summarily describes hierarchical activities as the celebration of Mass, the administration of the sacraments, and the preaching of sermons.[71] Elsewhere, however, he goes into more detail about their nature. The hierarchical activity of purgation is achieved primarily through the processes of excommunication and interdict in the external forum. In the realm of the internal forum, purgation is attained through the sacraments of

---

[70] *Ambulate dum lucem habetis*, G, 5, 40, "Siquidem in hoc constituti estis alios purgare, illuminare atque perficere, nunc maxime cum factus conventus iste sacrosanctus, dum adunatus est coetus, dum congregata est Ecclesia. . . ."

[71] *Responsio ad errores de orationibus privatis fidelium*, P, 2, 656 B. ". . . quae subinde suas orationes praeferant vel praeferri gaudeant, actibus hierarchicis saecularium, qui sunt missas celebrare, sacramenta ministrare, praedicationibus insistere."

baptism and penance which have as their primary purpose the removal of sin in the believer and his full restoration to fellowship with God.

Illumination takes place principally through the activities of preaching and doctrinal teaching. University sermons and disputations can especially serve to illumine the human intellect. The administration of the sacraments other than baptism and penance comprises the hierarchical activity of perfection. These sacraments bring their recipients to the fullness of Christian life: union with God in charity.[72] As will be seen in later chapters, Gerson frequently considers all the sacraments, baptism and penance as well, as instruments of perfection. Among the sacraments, the Eucharist holds a place of special importance. For Gerson, the immediate aim of all hierarchical activity is to lead the members of Christ's mystical body to his sacramental body as contained in the Eucharist.[73]

The specification of the hierarchical functions of purgation, illumination and perfection reveals, consequently, a strong sacramental orientation in Gerson's thought, especially in the areas of purgation and perfection. The role of Scripture is also of great importance since in the process of illumination primary emphasis is placed upon preaching the Word of God. Closely allied with Scripture, for Gerson, is the study of theology which he describes as an affective reflection upon the Scriptures in the spirit of faith, hope, and charity. This reflection must then be translated into action through preaching and the personal example of a virtuous life.[74]

---

[72] De potestate ecclesiastica, G, 6, 218-219. On the role of university sermons and disputations see Gratia tibi frater et pax, G, 2, 276.

[73] Responsio ad errores de orationibus privatis fidelium, P, 2, 654 B. "Valor et dignitas actuum hierarchicorum in Ecclesia principaliter attenditur per reductionem corporis mystici seu politici ad Corpus Christi verum quod in eucharistia sacramentaliter continetur, et quod usque in finem seculi permanebit nobiscum...." Gerson here exemplifies the tradition of using the term corpus mysticum to designate the church and corpus verum as applying to the Eucharist. The term corpus mysticum first came into use in Carolingian times and was applied to the Eucharist to distinguish it from the physical body of Christ, the corpus verum. At the same time, the church was designated as the corpus Christi. As a result of the Eucharistic controversies on transubstantiation in the mid-twelfth century, the Eucharist became designated as the corpus verum or the corpus Christi, while the term corpus mysticum was applied to the church. Thus the term corpus mysticum was transformed from a liturgical and sacramental idea into one with sociological content and implications. The entire history of this gradual transformation has been studied by Henri de Lubac, Corpus Mysticum (Paris, 1949).

[74] De consolatione theologiae, P, 1, 177 B.

4. FINALITY OF HIERARCHICAL ACTIVITY

The study of hierarchical activity in Gerson's thought has already given us some indication of its finality. In brief, the ultimate goal of hierarchical activity is to lead all members of the church to union with God. This aim is abstractly but succinctly expressed by Gerson in what can be called the principle of reduction: *"ut infima reducantur ad suprema per media."* [75] The *infima* refers primarily to the laity and religious; the *media* to the hierarchical orders of pope, bishops and priests to whom are entrusted the hierarchical activities of purgation, illumination and perfection. The *suprema* represents the celestial and angelic kingdom of which the church is a faithful image. In its full sense, the *suprema* refers to Christ and to the supercelestial hierarchy, i.e. the Holy Trinity. The ultimate purpose, then, of all hierarchical activity within the church is to lead its members to Christ and through Christ to the Trinity. For Gerson, therefore, hierarchical activity is essentially reductive in nature and is ordinarily achieved through intermediaries.

The importance that Gerson places upon intermediaries is manifested in a sermon given about 1392 for the feast of Saints Peter and Paul. Speaking of the miraculous revelation made to St. Paul on the road to Damascus which resulted in his conversion, Gerson proposes an objection that might be raised by one of his audience. If God revealed himself directly to all men as he did to St. Paul, everyone would be immediately converted. Gerson personally finds this suggestion scandalous. To demand such a course of action would be tantamount to denying the need for human intermediaries. In the normal course of events, conversions of faith take place through the human medium of preaching. He is undoubtedly referring to the Pauline notion of *fides ex auditu* in Rom 10:17. He compares God's proclamation of salvation through the mediation of human preachers to a king who promulgates his decrees through royal messengers. To ask that a king promulgate his legislation without the aid of

---

[75] *Quomodo stabit regnum*, G, 7, 981. I have been unable to find this phrase or its equivalent in *De divinis nominibus*, 7, as claimed by Gerson. The principle behind the phrase, however, is definitely Dionysian and can be found essentially in *De coelesti hierarchia*, 4, 3, MPG 3, 181 A: "...ὡς τῆς θεονομικῆς τάξεως ἐκεῖνο θεσμοθετούσης, τὸ διὰ τῶν πρώτων τὰ δεύτερα πρὸς τὸ θεῖον ἀνάγεσται." See also *De coelesti hierarchia* MPG, 3, 210 A-B; 8, 2, MPG, 3, 239 C-D, and *De ecclesiastica hierarchia*, 1, 2, MPG, 3, 373 A.

intermediaries is inconceivable. So too is it inconceivable that God would dispense with human intermediaries in his normal activities. Gerson considers such a possibility as destructive of human society and fellowship. He concludes his reflections on the issue of mediation by reasserting the basic Dionysian principle that the lowest must be led to the highest by intermediaries.[76]

Closely related to the idea of intermediaries is the notion of participated perfection. Just as in all hierarchical order there are gradations so too are there gradations in the various perfections within that order. The perfections involved in the exercise of hierarchical activity are possessed to the fullest degree by the highest members of the hierarchical order and are then found in the intermediate or lower members of the hierarchy according to their respective hierarchical rank. Thus it is that the virtue of wisdom is found in a more eminent degree in the angelic order of the Seraphim than in the Cherubim.[77] In the area of faith, Gerson clearly affirms that men must be brought to a better knowledge of their faith by those who are their superiors in such matters. Consequently the latter must have a fuller and firmer grasp on the essentials of their belief. He argues that his position has the support of St. Thomas Aquinas and Dionysius the Areopagite.[78]

The union with God which results from hierarchical activity is essentially a union of love. This union is most perfectly realized in heaven through the fullness of charity which is characteristic of the beatific vision. In heaven, the church fully reflects the order of the celestial hierarchies, truly becomes the new Jerusalem, and is completely united with its head, Christ. While on earth, however, the church is but a partial image of its celestial archetype. The union in love so characteristic of its final and heavenly state is on earth but inchoative and progressive.[79] That progress in charity is achieved through the proper functioning of hierarchical order within the

---

[76] *Nimis honorati sunt*, G, 7, 728.

[77] *Jacob autem genuit Joseph*, G, 5, 345. "Nam habet hoc hierarchicus ordo secundum Dionysium, ut inferiores virtutes sint in superioribus perfectiori modo repositae, quemadmodum sapientia perfectior est in seraphim quam in cherubin."

[78] *De protestatione circa materiam fidei*, G, 6, 159-160. "Notetur pro consideratione sanctus Thomas, 2, 2, q. 2, a. 6. Explicatio, inquit, fidei ad inferiores homines oportet quod veniat per majores; quod probat auctoritate Dionysii; concludens quod oportet eos pleniorem habere notitiam de credendis, et magis explicite credere." See *De coelesti hierarchia*, 12, 2, *MPG*, 3, 292 D-293 A.

[79] *Domine si in tempore hoc*, G, 5, 212.

church, primarily through the administration of the sacraments, which serve as the main channels of divine grace and love. As long as hierarchical order is preserved in the church, hierarchical activity will be properly exercised, and the consequence will be increased charity and progressive union with God.

The result of such union and love is peace. Although Gerson's concept of the church as a hierarchy reveals strong Dionysian influence, he relies more upon Augustine for his concept of peace. Dionysius describes the finality of hierarchical order principally in terms of love and union and does not explicitly develop the interrelationship of peace and the ecclesiastical hierarchy. Peace in Dionysius' thought, moreover, is primarily cosmic; it is the source of universal concord and harmony.[80] Gerson regards Augustine's concept of peace as more expressly formulated in terms of order and more personal and social in orientation. Following Augustine, therefore, he defines peace as the tranquility which comes from order.[81] Peace is the maintenance of proper hierarchical order within the church. As long as hierarchical order is preserved, the church will enjoy peace. Hierarchical order, moreover, can only exist and function in a context of peace. Such peace, finally, is salvific, for the hierarchical activities of purgation, illumination, and perfection result in union and love of God.[82]

The growth of love, union, and peace within the church is, in effect, the building up of Christ's mystical body. The peaceful functioning of hierarchical order, therefore, results in the growth of the church. As this growth continues the church becomes more unified with Christ and more reflective of its celestial archetype. The finality of all hierarchical activity, therefore, can also be expressed as the edification of Christ's mystical body. This finality is manifested in the fact that the grace which accompanies every hierarchical state within the church is a *gratia gratis data* or charism. As such it does not result primarily in the sanctification of the possessor but rather in the sanctification of others. Such grace has been given to the church's ministers for the common good and has for its ultimate purpose the

---

[80] *De divinis nominibus*, 11, 1-2, *MPL*, 3, 948 D-952 A.

[81] *Dedit illi gloriam regni*, G, 5, 185. "Est autem pax tranquillitas ordinis secundum Augustinum." Cf. *De civitate Dei*, 19, 13, *CCSL*, 48, p. 679. For a study of Augustine's concept of peace see Ernst Bernheim, *Mittelalterliche Zeitanschauungen in ihrem Einfluss auf Politik und Geschichtsschreibung* (Tübingen, 1918), pp. 1-23.

[82] *Apparuit gratia*, G, 5, 84.

growth and development of the church.[83] Every hierarchical office
and dignity exists solely for the building up of the church and for its
general welfare. All office exists for service and all service is directed
to the edification of the church as Christ's mystical body.[84]

Gerson's teaching on the edification of the mystical body is deeply
rooted in Pauline theology. The key scriptural passages upon which
he relies are 1 Cor 12 : 4-11, Eph 4 : 10-16 and 2 Cor 13 : 10. In 1
Cor 12 : 4-11 Paul enumerates the varieties of gifts within the church:
wisdom, knowledge, faith, healing, miracles, prophecy, discernment
of spirits, tongues, and their interpretation. Despite the plurality of
gifts, the same spirit works in each towards the attainment of the
common good. In Eph 4 : 10-16 Paul tells his readers that Christ has
established the various offices of apostles, prophets, pastors and
teachers primarily for building up the body of Christ. By these offices
Christians are to be so aided that they will grow into the fullness of
Christ who is the head of the church. This growth takes place in love
when each part of the mystical body is functioning properly. In 2
Cor 13 : 10 Paul explains to the Christians at Corinth that the
authority which he has from the Lord is for building up and not for
tearing down the mystical body.

Gerson adds his own orientation to the Pauline teaching on office
when he specifies that the highest form of ecclesiastical office is to be
found in the papacy and then in descending order through the ranks
of patriarchs, archbishops, bishops, archpriests, and curates. The
more charismatic offices stressed by St. Paul such as prophets,
discerners of spirits and interpreters of tongues are all subordinated to
the hierarchical structure of the church.[85] While transforming the
Pauline concept of office into one of a primarily hierarchical nature,
Gerson, nonetheless, situates the thrust of hierarchical order within
the context of the edification of the mystical body. Gerson, in effect,
has subordinated the Dionysian and Augustinian elements of his
thought to an overall Pauline orientation. His concept of the church,

---

[83] *De nobilitate*, P, 3, 213 C. "...omnis itaque potestas gratiarum gratis datarum
supernaturaliter ad aedificationem Ecclesiae per Christum, est eminentia quaedam
notabilis. ..."

[84] *De auferibilitate sponsi ab Ecclesia*, G, 3, 300. "Nullum quippe statum, nullum
gradum dignitatis, nullam ministrationis genus dedit Deus nisi in aedificationem suam
et utilitatem communem. Patet ad Eph. iv et I ad Cor. xii." Cf. *De modo se habendi
tempore schismatis*, G, 6, 31.

[85] *De nobilitate*, P, 3, 213 C-D.

therefore, emerges as a highly personal synthesis of Dionysian, Augustinian, and Pauline thought.

5. *Semen Vivificum et Reformativum*

The church for Gerson is primarily an image of a celestial archetype; its structure is hierarchically ordered with a distinct set of hierarchical functions whose aim is the production of love, union, and peace which terminate in the edification of the mystical body. The question now emerges as to what principles in his thought provide for the continual reform and renewal of the church? Fragmented by the Great Schism which had lasted since 1378, plagued by numerous heresies, especially those of Wyclif and Hus, submerged under extensive moral corruption, the church of Gerson's times was hardly a true image of its celestial archetype. Innumerable deformities in its hierarchical structure had occurred, notably the deformity introduced by the lack of a single head. The exercise of the church's hierarchical functions on the part of her ministers left much to be desired. The peace that should reign in its realms was nowhere to be found. The law of charity which was to rule its institutions was frequently violated. In short, instead of being built up, the mystical body of Christ was in the process of being torn down.

The calamities that befell the church were always regarded by Gerson essentially as perversions of the duly constituted hierarchical order. The disturbances within the church are such that it is unable to see in itself the celestial similitude from which it draws its life. The church is reduced to a *similitudo inferni* where chaos has replaced *ordo*. Whereas the order characteristic of its celestial archetype brings life to the church, chaos results in death. The order in which the church was established is rarely taught in the schools and much less is it observed in the domain of morality.[86] The sins of Lucifer and Adam, from whom stems all disorder in the world, are basically sins of persons who through pride transgressed their proper

---

[86] *Domine si in tempore hoc*, G, 5, 212-213. "Sed heu, quid de calamitate praesentium temporum querar misera, quibus pro coelesti ordine perturbor confusione et ex similitudine coelesti quae mihi vita est, ad inferni similitudinem ubi nullus ordo sed sempiternus horror inhabitat, quae mihi mors est, manibus impiis pertrahor. Denique ex distinctissima membrorum decentia in chaos anaxagoreum nisi manus conditoris retentaret, prope dilaberer. Siccine mi rex te sequor? Siccini coelos peto? Siccini matris coelestis veneratur imago? Vix jam ordo meus quem instituisti, legitur in libris, quanto minus in moribus."

order.[87] The trials of the present time are all caused by failure to observe due order. Too many are unwilling to be content with their state; too many refuse to remain within the just bounds of their order. They are impatient with limits set by their forefathers.[88]

The schism naturally remained the greatest deformity in the church's order since it affected all Christians whether good or bad.[89] Since the schism posed the greatest threat to the church's order, the removal of that deformity should be placed before all else.[90] Heresy, another major problem facing the church, is also seen in the context of order. Heretics and heresies corrupt hierarchical order. They profess that they are loyal to the principles of the faith but when challenged they resort to sophistries and subterfuge. Their replies are deceitful and they frequently use language as an escape. They have tainted the kingdom of England and destroyed the University of Prague. Gerson is here undoubtedly referring to the followers of Wyclif and Hus. The very principles of their teaching are destructive of the hierarchical structure of the church. The most serious charge that Gerson can lay against them is that they have violated one of the basic tenets of hierarchical order. By their attacks upon the hierarchy they are unwilling to recognize the principle: "*quod infima per media reducantur ad Deum.*" They prevent man from being led to God through the agency of the church's hierarchical order.[91]

In the realm of morals, Gerson complains that the beauty of the church's order which consisted in the virtues of its clergy has disappeared. No longer is the church an image of the heavenly hierarchy. Under its former clergy the church flourished in a spirit of great felicity, for the clergy preserved in its lives the celestial virtues of wisdom and faith; it was aflame with the love of God and rooted

---

[87] *Quomodo stabit regnum*, G, 7, 981. "Appert que s'aucun homme ou aucun estat veult sans raison ou necessite troubler cest ordre, on luy doit resister. Car ainsy fut fait ou ciel quant Lucifer ou les anges mauvais voulurent par orgueil passer leur ranc, leur ordre ou hierarchie."

[88] *Domine si in tempore hoc*, G, 5, 216. "Exinde confusionem praesentis temporis reduces ad distinctionem ordinis. Coges quemque suum tenere locum, suo gradu contentari, officium exercere ordinis suscepti, limites non excedere, non pertubare terminos positos a patribus."

[89] *De futuri summi pontificis electione*, G, 6, 282. "Item deformitas Ecclesiae in hoc quod vacet papa, est prae omnibus deformitatibus generalior quod tangit bonos et malos et omnes generaliter christianos."

[90] *De futuri summi pontificis electione*, G, 6, 280. "... quoniam aliter Ecclesia exponitur discrimini ut remaneat acephala a tali capite, quae est maxima deformatio Ecclesiae; cujus deformitatis reformatio prae ceteris est necessaria."

[91] *De sensu litterali sacrae scripturae*, P, 1, 7 A-B.

solidly in true hope. The establishment and expansion of the church was built upon the virtues of its clergy. The contemporary clergy, however, is characterized by carnal prudence, love of the world, and hope in false values. By their vices, clerics have brought ruin upon the church and considerably restricted its growth.[92] By their lack of humility they destroy the hierarchical order of the church.[93] Even archbishops ignore the rights of their ecclesiastical superiors. Though they appeal to custom or dispensation to justify their actions, these actions remain essentially unjust for they are a violation of hierarchical order. Suffragan bishops do not escape censure, for they too are charged with similar injustices toward their metropolitans.[94]

The continued controversy with the mendicants which had been raging in the church ever since their inception was looked upon by Gerson in terms of hierarchical order.[95] In his sermon against Alexander V's Bull of October 12, 1409, *Regnans in excelsis*, Gerson complained that the bull was destructive of hierarchical order. The concessions made to the mendicants in the areas of preaching and hearing confessions undermined the office of prelates and, consequently, the very structure of the church.[96]

Related to the issue of the mendicants was the question of what form of life was more appropriate for preaching God's Word: a life based on poverty or one which allowed material possessions. Gerson strongly criticizes those who applaud when preachers speak of depriving the church and her ministers of their wealth and property but suddenly become silent when the issue turns to such topics as the honor due prelates, the preservation of their liberties or their obligations to defend the faith with their own lives. When the former themes are discussed, no one seems to care how long the sermon runs; when the latter subjects arise, there is hissing, unrest, murmurs

---

[92] *Domine si in tempore hoc*, G, 5, 214. "Profecto ex foedis inquinamentis clericorum; unde quia periere virtutes ex quibus foecunda similitudo mea ad coelestem hierarchiam intemerata salvabatur, sublatus est simul omnis decor ordinis in quo prima fundabatur."

[93] *A Deo exivit*, G, 5, 21.

[94] *Domine si in tempore hoc*, G, 5, 214.

[95] On the history of the controversy between the secular and religious clergy see Y. M.-J. Congar, "Aspects ecclésiologiques de la querelle entre mendiants et séculiers dans la seconde moitié du xiiiᵉ siècle et le début du xivᵉ," *AHDL*, 28 (1961), 35-151. A brief summary of the controversy of 1409 is found in Connolly, *John Gerson*, pp. 108-110.

[96] *Quomodo stabit regnum*, G, 7, 983. "Nous pouvons bien dire en general que ceste escripture, s'elle passoit, troubleroit l'ordre hierarchique de prelas de saincte eglise, grans, moiens et petis qui sont les cures."

and often calls for an end to the sermon. Gerson warns the pastors of the church not to let such attitudes go unchecked; if they do the final result will be chaos and confusion within the hierarchical order of the church.[97]

He censures mendicants for not practicing the poverty appropriate to their religious state. Their failure, moreover, to live up to their proper place in the church is disruptive of hierarchical order. Mendicants should strive to imitate the charity of the Seraphim and the wisdom of the Cherubim, but their quest for wealth is such that the attainment of these virtues is rendered impossible. They avidly seek after hierarchical offices and the accumulation of benefices. In their pursuit of wealth they quickly outdistance others who do not even have a vow of poverty. They continually seek new privileges and exemptions from Rome with the result that the hierarchical structure of the church is considerably weakened.[98]

Hierarchical order is further threatened by the overcentralization of the church in the area of benefices, ecclesiastical appointments, reservation of sins and excommunication. The papacy has assumed such absolute control over benefices and appointments that it has usurped much of the power of the episcopacy. All cases are appealed from the local ordinary to Rome even when a diocese has a university where such matters can be settled locally. Hierarchical order is also weakened by the accumulation of benefices and territory. House is added to house and field to field; exemptions are so readily obtained that regulations prohibiting incompatible benefices are no longer effective. Income from benefices is collected whether or not one resides at the location of his benefice. Finally, the occupant of a benefice can both possess the income from his benefice and not be required to advance to sacred orders.[99]

Gerson's objection to the inauguration of new and private liturgical rites within the church is also based on the notion of hierarchical order. Private additions to the officially accepted liturgical rites cause sedition, partiality and superstition among the people. Priests do not have the right to institute new rites arbitrarily. The multifold composition of the church requires a stable and orderly liturgy, capable of accommodating itself to the young and old, the rich and the poor. Private initiative in the realm of liturgical rites only results

---

[97] *De nuptiis Christi et Ecclesiae*, G, 6, 202.
[98] *Domine si in tempore hoc*, G, 5, 213.
[99] *De potestate ecclesiastica*, G, 6, 239-240.

in the disturbance and confusion of the hierarchical order. Proper hierarchical order demands that all liturgical activities be performed according to the manner prescribed by competent ecclesiastical authority.[100]

The Roman Curia also comes under sharp criticism from Gerson. He compares the curia to the first angelic triad of Seraphim, Cherubim and Thrones. As an image of this triad the curia should be so ordered in all its activities that it reflects the charity of the Seraphim; it should be resplendent with the divine wisdom of the Cherubim. Finally in imitation of the Thrones, the curia should be most steadfast in the exercise of equity. Unfaithful to its celestial image and ignorant of the hierarchical order that should prevail within its ranks, the curia of Gerson's time was a far cry from its heavenly archetype. The confusion and disorder within the curia is such that it might better be called a *curia peccatorum* rather than the image of the first celestial hierarchy.[101]

Given Gerson's concept of the church with its stress on celestial archetypes, hierarchical order and hierarchical functions, the basic principles of his thinking on reform emerge clearly. Reform will entail a return to the celestial archetypes. The church, therefore, will be called upon to mirror more closely the model upon which it has been patterned. This return to celestial archetypes will consist primarily in the restoration of hierarchical order and the proper reorientation of all hierarchical activity. The primary end, moreover, of such reform is the union and peace of the church which, in turn, terminates in its growth as the mystical body of Christ.

For the general reform of the entire hierarchical order, the council emerges in Gerson's thought as the most effective instrument. To the council is to be entrusted the task of resolving the hierarchical disorder caused by schism, heresy, and moral decline. Gerson had learned from personal experience not to place his hopes for reform upon the papacy. The papacy, indeed, as an instrument of reform is conspicuously absent in Gerson's writing after 1408. This absence reflects the disillusionment he encountered in his personal endeavors in 1407 to convince Gregory XII and Benedict XIII to adopt the *via*

---

[100] *Contra sectam se flagellantium*, P, 2, 661 C.

[101] *Apparuit gratia*, G, 5, 77. "Sed et curia sua, curia Romana, quae ad similitudinem primae hierarchiae angelicae ordinanda erat et replenda viris caritate fervidis et contemplatione suspensis ut Seraphim, viris sapientia divina splendidis ut Cherubim, viris aequitate firmissimis ut Throni, nonne mutabitur in curiam peccantium?"

cessionis. Had both popes resigned the schism would have been resolved, the church restored to peace, and the path to reform opened.

Disappointed with the prospects of papal initiative in the area of reform, Gerson turned to the *via concilii* and became a strong proponent of the Council of Pisa in 1409. The election of Alexander V temporarily restored his hope in the papacy as a leader in the reform of the church but these hopes were soon shattered when he realized that the actions at Pisa had merely accentuated the schism and resulted in three contendants for the papacy instead of the single pope that Christendom so ardently desired.[102] Gerson then turned decisively towards the *via concilii* as a solution for the ills of the church and rejoiced at the convocation of the Council of Constance in December, 1413. Gerson's hopes for reform were again threatened by the departure of John XXIII from Constance on March 21, 1415. With the existence of the council jeopardized by the pope's action, Gerson rose in the council to deliver his famous address, *Ambulate dum lucem habetis*, which served to rally the spirit of the council and renewed the determination of the bishops to pursue their work of solving the schism and inaugurating the general reform of the church.

In this sermon, given before the Council of Constance on March 23, 1415, Gerson reminds the bishops that the church has no more efficacious means for its general reformation than that of continued councils.[103] He tells the bishops that after the settlement of the schism and the restoration of the papacy to its proper place in the hierarchical order of the church, they should strive to remove all heresy within the church. Heresy, as seen earlier, was considered an obstacle to proper hierarchical order. His call for the restoration of hierarchical order is to extend to bishops and parish clergy as well. Too long has the order of prelates been in chaos and disarray. Let all hierarchical order be reformed according to the likeness of the celestial hierarchy and the rules established at the beginning of the church's existence.[104] While Gerson does not clarify the exact nature

---

[102] *Domine si in tempore hoc*, G, 5, 204, 217.

[103] *Ambulate dum lucem habetis*, G, 5, 45. "Ecclesia non habet efficacius medium ad generalem sui ipsius reformationem quam si statuatur generalium conciliorum continuatio, celebrationem provincialium non omittendo."

[104] *Ambulate dum lucem habetis*, G, 5, 45. "Ecclesia seu generale concilium praecipue debet intendere cum prosecutione unius perfecte ad extirpationem errorum et emendationem errantium sine personarum acceptione; similiter ad hoc quod

of the rules which governed the early church, it is safe to conclude that he is referring here to divine law contained in the Scriptures. The Scriptures are, in effect, the constitution of the primitive church. This conclusion is further substantiated by the important role played by law in all conciliar attempts at reform.

The effectiveness of the council as an agent for the reform of the hierarchical order is rooted in the fact that the church has within itself the resources for its own reformation. Gerson maintains that the church is endowed with a *semen vivificum et reformativum* which has both a conservative and a reformative role in its life. At times he calls the *semen* a *vis insita spiritualis* or an *ars quaedam vivifica*. This *semen* permeates the entire body of the church and guarantees the continued existence of its hierarchical order through successive generations.[105] The reformative activity of the *semen* is manifested in the fact that it is capable of restoring proper order to the church whenever deformities occur in its hierarchical structure. Under its influence the church is restored to the unity that characterized the early days of its institution. Gerson sees this unity as one of faith, morals, and hierarchical structure. He argues that this is the unity to which St. Paul refers in Eph 4 : 4-6, 15-16 when he speaks of one Lord, one faith, one baptism and one body under one head.[106]

Gerson discovers scriptural evidence for his notion of the *semen* in Is 1 : 9 where the prophet proclaims that unless the Lord had left his people a *semen*, that is to say, a few survivors, they would have become like Sodom and Gomorrah. The survivors that Isaiah refers to are those that were left after the destruction of Judah by Sennacherib in 701 B.C. While the prophet does not seem to have used the term *semen* in the technical sense of the faithful remnant so prominent in Old Testament thought, it is highly probable that Gerson so interpreted the term and applied it to his teaching on the hierarchical

---

hierarchicus ordo ecclesiasticus praelatorum et curatorum multipliciter turbatus, reformetur ad similitudinem coelestis hierarchiae et conformiter ad regulas primitus institutas."

[105] *De auferibilitate sponsi ab Ecclesia*, G, 3, 297. "Hoc autem semen quid aliud debet intelligi quam vis insita spiritualis et ars quaedam vivifica per universum corpus Ecclesiae per quam hierarchicus ordo potest usque in finem subsistere."

[106] *Propositio facta coram Anglicis*, G, 6, 126. "Habemus praeterea causam quodammodo formalem, et ad hujus celebrationem concilii vivifice praeparantem; quae forma est semen Dei vivum et efficax, semen Spiritus Sancti habens virtutem formativam et reformativam totius unitatis, sub uno Deo et Domino, per omnem juncturam secundum deductionem apostoli ad Eph. iv."

order of the church.[107] In any case, Gerson's conclusion was that just as God had left Judah a *semen* which guaranteed its continuation after the destruction by Sennacherib so has he left the church a *semen* which will guarantee the continuance of its hierarchical order despite the disturbances occasioned by the prolonged schism.

Another scriptural example of the *semen* is seen in the Mosaic Law, for in that law the priestly caste is perpetuated either through the first born or through the hereditary succession of sons.[108] If such is the case in the Old Testament how much more fitting is it that the most perfect law of grace in which the church is constituted should have within itself the resources for the legitimate continuation of its hierarchical order? Gerson, moreover, understands Mt 24 : 34 to imply just that. When Christ said that this generation will not pass away, he was referring primarily to the apostles and disciples. These two groups constitute for Gerson the entire hierarchical order of the early church. The present hierarchical order is but the continuation of that established by the apostles and disciples. To all Christ promised in Mt 28 : 20 his presence and support until the consummation of time. Gerson also finds extra scriptural support for his notion of a *semen* in the law of nature. The Lord has endowed all his creatures with a *semen* which insures their continued generation according to their respective genus and species.[109]

While he clearly delineates the conservative and reformative function of the *semen vivificum et reformativum*, Gerson says relatively little about its nature. From what he does say, it is certain that the *semen* is directly related to the Holy Spirit, for it is implanted in the hierarchical order through the instrumentality of the Spirit.[110] To be more exact, the *semen* is the Holy Spirit. Under

---

[107] *De auferibilitate sponsi ab Ecclesia*, G, 3, 297. For the interpretation of the *semen* of Isaiah 1:9 see *Peake's Commentary on the Bible*, ed. Matthew Black and H. H. Rowley (London, 1963), p. 490 and *The Jerome Biblical Commentary*, ed. Raymond E. Brown, Joseph A. Fitzmyer, and Roland E. Murphy (Englewood Cliffs, 1968), p. 267.

[108] The reference to the Mosaic Law concerns the designation of Aaron and his sons as priests in charge of public worship. They were to be assisted by members of the tribe of Levi, who were to take the place of the first born of Israel. Cf. Ex 29:43-44: 30:30-31; Nm 3:5-10; 3:40-41; 18:1-7. The term *semen* is applied to the sons of Aaron in whom rests the succession of the priestly line. Cf. Nm 16:40; 28:43.

[109] *De auferibilitate sponsi ab Ecclesia*, G, 3, 297. For Gerson's exegesis of Mt 24:34 see *Nuptiae factae sunt*, G, 5, 384.

[110] *Ambulate dum lucem habetis*, G, 5, 44. "Ecclesia habet potestatem seu facultatem ex vivifico germine sibi insito per Spiritum Sanctum quod seipsam potest

the guidance of the Spirit, the church is assured that its hierarchical structure will continue through the ages. The Holy Spirit is also directly related to the functioning of the hierarchical order, for love, union, and peace are, in effect, the work of the Spirit. The church for Gerson is, in reality, a Spirit-directed hierarchy. The ecclesiastical hierarchy, moreover, possesses in the Spirit the power of self-reform which becomes operative whenever the church's integrity and unity are threatened. This reformative force is especially operative whenever the church is gathered in council, for it is in the council that the hierarchical order is most visible and the Spirit most active.[111] Working within the hierarchical structure, the Spirit forms and reforms the entire body of the church. This Spirit, with its conservative and reformative dynamism, will be with the church throughout history since in Mt 28 : 20 Christ promised the apostles that he would be with them until the end of time.[112]

Through the conservative and reformative power of the Spirit, therefore, the bishops gathered in council will be able to achieve the reformation of the hierarchical order. That order had been disturbed by the schism which has given the church three heads instead of the single head established by Christ. By means of the reformative power of the Spirit, the bishops in council can restore proper leadership within the church's hierarchy. The council, consequently, has the authority to restore the church to its one true head by the election of a sovereign pontiff. The authority to provide for the head of the church is rooted primarily within the hierarchical order itself and is not the sole prerogative of the sovereign pontiff. The council, moreover, is capable of determining the manner according to which the pope is to be elected. Unless the church possessed such powers over the papacy there is always the possibility that the church could permanently exist without a supreme head. Such a possibility is incomprehensible to Gerson because it is directly contrary to the present dispensation under which Christ has established his church

---

continuare in integritate et unitate membrorum suorum tam essentialium seu formalium quam materialium atque fluentium."

[111] *Prosperum iter faciat*, G, 5, 479. "... concilium generale est congregatio legitima auctoritate facta ad aliquem locum ex omni statu hierarchico totius Ecclesiae catholicae, nulla fideli persona quae audiri requirat exclusa, ad salubriter tractandum et ordinandum ea quae debitum regimen ejusdem Ecclesiae in fide et moribus respiciunt."

[112] *Nuptiae factae sunt*, G, 5, 384.

as hierarchically perfect.[113] With the aid of the Spirit, moreover, the bishops will be able to remove the forces of heresy which have threatened the proper balance of the hierarchical order. Finally, by its reformative activity in the area of morals, especially those of the clergy, the council will again insure the proper functioning of the hierarchical order.

Reform in all the above areas means, in effect, that the church will be restored to the image of its celestial archetype and will reflect the hierarchical order of that archetype. The restoration of the hierarchical order results in the harmonious exercise of hierarchical activity whose goal is internal peace and union. For Gerson the resolution of the schism is tantamount to a *reformatio pacis* within the church.[114] Peace and unity enable the church to accomplish more effectively its main task of sanctifying the faithful and building up the mystical body of Christ.

---

[113] *De auferibilitate sponsi ab Ecclesia*, G, 3, 297. "Et ex his protinus infertur quod Ecclesia vel Concilium eam repraesentans potest instituere vel eligere vel designare summum pontificem in sacra sede Petri. Potest insuper modum determinare vel immutare eum taliter vel taliter instituendi sive designandi, ita quod non spectat hoc ad solum pontificem summum; alioquin ipso vel mortuo vel nolente dare legem eligendi successorem, posset ecclesia permanere jugiter sine summo pontifice, quod nequit fieri lege stante."

[114] *Propositio facta coram Anglicis*, G, 6, 131. "Hoc est semen in quo conveniunt ambae obedientiae; quale si abstulisset schisma de pace reformanda actum esset prout alias scripsit ipsis Romanis Parisiensis Universitas."

CHAPTER TWO

THE CHURCH: LAW, COUNCIL, AND REFORM

The analysis of the preceding chapter has established the general nature of Gerson's ideas on the church and its reform. Order and hierarchy have been shown to be central to his thought. Hierarchical order, in turn, proceeds according to a set pattern of activity, namely, purgation, illumination, and perfection, and results in charity, union, and peace which terminate in the growth and edification of the church as Christ's mystical body. The potentialities of reform, moreover, lie within the church's very hierarchical structures, for the church has the power of self-reform through its intimate relationship with the Spirit. Our attention in the present chapter will be directed to the notion of law. Law is, indeed, closely related to order and hierarchy, for law governs the entire hierarchical order.[1]

Gerson maintained that the disturbances within the hierarchical order caused by the schism resulted from a malfunctioning of law. Hierarchical disorder, therefore, persisted because of legal disorder. The church was governed by several laws: divine, natural, and positive. When functioning properly and according to their respective role and importance, these laws contributed to and maintained the proper hierarchical order of the church. Once disorder and confusion had set in among the various laws that governed the church, the result could only be the disturbance of the hierarchical order. Such was the situation in the church at the time of the schism.

The present chapter will analyze first Gerson's conception of the legal confusion within the church as originating with the Donation of Constantine. After the varieties of law which govern the church have been analyzed, our investigation will study the legal confusion within the hierarchical order at the time of the schism and the means Gerson proposed for restoring the proper relationship among the various forms of law utilized by the church. In the correct

---

[1] The intimate relationship between hierarchical order and law is clearly established in Gerson's *De potestate ecclesiastica*, G, 6, 211. "Potestas ecclesiastica est potestas quae a Christo supernaturaliter et specialiter collata est suis apostolis et discipulis ac eorum successoribus legitimis usque in finem saeculi ad aedificationem Ecclesiae militantis secundum leges evangelicas pro consecutione felicitatis aeternae."

understanding of law lies the key to the convocation of the council and the reform of the church. Our analysis will conclude with a study of the finality of law and the manner in which the proper functioning of law contributes towards the removal of the disorders that have beset the church's hierarchical order and results in the growth of the mystical body.

1. DEVELOPMENT OF LAW

Gerson's understanding of the Donation of Constantine provides the necessary background for any study of his concept of law.[2] Gerson accepts the authenticity of the Donation without any doubt. He argues that during the reign of Pope Sylvester I (314-335) the Donation marked a critical turning point in the church's attitude to and use of law. According to Gerson, the early church neither had temporal possessions nor exercised temporal jurisdiction. He argues that Christ's words and actions tended more to prohibit than to permit temporal possessions, although at no time did he explicitly forbid them. Gerson finds the reason for Christ's attitude in the fact that the church was, at that time, extremely young and as such preoccupied with its own expansion and development. Temporal possessions and jurisdiction would only serve to impede the church in the execution of its mission.[3]

---

[2] The forgery known as the Donation of Constantine was most probably written in the second half of the eighth century either in France or in Rome. In this document, Constantine recognizes the universal primacy of Rome, grants the pope the Lateran palace, imperial titles and insignia, and appoints him ruler of Rome, Italy, and all the western regions. The Donation reflected the religious and territorial claims of the papacy in the eighth century but it is not fully certain whether it was directed against the Franks, the Lombards, or the Greeks. The medieval papacy frequently employed the Donation to justify its temporal and spiritual claims and even used it to support its claim to universal dominion in the West. Not until the fifteenth century did men such as Nicholas of Cusa and Lorenzo Valla doubt the authenticity of the document. Cf. W. Ohnsorge, "Die Constantinische Schenkung," in *Abendland und Byzanz* (Darmstadt, 1958), pp. 79-110; E. Ewig, "Das Bild Constantins des Grossen in den ersten Jahrhunderten des abendländischen Mittelalters," *HJ*, 75 (1956), 1-46; W. Gericke, "Wann entstand die Constantinische Schenkung?" *ZSSRk*, 43 (1957), 1-88, and H. Fuhrmann, "Constantinische Schenkung und Silvesterlegende in neuer Sicht," *DA*, 15 (1959), 523-540. For the history of medieval attitudes towards the Donation see Gerhard Laehr, *Die Konstantinische Schenkung in der abendländischen Literatur des Mittelalters bis zur Mitte des 14. Jahrhunderts* (Berlin, 1926), and Domenico Maffei, *La Donazione di Constantino nei giuristi medievali* (Milan, 1964). The text of the Donation can be found in H. Fuhrmann, ed., *Das Constitutum Constantini, MGH, Leges, Fontes Iuris Germanici Antiqui*, 10 (Hannover, 1968).

[3] *De concilio unius obedientiae*, G, 6, 54.

In the fourth century, he maintains, the church's situation was considerably altered by the Donation of Constantine which gave the church temporal power and possessions.[4] Gerson is not antagonistic towards the Donation, but regards it as part of the overall plan of divine providence. The Donation, moreover, as well as all subsequent temporal endowments, reflected the goodness and fidelity of their donors. By such endowments rulers also sought to reward the early Christians for their virtuous lives.[5] Finally, Gerson claims that temporal power and possessions had now become useful for the church's future expansion and development, especially after the period of persecution.[6] He does not explain why temporal possessions hindered the church in its early years and, nevertheless, aided in its expansion in the period after the persecutions.

Gerson feels, moreover, that the temporal endowment of the church was prefigured in the Old Testament. In the early days of his sojourn among his people, the Lord had no permanent place of residence. His abode was the ark of the covenant which was carried

---

[4] Gerson's uncritical acceptance of the Donation of Constantine leads him to an overly simple view of early church history. The church before Constantine certainly possessed property, especially in the form of cemeteries and places of worship. Early in his reign, the emperor Gallienus (260-268) implicitly acknowledged the church's right to possess such property. This right was rescinded during the Diocletian persecution but restored by Galerius' edict of toleration in 311. In 313 Constantine officially recognized the corporate legal existence of Christian communities together with their right to inherit and to possess property. Cf. Gerda Kruger, *Die Rechtsstellung der vorkonstantinischen Kirchen* (Stuttgart, 1935), and G. Bovini, *La proprietà ecclesiastica e la condizione giuridica della chiesa in età preconstantiniana* (Milan, 1949). The growth of the church's temporal power, moreover, especially as it relates to the rise of the papal states, dates not from the time of Constantine but from the eighth century. With the decline of Byzantine power in Italy and with the increasing Lombard threat to Rome, the papacy was forced to seek the support of the Franks. Pepin's defeat of the Lombards in 754 and 756 led to the formation of the papal states. Frankish protection continued under Charlemagne, who, after his defeat of the Lombards in 774, confirmed papal possession of the duchies of Rome, Spoleto, Benevento, the Exarchate of Ravenna, the provinces of Venetia and Istria as well as the island of Corsica. Additional adjustments in the size and extent of the papal states were made by Charlemagne in 787. The best and most recent survey on the rise of the papal states is that of P. Classen, "Karl der Grosse, das Papsttum und Byzanz," in *Karl der Grosse. Lebenswerk und Nachleben*, ed. W. Braunfels, 1 (Düsseldorf, 1965), 537-608. See also E. Griffe, "Aux origines de l'État pontifical," *BLE*, 53 (1952), 216-231; 55 (1954), 65-89.

[5] *Scriptum est melius*, G, 2, 114. "...quae scilicet Ecclesia prout ex virtutibus sanctorum patrum originem, bona et possessiones accepit, sic etiam per virtutes non aliter servanda est." Cf. *De nuptiis Christi et Ecclesiae*, G, 6, 201.

[6] *De comparatione vitae contemplativae ad activam*, G, 3, 75. "... potuit enim tunc dotatio hujusmodi esse utilis propter bonitatem et fidelitatem dispensantium et dilatationem Ecclesiae post adversitates habitas...."

about as the Jewish people moved from place to place. All that changed, however, in the time of King Solomon. Solomon constructed the Temple of Jerusalem and installed the ark there amid great riches and magnificence.[7] Gerson argues that a similar parallel existed in the church's history. In its very early days, the period of the *ecclesia primitiva*, the church was without temporal possessions but with the arrival of Constantine and the end of persecution, it entered a new period of history. The church was now officially recognized by the Roman Empire and received extensive lands, buildings and temporal honors.

Gerson recognizes that there are many who have taken a negative attitude toward the Donation of Constantine as well as towards all other grants of temporal possessions to the church. For them, the acceptance of such possessions on the part of the church was definitely wrong.[8] This negative attitude is reflected in many histories and sermons which maintain that when Constantine endowed the church with temporal possessions there was heard a voice in the heavens saying, "Today, a deadly poison has been poured out upon the holy church of God."[9] The endowment of the church, furthermore, has engendered such opposition in the minds of many that they do not hesitate to assert that from the days of Pope Sylvester until the present, every pope and prelate who received such

---

[7] *Diligite justitiam*, G, 7, 608.

[8] *Diligite justitiam*, G, 7, 608.

[9] *De comparatione vitae contemplativae ad activam*, G, 3, 75. "Juxta quod dicunt historiae et legi in postilla super Bibliam, quod dum dotata est Ecclesia bonis temporalibus per Constantinum, audita est vox in aere: hodie venenum effusum est in Ecclesia sancta Dei." Cf. *Diligite justitiam*, G, 7, 608. The account of the voice from heaven at the time of the Donation of Constantine enjoyed a long tradition among medieval writers. Gerald of Wales (1147-c. 1221) refers to the story in four of his works, *Gemma ecclesiastica*, 2, 38, *RBS*, 21, pt. 2, 360, *De principis instructione*, 1, 18, *RBS*, 21, pt. 8, 87-88, *De invectionibus*, 6, 27, *RBS*, 21, pt. 1, 192, and *Speculum ecclesiae*, 4, 39, *RBS*, 21, pt. 4, 350-351. According to Gerald the voice heard in the heavens was that of Satan but other writers made it the voice of an angel; cf. Walther von der Vogelweide (1170-c. 1228), 25, 11, ed. Karl Lachmann and C. von Kraus, *Die Gedichte Walthers von der Vogelweide* (Berlin, 1962), p. 82. Later, in the chronicles, the incident was simply referred to as a voice from heaven. Cf. Laehr, *Die Konstantinische Schenkung*, pp. 72-73; 172-175. Medieval canon lawyers frequently used the story in their arguments concerning the validity of the Donation. Pierre Jame d'Aurillac (1270-c. 1351-67), Alberigo da Rosciate († 1360) and Giovanni da Imola († 1436) mention the tradition. See Maffei, *La Donazione di Constantino*, pp. 154, 181, 284. Maffei, also indicates that the tradition was popular with the religious reformers of the fourteenth century. For Dante's pessimistic interpretation of the effects of the Donation, cf. *Inferno*, 19: 115-117 and *Paradiso*, 20: 55-60, ed. Giuseppe Vandelli, *La divina commedia* (Milan, 1955), pp. 156-157, 791-792.

possessions is in truth a member of the Antichrist. Gerson admits that many people in his own day are asking why prelates do not lead a life similar to the apostles in the early church.[10]

Although he makes no direct reference to Wyclif and Hus, he is undoubtedly referring to their attitudes towards the church and temporal possessions. He criticizes their followers for their overzealousness in attacking the vices of the clergy. They have gone so far as to suggest to rulers and the people that they would be fully justified in appropriating the temporal possessions of churchmen who were not leading morally good lives. In some cases they even asserted that such clerics could be put to death if they tried to defend their property. They argue that temporal goods are primarily a gift to the church and can only be possessed on the condition that members of the clergy live upright lives and use their temporal possessions properly. If those conditions are not fulfilled, then the clergy loses all legal title to temporal goods. Teaching of this nature, Gerson maintains, falls on receptive ears and there will always be those who use such arguments to cloak their avarice and hatred for the clergy.[11]

Gerson is fully aware that the endowment of the church has been a mixed blessing. Excessive concern for temporal goods and jurisdiction has led to its impoverishment not only in the temporal domain but, what is more important, also in the spiritual realm. Too often temporal values are preferred to spiritual ones. Churchmen frequently show more concern for temporal goods than do secular rulers. In short, the church has become very worldly in its outlook. Since material possessions were given to the church for the protection and promotion of spiritual values, many now maintain that once these values cease to be appreciated, the church forfeits her temporal rights. Gerson fears that if such an attitude continues the church will be deprived not merely of her temporal power but of her spiritual rights and privileges as well. Present trends within the church could easily lead to the complete destruction of ecclesiastical

---

[10] *Diligite justitiam*, G, 7, 608. "Et sont venus aucuns en tele fureur qu'ils ont dit que depuis saint Silvestre jusques au jourdui tous les papes et aultres qui ont receu et tenue telles possessions estoient membres de l'antecrist. Et les autres dient encores: cur non etiam episcopi sunt ut primi cristiani; pour quoi ne vivent les prelas comme les apostres?"

[11] *De nuptiis Christi et Ecclesiae*, G, 6, 201. For Wyclif's and Hus' theory on dominion see Gordon Leff, *Heresy in the Later Middle Ages*, 2 (Manchester, 1967), 546-549, 671. Cf. also John Stacey, *John Wyclif and Reform* (Philadelphia, 1964), pp. 62-71.

authority both in the temporal and in the spiritual realm. Excessive concern for temporal goods has, therefore, resulted in a reversal of the church's values and contributed considerably towards its spiritual impoverishment.[12] If the church's benefactors could only see the negative effects that such endowments have had upon prelates and theologians, they would hardly be tempted to repeat their actions.[13]

The endowment of the church has led to other less than beneficial effects especially in the area of law. For the *ecclesia primitiva* there was basically one law, the divine law, which was revealed in the Scriptures and ordered man's relationships to God and to his fellow men. What little positive law did exist regulated relationships among men in the area of temporal goods and possessions.[14] Gerson finds a parallel between the law of the *ecclesia primitiva* and that of the Old Testament. The Mosaic Law was essentially regarded as one even though it contained much legislation that concerned man's temporal well-being.[15] The union of divine and positive law lasted throughout the period of the *ecclesia primitiva*, which, according to Gerson, spanned the first four hundred years of the church's existence. During this time there was no distinction between theologians and canonists even though there were canons that went beyond the content of the Scriptures.[16] Such canons were relatively few and their formulation and interpretation were essentially entrusted to the theologians.[17]

With the endowment of the church, however, there began a proliferation of papal decrees concerned solely with temporal matters. By the time of Constantine, the church had spread throughout the empire and his donation had made it the equal of any secular power

---

[12] *Dum mentis aciem*, G, 2, 25. Cf. *De comparatione vitae contemplativae ad activam*, G, 3, 76.

[13] *De nuptiis Christi et Ecclesiae*, G, 6, 201.

[14] *Conversi estis nunc ad pastorem*, G, 5, 172. "... olim pro una voce lex evangelica et canonica haberentur. ..."

[15] *Conversi estis nunc ad pastorem*, G, 5, 172. "Quemadmodum praeterea lex vetus quae et mosaica dicitur, complectabatur cum divinis praeceptis ordinantibus immediate ad Deum, judicialia quae proximos in temporalibus regulabant, nec ob hoc plures leges sed una putabatur, non aliter Ecclesia primitiva legem evangelicam cum canonica conjungebat quamvis evangelica ad Deum et canonica magis ad proximum ordinaret."

[16] *Dominus his opus habet*, G, 5, 223. "Sic instituta videtur et gubernata fuisse sufficienter Ecclesia primitiva sub Apostolis, ac deinde per successiones varias usque ad doctores sanctos inclusive per quadringentos annos et amplius, quibus temporibus non erat distinctio theologorum et canonistarum. ..."

[17] *Conversi estis nunc ad pastorem*, G, 5, 172. "... nam decreta quales alii nisi theologi praecipui condiderunt, tradidierunt, promulgarunt?"

both in the size of its temporal possessions and in the extent of its secular jurisdiction. The immediate consequence of the endowment, as Gerson observed, was an increase within the church of litigation over riches, material needs, and property rights. Court cases and appeals multiplied. When speaking of the endowment, Gerson frequently repeats the proverb that he who possesses territory will also experience contention and war.[18]

The church, consequently, was faced with a new situation. It was no longer merely a spiritual institution but a temporal one as well. To cope with these changed circumstances, new legislation was increasingly necessary.[19] The result, in brief, was the emergence of another major body of law alongside the lex divina which became known as the lex canonica.[20] Since most theologians were unable to keep up with the increased canonical legislation and still devote themselves to their major task of meditating and speculating upon the divine law, there developed a whole new category of specialists known as canonists.[21] The governance of the church was thus no longer exclusively in the hands of the theologians but was now shared by the canonists as well. The growing distinction between theologians and canonists led eventually to the separation within the universities of the faculties of canon law and theology.[22]

Gerson does not regard the development of canon law and the

---

[18] Conversi estis nunc ad pastorem, G, 5, 172.

[19] Conversi estis nunc ad pastorem, G, 5, 172. "Hinc leges legibus, hinc constitutiones constitutionibus, hinc decretales decretalibus additae sunt. . . ."

[20] Gerson's reflections on the origin of canon law reveal a very restricted historical outlook. The early churches were governed by more than divine law. Each church also had its own local customs and traditions. These traditions are witnessed in the Didache (c. 100), the Traditio Apostolica of Hippolytus of Rome (c. 218), and the Didascalia Apostolorum (c. 250-300). The growth in canonical legislation from Constantine's time was not due exclusively or even primarily to his temporal benefactions but resulted from increased conciliar activity as well as from frequent provincial and local synods. Pronouncements from leading popes and bishops also became part of canon law. Canonical legislation, moreover, was concerned with more than temporal possessions; it was related to the functioning of the church as a religious body. As such it was principally concerned with church organization, ministerial office, sacramental life, liturgical activity, and church discipline. Gerson's view of canon law may well represent more the preoccupations of late medieval canon law than those of the Constantinian church. For the history of canon law see A. Van Hove, Commentarium Lovaniense in Codicem Iuris Canonici, 1, 1: Prolegomena (2nd ed.; Malines, 1945), H. E. Feine, Kirchliche Rechtsgeschichte, 1 (3rd ed.; Weimar 1955), and W. M. Plöchl, Geschichte des Kirchenrechts, 1 (2nd ed.; Vienna, 1953).

[21] Dominus his opus habet, G, 5, 224. Cf. also Conversi estis nunc ad pastorem, G, 5, 173.

[22] Diligite justitiam, G, 7, 609.

emergence of professional canon lawyers as an essential distortion in the church's nature. The church after the Donation of Constantine is just as much the work of the Holy Spirit as is the *ecclesia primitiva*. The new situation faced by the church after the Constantinian benefaction required the emergence of new institutions and new ways of dealing with problems. Gerson uses a succinct and favorite expression to describe such situations: *"ea quae de novo emergunt novo egent auxilio."* [23] He chides those who would demand that the prelates of his day imitate those of the *ecclesia primitiva* who made little use of canon law. [24]

What Gerson complains about, therefore, is not the emergence of canon law as such nor its existence and use in the church but rather the confusion between divine law and canon law that has resulted from the endowment. The church has failed to maintain the proper hierarchy between the two bodies of law. The proliferation of decrees and laws concerning temporalities has resulted in complete legal confusion within Christendom. Divine law had become identified with positive and human law. Many prelates give the impression that man's spiritual needs can be legislated in the same way as his temporal needs and that the same legal principles apply both in the temporal and in the spiritual domain. No greater confusion can befall Christendom than to believe that a spiritual institution can be governed in the same manner as a secular organization. [25]

As an example of this legal confusion, Gerson cites the church's use of excommunication and interdict. Excommunication and interdict have their origin in Mt. 18:15-17 and involve the case of a Christian sinning against another Christian. If the former fails to listen to the correction of the person sinned against or to others who admonish him, he is to be brought before the church. If he fails to listen to the church then he is to be put under the ban, that is, he is to be considered by his fellow Christians as being outside the fold of the church. Gerson argues that excommunication and interdict are essentially of divine law and were instituted by Christ primarily for the punishment of schismatics and heretics as well as the morally incorrigible. As a result, however, of the temporal endowment of the

---

[23] *Conversi estis nunc ad pastorem*, G, 5, 172. Cf. *Apparuit gratia*, G, 5, 85.

[24] *Conversi estis nunc ad pastorem*, G, 5, 173.

[25] *Pax hominibus bonae voluntatis*, G, 7, 772. "Car n'est choze qui plus trouble la police de toute crestienté que de vouloir gouverner par une meisme maniere l'espirituauté des hommes et la temporalité, et reputer que temporalité soit proprement espirituaute."

church excommunication and interdict began to be applied not only against those who disrupted the church's spiritual order but also against anyone who threatened its temporal welfare. The spiritual sword of excommunication and interdict was thus transformed into a temporal weapon to protect the possessions of the church.[26]

The consequences of such a transformation in the nature of excommunication and interdict have been several. First there has resulted a considerable amount of confusion within the church. This is naturally to be expected when spiritual punishment is applied to temporal transgressions. The natural tendency is to threaten excommunication or interdict on the slightest danger to the temporalities of the church. An even greater consequence is the lessened esteem for the church's authority in the area of excommunication and interdict. Misuse leads naturally to a lessening of appreciation. All spiritual censures are supposed to be medicinal as well as vindictive; their ultimate purpose is to restore the spiritual well-being of the person involved. Gerson feels that the misuse of excommunication and interdict makes them more a spiritual hindrance than a means for spiritual regeneration.[27]

Gerson does not claim that the church should be oblivious to all threats and attacks upon her temporal possessions. He does not advocate that the church should merely turn the cheek when its possessions are jeopardized. He accepts fully the fact of the church's endowment with temporalities and is also of the opinion that the church should have some means to protect those temporalities. What he insists upon, however, is that temporal possessions should be protected with temporal censures. He specifically objects to the use of spiritual means to protect temporal goods. In place of excommunication and interdict, he would propose other means to protect ecclesiastical property. Among those means, he cites physical punishment, monetary fines, corporal detention and the confiscation of temporal goods. He proposes, in effect, temporal punishments for all infractions against the church's possessions, thereby leaving the more spiritual means of excommunication and interdict for spiritual

---

[26] *De potestate ecclesiastica*, G, 6, 218.

[27] *De potestate ecclesiastica*, G, 6, 218. "Haec autem applicatio gladii spiritualis ad defensionem temporalium si confusionem magnam in Ecclesia, si vilipensionem vel contemptum evangelicae hujus censurae suae quae est excommunicationis gladius extreme formidabilis, si denique laqueos animabus multorum magis quam salutem spiritualem induxerit vel inducat, experientiam testem voco."

infractions, as was, in his view, the intent of Christ when he
instituted these forms of censure.[28]

2. Varieties of Law

Any study of the relationship between law and reform in Gerson's
thought must first begin with his classification of the various forms of
law. Highest in the hierarchy of law is the *lex divina* which, for
Gerson, has four distinguishing notes. The first is that it is a true sign
revealed to a rational creature. Secondly, this sign is indicative of
God's right reason. Thirdly, it represents God's right reason as willing
that the creature be obligated to perform or refrain from a particular
action. Finally, the whole purpose of such obligatory action is to
obtain eternal life and to avoid damnation.[29] With regard to the
question of whether divine law is to be attributed primarily to the
divine intellect or to the divine will, Gerson refuses to take sides in
this controversy between realists and nominalists. He deliberately
leaves this point vague in his definition. Interestingly, however, he
refers his readers to St. Thomas on the question and not to
Ockham.[30]

In a series of corollaries, Gerson elaborates upon his notion of
divine law. The fact that God is ultimately the source of all obligation
and the power behind all law does not mean that every law belongs
specifically in the category of divine law in the strict sense of the
term. Secondly, the mere fact that a law has been revealed does not
necessarily make it part of divine law. In the Old Testament God
revealed many laws which were primarily of a political and social
nature. Such laws provided for man's temporal felicity. As a

---

[28] *De potestate ecclesiastica*, G, 6, 218. "Itaque sicut temporalitas addita est
Ecclesiae pro dote sua, videri potest aliquibus quod ad ejus defensionem similiter
addere suffecerat adversus impeditores poenam vel censuram temporalem, ut est
mulctatio pecuniaria vel corporalis detentio vel arrestatio bonorum propriorum."

[29] *De vita spirituali animae*, G, 3, 130. "Lex divina praeceptoria est signum verum
revelatum creaturae rationali quod est notificativum rectae rationis divinae volentis
teneri illam creaturam seu ligari ad aliquid agendum vel non agendum pro
dignificatione ejus ad aeternam vitam consequendam et damnationem evitandam." Cf.
De potestate ecclesiastica, G, 6, 244.

[30] *Dedit illi gloriam regni*, G, 5, 184. "Utrum vero lex aeterna dicatur prius de
intellectu divino quam de voluntate, discussionis onus non hic suscipio quia de hoc in
Summa multa locutus est et faciliter homo se resolvit si propriam vocem et conceptum
cognoverit et si non se per chimerinas phantasias gratis involverit." Cf. *Summa
Theologiae*, 1, 2, q. 90, a. 1 and 1, 2, q. 17, a. 1 (Rome: Marietti. 1952) pp. 410-411,
80-81. Pierre d'Ailly's notion of law was decidedly Ockhamistic. See Francis Oakley,
The Political Thought of Pierre d'Ailly (New Haven, 1964), pp. 172-197.

composite creature, man has a twofold orientation in life. Insofar as he has a body, he possesses a distinct natural finality which is primarily political and civic. To the spiritual side of his nature corresponds a supernatural end and it is towards the achievement of that end that divine law is ordered. Gerson does not argue that both ends of man are unrelated. Man's temporal end is ultimately related to his goal of eternal beatitude. What Gerson does contend is that laws concerned with man's temporal felicity do not have a direct influence upon his supernatural end and, consequently, are not essentially part of divine law.

Thirdly, he denies that all decrees of the sovereign pontiffs belong to the category of divine law. Many papal decrees apply only to the temporal possessions of the church. Such possessions can be called spiritual only in the sense that they exist to promote the spiritual work of the church. Papal decrees related to the church's temporalities are called divine law only in an improper sense. Fourthly, Gerson denies that a law belongs to divine law simply because it has been derived from the principles of that law. He draws an analogy with the area of faith. Not every truth inferred from Scripture is said to pertain to the faith but only those that have a direct relationship to man's final beatitude. The same norm applies in the area of divine law. The mere fact that a law is deduced from the principles of divine law does not make it a part of divine law, unless it can be shown that it bears a direct relationship to man's eternal beatitude.[31]

Gerson next establishes four categories of divine law. The first category contains those laws which have been directly revealed by God for the whole community of mankind and are contained in the Bible, especially in the Gospels. These laws have been revealed to enable man to attain eternal beatitude. As always Gerson is careful not to equate revealed truth with divine law. Revealed truth is more comprehensive than divine law since it contains many truths which do not carry with them an obligation to action. The second category of divine law contains those laws which are evident and immediate deductions from the first category of divine law or have been determined as such by the church. In the third category are contained those laws which have been given directly by Christ to his apostles and disciples. These laws have been communicated to us

---

[31] *De vita spirituali animae*, G, 3, 133-134.

through apostolic succession and are on the same level as canonical scripture. They are, moreover, an essential part of the apostolic traditions. The fourth and final division of divine law is comprised of laws which have been revealed directly to certain private persons.[32] As a result of the third and fourth categories, the *ecclesia primitiva* enjoys a special authority shared by no other period of the church's history. The authority of the *ecclesia primitiva* is such in the area of divine law that neither pope, council, nor church is able to change the apostolic traditions.[33]

Turning next to natural law, Gerson defines that law as a sign with which every man is endowed who possesses the normal use of his reasoning power. As a sign it is indicative of the divine will which obliges him to perform or abstain from a certain action insofar as it is conducive or not to the attainment of his natural end. He defines the natural end of man in terms of human happiness, which consists primarily in proper domestic and civil relations. For Gerson natural man is essentially a civic animal.[34]

Gerson finds two essential differences between divine and natural law. First, divine law relies primarily upon divine revelation whereas natural law rests principally upon the dictates of human reason. Natural law, therefore, requires the normal use of man's reasoning powers. The proper functioning of man's reason can, however, be impeded by the excessive influence of his sensitive faculties. Any impairment of man's sense faculties, moreover, hinders the proper use of his reason by not providing adequate and correct sense data with which the mind can work. Finally, human reason can be impeded by moral defects rooted deeply in the human soul.[35] The second major difference between divine and natural law lies in the area of their respective finality. Divine law looks towards man's supernatural destiny while natural law is concerned primarily with his natural end.[36]

---

[32] *De vita spirituali animae*, G, 3, 137-138.

[33] *De vita spirituali animae*, G, 3, 139.

[34] *De vita spirituali animae*, G, 3, 135. "Lex vero naturalis praeceptiva appropriate talem habet rationem quod est signum inditum cuilibet homo non impedito in uso debito rationis, notificativum voluntatis divinae volentis creaturam rationalem humanam teneri seu obligari ad aliquid agendum vel non agendum pro consecutione finis sui naturalis, qui finis est felicitas humana et in multis debita conversatio domestica et etiam politica; homo enim natura animal civile est." Cf. *De potestate ecclesiastica*, G, 6, 244.

[35] *De vita spirituali animae*, G, 3, 135.

[36] *De vita spirituali animae*, G, 3, 136.

The distinction, however, between natural and divine law in Gerson's thought must not be drawn too closely. He regards both laws as having their origin ultimately in the divine will which manifests itself through the Scriptures as well as through the dictates of human reason. God, therefore, both reveals his divine will through the Scripture and implants it within human hearts. The result of this common foundation in the divine will is that all the principles of the natural law are essentially contained in the dictates of the divine law. The Old and New Testaments contain, therefore, all the essentials of the natural law. In a qualified sense, then, it can be said that for Gerson natural and divine law are identical, for the God of divine law is also the author of natural law. Through inspiration man is able to discern the principles of God's will within the Scriptures and through divine illumination he is able to see that same will as inscribed upon his heart. In making explicit the common origin and content of both divine and natural law, Gerson feels that he is but following the tradition of Augustine, Thomas and Bonaventure.[37]

After divine and natural law comes canon law which Gerson defines as a sign resulting from human tradition. This sign is indicative of divine right reason willing that a human and rational creature be obligated to perform or abstain from a certain action insofar as it is principally conducive or not to his eternal felicity. Canon law, therefore, shares with divine law, the common goal of eternal beatitude and in this respect it differs from natural law whose finality is primarily human and temporal happiness. On the other hand, canon law differs from both divine and natural law in that its knowledge and authority come from human tradition and are not obtained from revelation or natural evidence.[38]

Gerson regards canon law as a composite of divine, natural and positive law. The elements of divine law which are included in canon law are articles of faith, the sacramental tradition and the teachings of the doctors of the church on Sacred Scripture. In the area of natural

---

[37] *De vita spirituali animae*, G, 3, 136-137. For the Augustinian tradition see *De libero arbitrio*, 2, 14, 38, *CCSL*, 29, p. 263 and *De vera religione*, 31, 58 and 39, 72, *CCSL*, 32, pp. 225-226, 234. Thomas' ideas on the relationship between divine and natural law can be found in his *Summa Theologiae*, 1, 1, q. 91, a. 2 and q. 93, a. 2 and 3, Marietti, pp. 413-414. For Bonaventure, see *Itinerarium mentis ad Deum*, 2, 9; 3, 3; 3, 4; 3, 7, *Opera omnia*, 5 (Quaracchi, 1891), 302-306.

[38] *De potestate ecclesiastica*, G, 6, 244. "Lex canonica describitur quod est signum habitum per humanam traditionem notificativum rectae rationis divinae volentis creaturam rationalem humanam teneri seu ligari ad aliquid agendum vel non agendum principaliter pro consecutione felicitatis aeternae."

law, canon law incorporates moral precepts as well as the moral teachings of philosophers which have been established solely on the basis of human reason. Canon law also comprises elements of positive ecclesiastical law drawn from statutes of provincial councils, decrees of the church and liturgical practices. Finally, canon law also embraces ecclesiastical censures and punishments.[39]

Frequently Scripture or natural law will give general principles of action which in turn must be further specified by human authority. Such specifications neither flow directly from Scriptural or natural principles nor are they necessarily opposed to those principles. Gerson cites sacramental confession as an example of the manner in which different laws are interwoven into the fabric of canon law. The obligation of sacramental confession comes, strictly speaking, from divine law. Divine law, however, does not specify the manner and circumstances under which that obligation is to be fulfilled. The positive law of the church must further determine what divine law has decreed and this it does, in the case of confession, when it ordains that confession be made at a particular time of the year and to a determined priest, such as one's pastor.[40]

Given the various types of law that comprise the body of canon law, Gerson contends that for the perfect study of canon law there is needed a threefold *conversio: retrorsum, introrsum* and *deorsum*. There must be a conversion to God, a conversion towards oneself and finally a conversion towards one's neighbor.[41] Conversion, therefore, represents the effort that must be expended to determine distinctly what elements of canon law pertain to divine, natural and positive law respectively.[42] To ascertain what aspects of canon law are rooted in the divine law there must be a conversion back to God, the principle of all law. That is to say, the canonist must determine what laws proceed from God through the medium of the Scriptures, for Scripture is the *vestigium Dei* in the church.[43] The process of inward

---

[39] *Conversi estis nunc ad pastorem*, G, 5, 174. "Est autem haec communis distinctio quod doctrina canonica tres in se juris species aggregatas complectitur: jus divinum, jus naturale, jus positivum."

[40] *Dominus his opus habet*, G, 5, 224-225.

[41] *Conversi estis nunc ad pastorem*, G, 5, 177-178. "Ex his omnibus lucide deducitur id quod praemisimus, quod ad perfectam canonicae scientiae cognitionem triplex exigitur conversio: conversio retrorsum ad Deum, conversio introrsum ad cor suum, conversio deorsum ad proximum et statum ejus varium."

[42] *Conversi estis nunc ad pastorem*, G, 5, 178.

[43] *Conversi estis nunc ad pastorem*, G, 5, 175. "... pro intellectu juris divini

conversion allows the canonist to determine what legislation has been derived from the natural law. This conversion is achieved by self-analysis and reveals the principles of the natural law which have been inscribed in the human heart. Natural law is also seen as a *divinum vestigium*.[44] The third manner of conversion required by the canonist is the conversion towards one's neighbor. This mode of conversion determines those aspects of positive law contained in canon law. In this process of conversion the canonist should pay close attention to the instability of the human condition. The concrete human situation varies considerably according to circumstances of time, place, and person. Positive law therefore must be formulated, interpreted, and modified in the context of changing circumstances. In this respect positive law does not share the immutability of divine and natural law.[45] As a result of the variability of positive law, Gerson considers it a *remotum et imperfectum Dei vestigium*.[46]

Gerson strongly insists on the need for this triple conversion in any serious study of canon law. Failure to discern what aspects of canon law pertain to divine, natural or positive law can lead to insurmountable confusion within the church. Only by discerning the various laws at work within canon law can one distinguish the essential from the nonessential. Confusion of the various laws can turn unimportant matters into issues of strict obligation; it can frequently cause mutable laws to be considered as unchangeable. Such situations occur when a particular case is considered as falling under the category of divine or natural law while in fact it is only a matter of positive law. Using mineralogy as an example, he compares the inability to discern the various forms of laws to the inability to separate lead from silver, and copper ore from gold.[47] The confusion

---

comprehensi in decretalibus et decretis, necessaria est conversio retrorsum ad Deum fontale principium et ad suum evangelicae legis revelatae vestigium. . . ."

[44] *Conversi estis nunc ad pastorem*, G, 5, 177. "Pro intelligentia juris naturalis commemorati in decretalibus et decretis exigitur conversio introrsum ad cor, hoc est ad naturale scrutinium et ad divinum naturalis legis inditae vestigium."

[45] *Conversi estis nunc ad pastorem*, G, 5, 177. "Pro intelligentia juris humani positivi utilis est conversio deorsum ad conditionis humanae multiplicitatis statum varium."

[46] *Conversi estis nunc ad pastorem*, G, 5, 175.

[47] *Conversi estis nunc ad pastorem*, G, 5, 178. "Istis siquidem ignoratis confusionis sequi errorem necesse est dum non separatur pretiosum a vili, indispensabile a dispensabili, incommutabile a commutabili, obligans lex a non obligante, necessarium a non necessario, et ita de similibus ex quibus oritur deceptio quemadmodum si non separetur plumbum ab argento vel aurichalchum ab auro." On the *separatio pretiosi a vili* see Jer 15:19.

of law, which originated with the Constantinian Donation, has brought irreparable harm to the church and is primarily responsible for the prolongation of the schism that has splintered Christendom for so many years. In three extant exhortations given by Gerson as chancellor to students about to receive the licentiate in canon law, he always reminds the graduates that canon law is not all of one piece. Their task as lawyers is to recognize the varieties of law contained in canon law and to attribute to each its respective authority. In this recognition lies the proper order and peace of the church.[48]

In his enumeration of the various types of law, Gerson places positive law last. He describes positive law as a sign established through the medium of human authority which indicates that a man is obligated to perform or abstain from a certain action insofar as it is principally conducive or not to his temporal happiness.[49] The three areas of temporal happiness listed by Gerson are personal, domestic and political. Since positive law rests primarily upon human authority, it is not deduced from divine or natural law.[50]

Gerson lists four divisions of positive ecclesiastical law. The first division contains laws which may have been revealed immediately by God or by others authorized by him but cannot be substantiated except by hearsay or private revelations. Despite their uncertainty, such laws cannot be denied without scandal or rashness. An example of this category would be the tradition that the election of St. Clement (c. 88- c. 97) as pope was due to St. Peter. Gerson is unaware of the chronological factors that would militate against the veracity of such a tradition but evidently it must have been widely accepted if he selects it as an example. He considers it rash to deny such a statement but the person who does, nevertheless, cannot be accused of heresy.[51]

The second category of positive ecclesiastical law includes laws which have not been directly revealed by God but which have been

---

[48] These exhortations are: *Conversi estis nunc ad pastorem*, G, 5, 168-179, *Pax vobis*, G, 5, 435-447, *Dominus his opus habet*, G, 5, 218-229 and were delivered in 1406, 1408, and 1410 respectively.

[49] *De vita spirituali animae*, G, 3, 135. "Lex humana sive positiva praecepta pure et appropriate describitur quod est signum verum humana traditione et auctoritate immediate constitutum, aut quod non infertur necessaria deductione ex lege divina et naturali, ligans ad aliquid agendum vel non agendum pro consecutione finis alicujus humani."

[50] *De potestate ecclesiastica*, G, 6, 244-245.

[51] *De vita spirituali animae*, G, 3, 139-140.

deduced rationally from purely divine laws. Laws regulating the election of the pope fall into this category. Divine law dictates that when the see of Peter is vacant an election ought to be held to choose a successor, but divine law does not specify that this obligation falls necessarily upon the college of cardinals. Laws entrusting the election of the pope to the cardinals are merely rational deductions made by the church. To deny, consequently, that the cardinals' right to elect the pope rests immediately upon divine law, however rash, would still not be heretical.[52]

A third category of positive ecclesiastical law comprises laws whose basis in divine law is rather uncertain but which do have the effect of stirring up religious devotion. Papal decretals abound with laws of this category. They claim to rest their authority upon principles drawn from divine law such as Lk 10:16: "he who hears you hears me"; Heb 13:17: "obey your leaders"; and Mt 23:3: "observe what they tell you." The concrete deductions made from such principles of divine law either do not fall into the category of divine law, or are, at the least, extremely doubtful. While denial of such laws would not entail heresy, it is safer to observe them than to deny their validity. Examples of such laws include those related to the Lenten fast and to excommunication.[53] The fourth and final category of positive ecclesiastical law includes those laws which cannot be deduced from divine law with any reasonable degree of probability. Laws which involve the payment of taxes to a secular lord would be an example of this category.[54]

Closely associated with positive law in Gerson's thought is the principle of *epikeia*.[55] Gerson understands *epikeia* as an interpretation of law not according to its strictly litteral sense but according to the intention of the lawgiver.[56] Since the circumstances in which a law is formulated may change considerably the application of the law may well go contrary to the original purpose intended by the legislator. *Epikeia*, therefore, considers not only the

---

[52] *De vita spirituali animae*, G, 3, 140.
[53] *De vita spirituali animae*, G, 5, 140.
[54] *De vita spirituali animae*, G, 5, 140.
[55] For an historical analysis of the principle of *epikeia* as well as the closely related idea of *aequitas* see Charles Lefebvre, "Epikie," *DDC*, 5, 364-375, and "Equité," *DDC*, 5, 394-410, and especially Van Hove, *Commentarium Lovaniense*, 1, 2: *De Legibus Ecclesiasticis* (Malines, 1930), 274-304.
[56] *De unitate Ecclesiae*, G, 6, 143.

text of the law but particular circumstances as well. *Epikeia* thus harmonizes rigorous justice with mercy and indulgence.[57]

Gerson draws heavily upon Aristotle for his understanding of *epikeia*. In Aristotle's writings *epikeia* involves a correction of the law in cases where circumstances are different from those for which the law was conceived. *Epikeia* determines what the legislator would have said had he been present and understood the circumstances.[58] With the revival of Aristotelian studies in the West during the thirteenth century, the notion of *epikeia* made its appearance in the writings of scholastic theologians, especially Thomas Aquinas. Aquinas, however, restricted the use of *epikeia* to those cases where the application of a law would go contrary to the common good. He also required recourse to the legislator, if possible, in cases of doubt. Although Aquinas also uses the term *aequitas*, he understands that term primarily in the Aristotelian sense of *epikeia*. Gerson too uses *aequitas* and *epikeia* interchangeably.[59]

Strictly speaking, *aequitas* is a legal term drawn originally from Roman law and refers to the justness of law. *Aequitas* can also refer to a benign interpretation of law which corrects whatever is excessively strict and contrary to justice. In this latter sense, *aequitas* approaches the notion of *epikeia*. *Aequitas* and *epikeia* are further related in that both flow from a spirit of justice, humanity, and benignity. Before the revival of Roman Law in the twelfth century, the spirit of *aequitas* was generally expressed in canon law by such terms as *dispensatio*, *misericordia, indulgentia*, and *caritas*. With the rediscovery of Roman Law, *aequitas* appeared frequently in papal decretals and in canonical writings throughout the middle ages.[60]

While Gerson frequently mentions Aristotle as his major source for the doctrine of *epikeia*, he also contends that it is a principle

---

[57] *De vita spirituali animae*, G, 3, 189. "Exhinc elicitur evidens necessitas virtutis illius quam Aristoteles epikeiam, hoc est interpretativam legum appellat; cuius est considerare non nudum de se praeceptum sed circumstantias omnes particulariter ipsum vestientes. Ex hoc consequenter habetur modus concordandi rigorem justitiae atque severitatem disciplinae cum lenitate misericordiae et favorabilis indulgentiae."

[58] Aristotle's doctrine of *epikeia* can be found in the *Nicomachean Ethics*, 5, 10, 1137a, 31-1138a, 3, and 6, 11, 1143a, 19-1143b, 17, ed. I. Bywater (Oxford, 1894), pp. 110-111, 125-126, and in his *Rhetoric*, 1, 13, 1374a, 25-1374b, 23, ed. W. D. Ross (Oxford, 1959), pp. 59-61.

[59] For the Thomistic teaching on *epikeia* see *Summa Theologiae*, 1, 2, q. 96, a. 6 and ad. 2, Marietti, p. 439; 2, 2, q. 60, a. 5, ad 2; 2, 2, q. 120, a. 1, Marietti, pp. 297, 547.

[60] Van Hove, *Commentarium Lovaniense*, 1, t. 2: *De Legibus Ecclesiasticis*, pp. 277-281.

ascertainable from mere human experience. Any prudent man, unhindered by inordinate affections, realizes that there are many circumstances which have not been provided for in the existing body of positive law.[61] This realization should not come as a surprise since there are always many more problems affecting an institution than there are laws providing for their solution. Positive law by its very nature is imperfect and can never provide for the infinite number of possibilities that occur in the human situation. In such circumstances recourse must be had to the principle of *epikeia*.[62]

The notion of *epikeia*, furthermore, is related to divine and natural law. When Gerson speaks of *epikeia*, he not only stresses the need to recur to the intention of the legislator but he also emphasizes the fact that the legislator's intent is rooted in the eternal and immutable principles of divine law.[63] The design of the legislator is based upon divine and natural law in the sense that it shares in the purpose of all law which is love, unity and peace.[64] If positive law fails to achieve these qualities then it is the function of *epikeia* to restore the law to its proper direction. This is especially the case when strict literal observance of the law would vitiate its very purpose. Correctly understood, then, *epikeia* does not denigrate positive law but brings it to its proper fulfillment.

Gerson finds verification for his position on *epikeia* in the life of Christ whom he considers as the supreme legislator. When Christ said that he came not to destroy the Law but to bring it to fulfillment, he was in effect employing the principle of *epikeia*. Through his words and actions, he brought Old Testament Law to a greater participation in the purpose of all law which is charity, union and peace. Christ's life, therefore, serves as an example to all princes and prelates of the proper use of *epikeia*.[65]

---

[61] *De unitate Ecclesiae*, G, 6, 143. Cf. *De auferibilitate sponsi ab Ecclesia*, G, 3, 301.

[62] *De unitate Ecclesiae*, G, 6, 143.

[63] *De unitate Ecclesiae*, G, 6, 143. "Unitas Ecclesiae ad unum certum Christi vicarium nequit modo procurari commode sine recursu ad epikeiam seu bonam aequitatem, quae interpretatur litteram jurium positivorum secundum intentionem legislatorum radicatam in regulis aeternis ac immutabilibus divinae legis; per quam legum conditores justa decernunt atque secundum dictamen legis naturalis."

[64] *De auferibilitate sponsi ab Ecclesia*, G, 3, 301. "Haec autem lex semper habet locum in interpretatione legum aliarum particularium, ubi deficere cernitur ratio et finis institutionis ipsarum. Finis autem legum omnium, nedum humanarum sed divinarum, est dilectio quae unitatem operatur. Sit igitur casus ubi legis alicujus observatio dissiparet unitatem et adversaretur publicae saluti; quis ratione utens diceret tunc eam tenere oportere?"

[65] *Apparuit gratia*, G, 5, 73.

Gerson sharply criticizes those, especially canonists, who spurn the use of *epikeia* and cling to the dead letter of the law. Following Aristotle, he refers to such persons as immovably fixed in their own opinions.[66] They adhere to positive law with the same tenacity as if it were the Gospel. Christ referred to people of this mentality when he accused the Pharisees and Scribes of so strongly adhering to their legal tradition that they vitiated the law of God.[67]

Gerson does not advocate unrestricted use of the principle of *epikeia*. Indeed, he maintains that the normal administration of any institution should not be based upon *epikeia*. *Epikeia* should be used by an institution only in extraordinary cases when exceptions to the general norm of action are clearly required. If standard legal procedures and interpretation of the law are too frequently bypassed in favor of *epikeia*, all law will lose its stability. Once the stability of law has been threatened, no institution, whether church or state, can long stand but will soon be reduced to a condition of constant inner turmoil.[68]

3. Law and the Schism

Gerson's clarification of the various forms of law and their respective degrees of authority is closely related to his thought on schism and reform. For Gerson, the settlement of the schism holds first place in any reform of the church. The resolution of the schism, moreover, rests primarily upon a proper understanding of divine, natural, and positive law. Divine and natural law must be disentangled from human law and restored to their rightful position within the church's legal structure. Correctly conceived, therefore, divine and natural law are essential for the resolution of the schism. All efforts to end the schism have had this failure in common: they have sought the settlement of the schism principally through means of positive law. The principle of *epikeia*, moreover, must be applied to all positive ecclesiastical legislation which has impeded the settlement of the schism. The prolonged nature of the schism clearly merits the use of extraordinary means.

Even before his firm commitment to the *via concilii* Gerson, in a sermon given before Benedict XIII at Tarascon in January, 1404,

---

[66] *Apparuit gratia*, G, 5, 85.
[67] *Dominus his opus habet*, G, 5, 228. Cf. Mt 15:6.
[68] *De unitate Ecclesiae*, G, 6, 145.

clearly asserted that the principles for the resolution of the schism and the reform of the church were to be found in divine law.[69] Human laws have clearly been shown to be insufficient. No solution to the schism is possible unless the church turns to divine law.[70] No way which might lead to the solution of the schism is to be neglected regardless of how contrary it might be to positive law. The only restriction that Gerson would place on the means utilized for settling the schism is that they be in accord with the principles of divine law.[71] He berates those who have so encumbered divine law with human inventions that they are unable to see the superior principles of that law. He attributes this inability to insufficient education, maliciousness and laziness. They should long ago have realized that human laws are incapable of ending the schism and that the only possible recourse is to divine law. The consciences of those seeking a solution to the schism should be formed more by the principles of divine law than by those of positive law.[72]

In an address given in 1406 to those who were about to receive their licentiates in canon law, Gerson again mentions the insufficiency of positive law to provide a viable solution to the schism. He admonishes the graduates to remember always that divine law is and remains the principal source and norm for all other forms of law. Conversion to divine law must always be a part of their legal experience. Only in this way will they truly recognize and acknowledge Christ who is the true pastor and bishop of their souls.[73] Writing in 1407, Gerson reviews the long period of time that has elapsed since the beginning of the schism and the confusion that it has created in the hearts of so many people. Throughout all these years men have sought to resolve the schism through human and positive law. All their efforts, however, have been in vain. With the church at such an impasse, Gerson sees no other alternative than to

---

[69] *Apparuit gratia*, G, 5, 84. "Dic tu, studiositas, radices aliquas ex jure divino sub generalibus principiis utiles ad sedandum pestiferum schisma, quoniam illud primum et principalius occurrit in Ecclesia reformandum."

[70] *Apparuit gratia*, G, 5, 73. "Et hoc documentum non mediocriter spectat ad schisma praesens cujus sedationem invenire non sufficerent leges humanae jam conditae nisi superior lex divina viva et architectonica consulatur . . . ."

[71] *Apparuit gratia*, G, 5, 85. "Ex quibus elicitur conclusio quod nulla via proficiens ad sedationem schismatis repudianda est quantumcumque jura vel leges humanae videantur opponi, ut de electione Summi Pontificis sic et sic celebranda et similes, dummodo jus divinum maneat inviolatum. . . ."

[72] *Apparuit gratia*, G, 5, 74.

[73] *Conversi estis nunc ad pastorem*, G, 5, 178.

turn to natural and divine law. The church has too long sought the settlement of the schism with improper means. Only by the implementation of natural and divine law will the church prevent the extension of the schism.[74]

Gerson developed a similar theme in his address to those who had received their licentiates in canon law in 1410. At that time he might well have irritated their sensitivities because he firmly declared that it was not God's intention that the church be governed principally by positive law. He argued against those who would make the principles of positive law as permanent as those of divine law. He censured those who consider positive law as indispensable and as binding upon the church as divine law. This tendency to place positive law on a parity with divine law has given rise to innumerable scandals and disturbances within the church.[75]

When he addressed Benedict XIII at Tarascon in 1407, Gerson listed some of the conclusions drawn from positive law which had delayed the resolution of the schism. He objected that such conclusions prohibited any discussion on the powers of the papacy. The papacy, consequently, could never be held accountable for its actions. Under no circumstances, moreover, could a general assembly of the church be convoked without the presence of the pope and the pope could never be summoned to appear before such a council. Gerson further complained that statements such as Benedict is the true pope are declared to be articles of faith. Finally, he expressed his opposition to the principle that without the pope there can be no salvation.[76]

In January 1409 Gerson wrote a brief defense of the convocation of the Council of Pisa in which he listed other objections of the canonists. Foremost among such objections was that only the pope could summon a general council. The canonists challenged the union of the cardinals from the Avignon and Roman lines soon to meet in council at Pisa without papal authority. Before any pope could be deposed moreover, they demanded clear proof that he was heretical or schismatic and had thereby ceased to be pope. Even if the deposition of the pope were legally possible, they raised questions as to the manner in which this was to be accomplished: through accusation, inquisition or denunciation? They asked, finally, how was

---

[74] Acta de schismate tollendo, G, 6, 97.
[75] Dominus his opus habet, G, 5, 228.
[76] Apparuit gratia, G, 5, 85.

the council to resolve the innumerable excommunications hurled by both sides against one another?[77]

Gerson maintained, however, that such objections against the convocation of the council arose from an excessive emphasis upon positive law; he would resolve these difficulties by the application of epikeia. Gerson, indeed, considered the general council as the primary agent for the application of epikeia within the church. In a treatise written shortly before the Council of Pisa, he stresses the point that the church's search for unity under the one true vicar of Christ need not proceed according to the strict and literal observance of positive ecclesiastical law. The Council of Pisa, consequently, can congregate and begin its work on the basis of epikeia. Utilizing epikeia, the council has the power to interpret and to adapt all positive ecclesiastical legislation for the attainment of church unity. The church also has the right to disregard positive legislation which hinders the attainment of unity.[78]

Similar thoughts were expressed by Gerson at the time of the Council of Constance. He repeatedly states that the general council is the supreme legislator in the church and, therefore, enjoys full power to utilize the principle of epikeia. The council should be considered by all Christians as the legitimate representative of the whole church since it has been convoked with the consent of all.[79] Gerson admits the use of epikeia for the resolution of the schism because the schism does not represent a normal state within the church. Under such circumstances, the only recourse against the restrictive nature of positive law is that of epikeia. Epikeia removes obstructive positive law and allows divine and natural law to operate freely.[80]

Divine and natural law, indeed, make possible the convocation of a council without the pope not only when there is a question of heresy or death but even when one of the contendants has valid rights to the papal office.[81] Those rights can be nullified by an authoritative decree of a council whenever they prove detrimental to the desired unity of the church.[82] After the flight of John XXIII from Constance, moreover, Gerson argued that the continuation of the council was justified by divine law. In his sermon on March 23, 1415, Gerson

---

[77] Pro convocatione concilii Pisani, G, 6, 124.
[78] De unitate Ecclesiae, G, 6, 138.
[79] Prosperum iter faciat, G, 5, 478-479.
[80] De auferibilitate sponsi ab Ecclesiae, G, 3, 301.
[81] De unitate Ecclesiae, G, 6, 137.
[82] De unitate Ecclesiae, G, 6, 138.

assures the members of the council that despite the departure of
John XXIII they still walk in the light of divine law which
enlightens the whole church gathered in council. He recalls Mt 5:15
where Christ states that men do not light a lamp to place it under a
basket but put it on a stand so that it might give light to all in the
house. That light for Gerson is the divine law and the house which it
enlightens is the church. Gerson also draws upon 2 Pt 1:19 where the
author says: "You will do well to pay attention to this as to a lamp
shining in a dark place, until the day dawns and the morning star
rises in your hearts." The lamp shining in the darkness is the divine
law which illuminates the darkness of spirit caused among the
bishops by the flight of John XXIII.[83]

If the reformation of the church lies first and foremost in the
resolution of the schism, and if that resolution is to be found
primarily in a return to the principles of divine and natural law, then
it is most important to determine what those principles are. Gerson
lists them in a treatise written in January 1409 for the convocation of
the Council of Pisa.[84] Canonists have neglected these principles and
their stress upon positive law has resulted in the impasse in which
the church found itself at the time of the schism. Gerson finds
justification for his appeal to divine and natural law in Acts 5:27-30,
where Peter is commanded by the high priest not to teach in Christ's
name. Peter's reply was: "We must obey God rather than men."
Gerson argues from Peter's statement that the church must follow the
dictates of divine and natural law which have their origin directly in
God and not the precepts of positive law which depend upon human
authority.

The principles from divine and natural law utilized by Gerson can
be classified according to three groups. The first group centers
around the notion of finality. The first principle in this group is
contained in 2 Cor 10:8, where Paul narrates that his authority has
been given to him by the Lord to build up and not to destroy the
church in Corinth. Gerson deduces from this statement that all
ecclesiastical authority exists for the edification of the church and not
for its destruction. This principle became for him the norm for the
valid or invalid exercise of church authority, especially papal
authority. A second and closely related principle states that the

---

[83] *Ambulate dum lucem habetis*, G, 5, 43.
[84] *De unitate Ecclesiae*, G, 6, 143-144. Cf. *Trilogus in materia schismatis*, G, 6, 81-82.

finality of all ecclesiastical authority is charity. The importance of this principle has already been seen in Gerson's concept of hierarchical order and activity. Gerson gives no exact scriptural reference for this principle but it recalls Eph 4:15-16, where Paul describes the growth of the church as Christ's body in terms of love. Gerson would argue, therefore, that if ecclesiastical authority has been given for the edification of the church, and if such growth takes place primarily through charity, then charity is the goal of all ecclesiastical authority.

Another principle related to the idea of finality concerns law. Gerson describes that principle accordingly: The fulfillment and end of all law is charity. Gerson draws here upon Rom 13:10 where Paul sums up the commandments of the Mosaic Law in terms of love, but he adds to the Pauline idea of fulfillment the specific note of finality. Like Paul, whose notion of law and its fulfillment in charity extends not only to Mosaic Law but to law in general, Gerson regards all law as enjoying the same finality.[85] Divine, natural, canon and positive law, therefore, all have their fulfillment in charity. The last principle in the area of finality is concerned with the effects of charity. Charity has as its direct effect the creation of union and peace. This principle recalls Paul's farewell in 2 Cor 13:11 where he urges the Corinthians to live in union and peace, for by so living the God of love and peace will be with them.

A second group of principles which Gerson claims to draw from divine and natural law is related to the ideas of *necessitas* and *epikeia*. The first of these principles has its origin in natural law and states that the attainment of the end requires the necessary means, that is to say, everything should be moderated according to the exigenicies of the end.[86] Gerson insists, however, that this principle does not claim

---

[85] For this interpretation of Paul's notion of law see *The Jerusalem Bible*, ed. Alexander Jones (London, 1966), p. 287, n. 13c.

[86] The scriptural antecedents of *necessitas* are found in Mk 2:25-26 and Mt 12:5-8 where Christ answers the charge of the Pharisees against his disciples by stating that they were picking ears of corn on the Sabbath because they were hungry and in need of food. The principle was incorporated in Gratian's *Decretum*, De Consecr., Dist., 1, c. 11, ed. A. Friedberg, *Corpus Juris Canonici*, 1, 1297. This canon is, in reality, a pseudo-Isidorian decretal. From the end of the twelfth century the maxim became a commonplace in the works of most decretists and decretalists. See Gaines Post, *Studies in Medieval Thought* (Princeton, 1964), pp. 21, 318 n. 21. For a study of the notion of *necessitas* in the medieval canonists cf. Stephan Kuttner, *Kanonistische Schuldlehre von Gratian bis auf die Dekretalen Gregors IX* (Città del Vaticano, 1935), pp. 291-298. The Fourth Lateran Council in its fiftieth canon considered *necessitas* as a valid basis for changing ecclesiastical legislation. Cf. Alberigo, *Decreta*, p. 233. The Council of

that the end justifies the means but that there must be a due proportion between means and the end. The attainment of the end, therefore, requires the use of appropriate means.[87] Gerson argues, consequently that if hierarchical order is to be restored to its proper finality, the church must take the necessary means. These means Gerson identifies primarily with the convocation of a council. Another principle used by Gerson states that necessity knows no law. Necessity is to be praised when it leads one toward higher goals. Gerson quotes Gregory the Great († 604) in support of this principle. Here too, Gerson does not maintain that the end justifies the means. The correct interpretation of this principle is related to the notions of *epikeia* and positive law. Necessity may demand the temporary abrogation of a positive law. All human law admits of exceptions under certain circumstances. This principle was of great importance in Gerson's thought on the schism and he regarded it as the only way out of the maze of positive laws which prohibited the convocation of a council.

Also closely related to the ideas of *necessitas* and *epikeia* is the principle that what is instituted for the sake of charity ought not to militate against charity. This principle is, in reality, another way of expressing the notion of *epikeia*. All law has charity as its goal and any law which militates against charity is self-destructive. Gerson, therefore, regards those positive laws which prohibit the solution of the schism through conciliar means as frustrating the very finality of law and by this very act invalid. A final and most important principle is that the spiritual man judges all things. Gerson quotes here directly from 1 Cor 2:15 where Paul declares that it is only the Spirit of God which allows man to understand the ways of God. The mature Christian receives the Spirit while the natural man neither possesses nor understands it. This principle is directly related to *epikeia*, for it is only the spiritual man who can discern when circumstances in the church are such as to require the application of *epikeia*. This principle also carries strong reminiscences of Aristotle's wise man who judges all things according to equity.[88] As seen in Gerson's mature thought, it is the general council which is the primary agent

---

Vienne also referred to the same principle in its decree on the Templars, cf. Alberigo, *Decreta*, p. 319.

[87] *Trilogus in materia schismatis*, G, 6, 82.

[88] Cf. *Nicomachean Ethics*, 6, 10, 1143a, 19-6, 11, 1143b, 17, ed. Bywater, pp. 125-126.

for the application of *epikeia* within the church. The council should represent the gathering of truly spiritual bishops and theologians to whom is entrusted the responsibility of deciding when and where *epikeia* is to be used.

The third set of principles drawn from divine and natural law is concerned primarily with the relationship of the part to the whole. The first of these principles contains the self-evident truth that the whole is greater than the part. The second and closely related principle embodies the idea that the part can be sacrificed for the good of the whole. In brief, the public good is to be preferred to the good of the individual. While acknowledging Aristotelian influence, Gerson frequently describes these principles in biblical terms.[89] He finds them reflected in Mt 18:8 which states that if a person's hand or foot causes scandal he is justified in cutting them off. While Matthew speaks only of the hand or foot, Gerson expands the statement to include the head. In this way he is able to apply the principles to the various papal rivals. The schism has been a scandal to Christendom, and, consequently, the entire hierarchical order of the church gathered in council is justified in casting out the papal claimants. Another scriptural manifestation of the same principles is found in Mt 18:17 which states that the person who does not listen to the church is to be considered as a pagan or tax gatherer and therefore cut off from the church. Gerson here contrasts the corporate power of the hierarchical church gathered in council with the individual power of the papacy. If the various papal contenders fail to listen to the church's aspirations for unity, then they should be considered as outside the church. A similar theme is found in Jn 10:11 where it is stated that the good shepherd lays down his life in order to save his sheep. The pope as shepherd is only part of the church and,

---

[89] In his *De potestate ecclesiastica*, G, 6, 221, 233, Gerson cites Aristotle when treating of the manner in which the part is contained in the whole. The passage to which Gerson refers, however, is not in the *Metaphysics*, as he claims, but in the *Physics*, 4, 2, 210a, 14-24, ed. W. D. Ross (Oxford, 1950). Aristotle's ideas on the priority and superiority of the whole to the part can be found in his *Politics*, 1, 3, 1253a, 20, and 3, 16, 1288a, 28-29, ed. W. D. Ross (Oxford, 1957), pp. 4, 108. For the Aristotelian categories of causality see *Physics*, 2, 3, 194b, 32-39, and *Metaphysics*, 5, 2, 1013a, 24-1013b, 2, ed. W. Jaeger (Oxford, 1957), pp. 86-88. Aristotle's historical survey of the types of causality is contained in the *Metaphysics*, 1, 2, 982a, 5-1, 10, 993a, 22, Jaeger, pp. 5-32. Gerson described the Council of Pisa in terms of Aristotle's fourfold division of causality, cf. *Propositio facta coram Anglicis*, G, 6, 126. For the primacy of finality in the Thomistic hierarchy of causes see *Summa Theologiae*, 1, 2, q. 1, a. 2, Marietti, p. 3.

consequently, should be willing to abdicate in order to save the entire church from the chaos of disunity. The individual good of the papacy is clearly subordinate to the good of the entire church.

The complex of principles drawn from divine and natural law represents the essence of Gerson's thought on the resolution of the schism. All the various arguments he used for the settlement of the schism were taken in varying degrees from this body of principles. Since these principles had their origin in divine and natural law, at least in so far as Gerson conceived them, they took precedence over positive law which he saw as one of the major obstacles to the resolution of the schism. These principles, moreover, reveal a strong Pauline influence, especially the ideas of love, union, and peace. The incorporation of these ideas into a hierarchical context, moreover, reflects the thought of Dionysius who described hierarchical order in similar terms.[90] The stress on finality, *epikeia*, and the relationship of the part to the whole discloses Gerson's indebtedness to Aristotle.

4. FINALITY OF LAW

Our analysis thus far has revealed Gerson's ideas on the development of law, its varieties as well as its relationship to the schism. Attention will now be directed towards the general finality of law in Gerson's writings. The subject has already been touched upon to some degree in the study of the principles of divine and natural law as well as in the analysis of *epikeia*. The finality of law is a datum of the divine law and is most succinctly expressed in Rom 13:10: *"Plenitudo ergo legis est dilectio."* Gerson modifies the Pauline principle by identifying the notion of finality with the idea of plenitude. He thus expresses the divine law as: *"Plenitudo legis atque finis ejus est dilectio."* [91]

From the context of his writings, it becomes clear that when Gerson speaks of *lex* he does not restrict the term to divine law but includes natural and human law as well. He explicitly states that the end of all law, not only human but divine as well, is charity.[92] He also clearly asserts that all law has goodness and stability only to the degree that it participates in charity. Charity is thus the end and

---

[90] *De ecclesiastica hierarchia*, 1, 3, *MPG*, 3, 376 A.

[91] *De unitate Ecclesiae*, G, 6, 143. Cf. *De desiderio episcopatus*, G, 3, 328.

[92] *De auferibilitate sponsi ab Ecclesia*, G, 3, 301. "Finis autem legum omnium, nedum humanarum sed divinarum est dilectio quae unitatem operatur."

measure of all law.[93] Theology, therefore, is the highest of the sciences not only because it deals primarily with divine law but also because it has as one of its functions the interpretation of all lower forms of law according to the norm of charity.[94] This interpretation of all law in accordance with charity is, in effect, the exercise of *epikeia*. Through the exercise of *epikeia*, theology seeks to restore all positive law to its proper finality.[95]

Closely allied with law and charity in Gerson's thought are the notions of unity and peace. Unity and peace are related to charity as effect to cause. Charity results directly in the creation of union and peace. This causal relationship of charity to union and peace is also a principle of divine law.[96] He finds this principle operative as well in the writings of Dionysius.[97] The relationship between charity, union and peace is so intimate that all three can be said to belong to the finality of law. Gerson, indeed, uses the terms interchangeably when speaking about law. In this respect, he feels that he is merely following the example of St. Paul.[98]

Although he adopts Augustine's description of peace as the tranquility that results from order, Gerson understands the definition in terms of the mystical body. He is primarily concerned with the peace of the entire mystical body. This peace, moreover, is not ordinary peace but *pax salutifera*; it is a peace which brings salvation. Salvific peace, therefore, is the end of all law governing the church, and is rooted in and results from the love of Jesus Christ. The finality of all law, therefore, and above all of divine law, is love and union with Christ and the consequent result of such love and union is

[93] *De vita spirituali animae*, G, 3, 170. "Attamen omnis lex tantum praecise habet de bonitate et stabilitate quantum participat de charitatis lege quae est finis praecepti et secundum quam debent cetera moderari."

[94] *Acta de schismate tollendo*, G, 6, 102. "Ad quid enim diceretur theologia, quae tractat de jure divino, superior et architectonica nisi quia interpretari habet jura omnia inferiora secundum ordinem et finem caritatis et unitatis, quae caritas est finis praecepti secundum Apostolum."

[95] *De unitate Ecclesiae*, G, 6, 142. "Unitas Ecclesiae ligatur quadruplici lege, divina scilicet vel evangelica, naturali, canonica et civili; quarum duas extremas regulare necesse est per primas secundum epikeiam...."

[96] *De unitate Ecclesiae*, G, 6, 143. "Dilectio est causa unionis et pacis."

[97] *Poenitemini...Repentez vous car penitence donne*, G, 7, G, 7, 944-945. Although this principle is essentially Dionysian it is not found in the *De divinis nominibus* exactly as stated by Gerson. Cf. *De divinis nominibus*, 4, 12, *MPG*, 3, 709 D.

[98] *Apparuit gratia*, G, 5, 85. "Nullo pacto igitur servatur lex non observato legis fine qui est pax." For his interpretation of St. Paul's use of charity, union and peace, cf. G, 5, 84.

peace and salvation.[99] Hierarchical order and law exist precisely for the promotion of salvific peace.[100]

Gerson regards the schism as the greatest obstacle to the attainment of salutary peace. The schism has been prolonged to the detriment of Christendom by men who have neglected the divine law and its precepts and have refused to apply *epikeia* to the maze of positive ecclesiastical legislation which prevents the summoning of a general council. All those who have neglected divine law and *epikeia* in their attempt to settle the schism are incapable of achieving peace within the church. He censures ecclesiastics who are so fixed in their attitude toward law that they can only admit the value of positive law. Such men hardly deserve to be called ecclesiastics. They spurn and reject the opinions of those who are learned in the divine law. At times their disdain of divine law verges on the realm of the sacriligeous. Their attitude toward divine law and *epikeia* has given rise to innumerable errors, presumptuous assertions, and insoluble legal perplexities and has resulted in the destruction of the church and that salutary peace towards which it is ordered.[101]

Gerson, moreover, conceives the entire resolution of the schism in terms of peace. As early as 1395, while still an advocate of the *via cessionis*, Gerson referred to his efforts to resolve the schism as *pro pacis reformatione*.[102] The schism has resulted from the spirit of discord and ambition and has destroyed the salvific peace of the church. The schism has also provided conditions conducive to heresies which have further disturbed the church's peace. True peace can never come to the church as long as it is torn by schism and heresy. Gerson's address of 1409 in Paris to the English delegation on its way to the Council of Pisa was also presented in terms of a *reformatio pacis*. In his speech he describes the basis upon which the union of the Avignon and Roman obediences can be achieved. This basis is the unifying bond of the Holy Spirit which is the *semen vivificum et reformativum* within the church. The Spirit binds both obediences under the one head which is Christ. The Spirit, moreover,

---

[99] *Apparuit gratia*, G, 5, 85. "Finis politiae ecclesiasticae et cujuslibet legis eam regulantis est pax salutifera. Hoc satis expressit divinus noster philosophus Paulus qui finem legis et praecepti nunc dilectionem esse dixit nunc Jesum, intelligens in dilectione pacem, in Jesu salutem ut sit finis pax salutaris."

[100] *Apparuit gratia*, G, 5, 86. "Quaelibet in ecclesiastica hierarchia potestas in pacem salutiferam ordinatur."

[101] *Apparuit gratia*, G, 5, 85.

[102] *Ante diem festum Paschae*, G, 5, 52.

is the source of those dispositive and life-giving qualities of the mystical body which he describes as the theological virtues of faith, hope, and charity, the sacraments, and the various individual charisms. If this reformative force within the mystical body were allowed to have its effect, the schism would be resolved and the result would be a true *reformatio pacis*.[103]

Speaking before the Council of Constance on March 23, 1415, Gerson set forth the aims of the university delegation, of which he, as chancellor, was a most prominent member. Foremost among those aims was the resolution of the schism which had plagued the church for several decades. Rather than describe the aims of the delegation in terms of resolving the schism, Gerson speaks of the means necessary to achieve the peace of the church.[104] He portrays the delegates to the council as fellow citizens of the apostles and servants of the Lord who have been appointed to bring peace and freedom to the people of the Lord.[105]

Our analysis of the finality of law reveals its identity with that of hierarchical order, namely, charity, union, and peace, and clearly demonstrates the close relationship between hierarchical order and law. The maintenance of hierarchical order depends upon the right relationship of divine, natural and positive law. Law in turn can only function effectively within the context of hierarchical order. The harmonious cooperation of hierarchical order and law terminates in charity, union, and peace within the church and contributes towards the growth and edification of the church as Christ's mystical body. In the final analysis, the growth and development of the mystical body is the ultimate goal toward which all hierarchical order and law are directed. In this goal, they find the fullest realization of their inner dynamism.

---

[103] *Propositio facta coram Anglicis*, G, 6, 131. "Hoc est semen in quo conveniunt ambae obedientiae; quale si abstulisset schisma, de pace reformanda actum esset prout alias scripsit ipsis Romanis Parisiensis Universitas."

[104] *Ambulate dum lucem habetis*, G, 5, 40-41.

[105] *Ambulate dum lucem habetis*, G, 5, 40. "Cives apostolorum et domestici Dei advenerunt hodie portantes facem et illuminantes patriam, dare pacem gentibus et liberare populum Domini." For the Pauline source of the titles *cives apostolorum* and *domestici Dei* see Eph 2:19-22.

CHAPTER THREE

THE THEOLOGIAN AND REFORM

The theologian holds a position of prominence in Gerson's thought on reform because he is primarily occupied with divine law. His function is to ascertain the various elements of divine law in the Scriptures and spread that knowledge through teaching and preaching. Our study will begin first with the milieu in which the theologian lived and taught, namely the university. Among the universities of Europe, Paris still maintained the position of highest importance, especially in the area of theology. The second area of study will center upon Gerson's concept of the theologian and his office, especially the relationship of the theologian to Scripture and divine law. If divine law is to provide the key for the reformation of the church's hierarchical order, then the theologian emerges as a major instrument of reform since the interpretation of divine law falls primarily within his sphere of competence. Although he had the highest esteem for the office and function of the theologian, Gerson felt that many of the theologians of his day fell considerably short of their professional ideals. His analysis of the state of theology at Paris and his program of theological reform, especially as it relates to the Scriptures and the *lex divina*, constitutes the third part of this chapter.

1. The University of Paris

Before beginning the study of Gerson's concept of the theologian, it will be profitable to investigate his attitude towards the University of Paris since, for him, this institution is the home par excellence of the theologian.[1] The university, indeed, provided the best milieu for

---

[1] For the history of the University of Paris and its theological faculty see C. E. Du Boulay, *Historia Universitatis Parisiensis*, 6 vols. (Paris, 1665-1673), H. Denifle, *Die Entstehung der Universitäten des Mittelalters bis 1400* (Berlin, 1885), pp. 40-132, Stephan d'Irsay, *Histoire des universités françaises et étrangères*, 1 (Paris, 1933), 53-74, H. Rashdall, *The Universities of Europe in the Middle Ages*, ed. F. M. Powicke and A. B. Emden, 1 (Oxford, 1936), 269-584, Gordon Leff, *Paris and Oxford in the Thirteenth and Fourteenth Centuries* (New York, 1968), Pierre Féret, *La faculté de théologie de Paris au moyen âge et ses docteurs les plus célebres*, 4 vols. (Paris, 1894-1897), and Palémon Glorieux, *Aux origines de la Sorbonne*, 2 vols. (Paris, 1965-1966). The most

theological speculation. In the University of Paris, moreover, the theological faculty was always considered foremost among her four faculties. If the University of Paris was dear to France and, indeed, to all Christendom, it was especially dear to Gerson, for he served as its chancellor from 1395 until his death in 1429. To the extent that any institution can be said to be his home, it was the University of Paris. All prolonged absences from Paris, especially the period after the Council of Constance, can and must be seen primarily as exiles. Since such a close relationship existed between Gerson and the university, it is most beneficial to study the various images which he used to describe this institution.

Without a doubt Gerson's favorite way of describing the university was to designate her as *filia regis*, the daughter of the king. By the use of this term, Gerson does not imply that the relationship between king and university is one of subservience or extreme paternalism. As *filia regis*, the primary function of the university is to enlighten the king as to the proper use of the power entrusted to him. Political authority no less than ecclesiastical must submit to the same finality that Paul describes in 2 Cor. 10:8 when he states that all power has been given for edification and not destruction.[2] The function of the university is to so guide and illumine the king that he will never exercise that power tyrannically. The primary obligation of the university, therefore, is to prevent the king from becoming a tyrant.

As tyrant, the king would vitiate the aim of all political power, namely, that those subject to his power should develop themselves according to the image of the Trinity in which they have been created. As will be seen in more detailed fashion in the chapters on episcopal and on personal reform, Gerson describes the image of God in man in several different ways. He frequently identifies the image with man's natural faculties of intellect and will. At other times he describes the image according to these same faculties in so far as they operate under the influence of the theological virtues of faith, hope, and charity. Whether portrayed in terms of natural faculties or the theological virtues, the image of God reflects the trinitarian characteristics of *potentia, sapientia*, and *bonitas*.

important collection of documents pertaining to the history of the university is that of H. Denifle and E. Chatelain, *Chartularium Universitatis Parisiensis*, 4 vols. (Paris, 1889-1897). For a comprehensive analysis of the methodology employed by the University of Paris in the teaching of theology see Glorieux, "L'enseignement au moyen âge," *AHDL*, 35(1968), 105-161.

[2] *Contre les fausses assertions des flatteurs*, G, 7, 361-362.

The tyrant does not seek the good of his subjects but converts everything to his own advantage. By so acting he creates an unnatural situation within the body politic and frustrates the development of the image of the God within his subjects. He restricts their *sapientia* with the result that they will know relatively little about events and happenings within the kingdom. The tyrant, moreover, weakens the *potentia* of his subjects since by the distorted use of his power he causes them to lose all hope and confidence in themselves. Finally he reduces his subjects to a state of indigence hardly in harmony with their intrinsic *bonitas*. In general, Gerson draws his description of the tyrant from the fifth book of Aristotle's *Politics* but he modifies Aristotle's teaching by situating it within the ideological framework of the divine image in man.[3]

Gerson warns that the king should be especially cautious of advisors who malign the reputation of university preachers. While they may not directly attack the content of university sermons, they frequently insinuate that the motivation behind those sermons is prejudicial to the king's rights. Gerson admonishes the king to avoid such advisors; indeed, there is no class of men more dangerous in the entire realm. He feels that such men are a special threat to the king because they can prevent him from following the way of truth. To hinder the king in the pursuit of truth is, in effect, to turn him into a tyrant. Through the agency of tyrants, great evils have befallen Christianity in the past. Gerson argues that France's strongest protection against the rise of tyrants lies in her universities; such institutions educate preachers and teachers dedicated to the truth and wisdom so necessary if the king is to govern his realm efficiently.[4] There is no doubt in Gerson's mind that Paris is the most outstanding university within Christendom and as such most capable of guiding the king in the pursuit of truth.

In addition to the idea of *filia regis* Gerson employs other descriptions of the university. Writing to the students of the College of Navarre during his stay at Bruges in 1400, Gerson depicts the University of Paris as a glittering sun which spiritually illuminates the entire ecclesiastical world and disperses the dark clouds of error by the pure brightness of its light.[5] In that same letter, Gerson compares

---

[3] *Vivat rex*, G, 7, 1158 Cf. Aristotle, *The Politics*, 5, 1314a, 14-29, ed. W. D. Ross, *Politica* (Oxford, 1957), p. 183.

[4] *Pax hominibus bonae voluntatis*, G, 7, 772-773.

[5] *Ecce pareo*, G, 2, 36. "Aspicitur quippe tamquam coruscus quidam sol spiritualis

the university to the river of Paradise described in Gn. 2:10. Just as the river of Paradise separated into four streams, so is the University of Paris divided into the four faculties of medicine, canon law, arts and theology. Continuing the analogy between the university and the Garden of Eden, Gerson conceives the university as intellectually irrigating the whole surface of the earth in a manner similar to the way in which the four streams of Eden watered the four corners of the known world.[6] Gerson also compares the university to the tree representing the knowledge of good and evil which, according to Gn. 2:9, God planted in the Garden of Eden.[7]

The University of Paris, therefore, is to be the font of all knowledge within Christendom. Through its faculties the university reaches out to the four corners of Christendom and revitalizes the entire world. Gerson regrets, however, that this universal revitalization of Christendom has been considerably impeded by the numerous factional squabbles that have resulted from the diverse schools of thought struggling for supremacy within the university. Gerson is undoubtedly refering to the controversies between Nominalists and Scotists. These controversies have impeded the university in its quest for truth. They have, moreover, turned the university into a place of unrest, thereby making it a faint image of its prototype, the Garden of Eden.[8]

At times Gerson varies his symbolic description of the Garden of

---

ecclesiasticam machinam irradiens, errorum quoque tenebrosas caligines suo nitenti puroque fulgore dispergens."

[6] *Ecce pareo*, G, 2, 36. "Videtur insuper quasi fluvius ille paradisi in quattuor partes divisus, irrigans universam superficiem terrae." A similar comparison was utilized by Gregory XI in 1377. See H. Denifle and E. Chatelain, *Chartularium Universitatis Parisiensis*, 3 (Paris, 1894), viii. In medieval biblical exegesis the four rivers of Paradise and the four corners of the earth were normally interpreted as the four evangelists or as the four leading doctors of the western church, generally Jerome, Augustine, Ambrose, and Gregory. Cf. Henri de Lubac, *Exégèse médiévale*, 1, 1 (Paris, 1959), 29.

[7] *Benedic haereditati tuae*, G, 5, 118. "Et bene ager plenus est filia tua Parisiensis Universitas; immo nihil erravero si eam appellavero paradisum voluptatis in quo est lignum scientiae boni et mali, et fons scientiae in quatuor facultatum flumina condivisus, irrigans universam superficiem terrae."

[8] *Ecce pareo*, G, 2, 36-37. Among those whom Gerson especially criticizes for having disturbed the theological peace of the university are the followers of Duns Scotus (1266-1308) whom he designates as *formalizantes* because of their *distinctio formalis ex parte rei*. Foremost among the members of the Scotistic school criticized by Gerson was the fourteenth-century theologian, John of Ripa. Gerson reacted especially against the application of the *distinctio formalis* to the divine ideas in God. Cf. *Contra curiositatem studentium*, G, 3, 242-243. See also Combes, *La théologie mystique*, 1, 58 and E. Gilson, *History of Christian Philosophy in the Middle Ages* (New York, 1955), 469, 772-773.

Eden. In one of his sermons he identifies the Garden of Eden with the French kingdom. France is the new Garden of Paradise, glittering with aetherial splendor and abounding in lilies which symbolize the people of the realm. The University of Paris is still compared to the river of Paradise which divides into four streams. As before, those streams are identified with the four faculties of medicine, canon law, arts and theology. The university, however, now intellectually irrigates the kingdom of France. He describes the waters of the river of Paradise as silvery clear, such as one would find in streams formed by newly melted snow. This clarity symbolizes the purity which should characterize the university's teaching.[9]

Gerson builds his description of the University of Paris not only on Scriptural but upon classical sources as well. Inspired by Vergil's *Georgics*, he compares the University of Paris to a farm. He interprets Vergil's ideal farm in terms of four fields which symbolize the four faculties of the University. The first field is to be uncultivated and filled with flowers which are to aid the bees in the production of honey. This field symbolizes the university's theological faculty and the bees represent the theologians, whom he refers to as *apes intellectuales*. Just as the activity of the bees results in wax and honey, so do theologians produce the wax which illumines the human intelligence and the honey which delights the human affections. He draws this comparison with wax and honey from Sir 24:27 where wisdom describes herself as *"super mel et favum."* The illuminative activity of the theologians is further portrayed in Ps 18:9. There the psalmist describes the divine law, which is the major concern of the theologian, as pure and enlightening to the eyes. Gerson understands the eyes here to refer to the intellect.[10]

The second portion of Vergil's ideal farm is dedicated to pastureland where cattle and domestic animals graze. Gerson compares this field to the faculty of canon law. The third field is to be fruit-bearing so as to sustain human life and is synonymous with the faculty of medicine. The fourth field contains vineyards which Gerson identifies with the faculty of arts.[11] Gerson does not develop his analogies between the last three fields and the faculties of canon

---

[9] *Considerate lilia agri*, G, 5, 156.

[10] *Benedic haereditati tuae*, G, 5, 118. The different types of fields are in reality the various aspects of farming depicted in each book of Vergil's *Georgics*: crops, vineyards and orchards, animal husbandry and bee culture.

[11] *Benedic haereditati tuae*, G, 5, 118.

law, medicine and the arts with the same detail that he describes the first field and the faculty of theology. This failure is understandable since Gerson was first and foremost a theologian; his primary concern was always the faculty of theology.

The prestigious position of the University of Paris in France and throughout all Christendom is considerably enhanced by the rich history and tradition which he attributes to it. He sets the university's origin as far back as the time of Adam. Adam, according to Gerson, was privileged with a special revelation and was entrusted with inspired knowledge. Through successive generations, this body of inspired knowledge was transferred and renewed in Egypt by Abraham and other successors of the children of Noah. This knowledge was then transmitted to Athens and subsequently to Rome from where it was carried across the Alps to France through the efforts of Charlemagne and planted with great labor in the city of Paris, where it became embodied in the University of Paris.[12]

What Gerson has thus presented is basically a detailed theory of the *translatio studii*, a notion which in the times of Charles the Bald (843-877) gradually became associated with the earlier Carolingian notion of the *translatio imperii*.[13] Gerson's theory of the *translatio studii* is of special interest because he does not regard the *translatio* as the mere transference of Greco-Roman culture and civilization to the Christian West. He attributes to Adam a special primitive revelation. Rome and Greece are but heirs to this body of inspired knowledge and not its first recipients. For Gerson, therefore, the Parisian

---

[12] *Pour exposer a vous, Messeigneurs,* G, 7, 329. "Helas, je suis celle qui en Adam fus premierement inspiree en sa nouvelle creation; je suis celle qui depuis par successions feu fondee et renouvelee en Egypte par Abraham et autres filz de Noe, puis feus transposee a Athenes et nommee Pallas ou Minerve; puis vins a Rome quant la chevallerie y seignorisoit. Puis par Charles Magne le grand, feus plantee a grans labeurs en France en la cité de Paris et tant amee et chier tenue que les tres nobles roys de France ont voulu que je soie nommee fille du Roy par civile adoption." See also *Vivat Rex,* G, 7, 1138.

[13] Ernst R. Curtius, *Europäische Literatur und lateinisches Mittelalter* (2nd ed. Bern, 1954), pp. 388-390. Cf. Etienne Gilson, *Les idées et les lettres* (Paris, 1932), pp. 182-187. On the basis of Gilson's analysis, it does not seem that the Carolingian notion of *translatio* either goes back to the time of Adam or involves a body of inspired knowledge but is concerned primarily with the transfer of Greco-Roman culture. For a study of the *translatio studii* as well as the relationship of *sacerdotium, regnum* and *studium* in the thirteenth century see Herbert Grundmann, "Sacerdotium, Regnum, Studium," *AKG,* 24 (1951), 5-21. On the *translatio studii,* see also the detailed study of F. J. Worstbrock, "Translatio artium," *AKG,* 47 (1965), 1-22. In Gerson's time, the notion of *translatio studii* was also utilized by Nicholas of Clémanges. Cf. Denifle, *Chartularium,* 3, xxxi.

studium generale goes back through the classical and Hebraic traditions to Adam. Gerson does not specify the nature of the inspired knowledge given Adam nor does he speculate on its relationship to the writings of the Old and New Testaments. Gerson also fails to describe the manner in which this inspired knowledge existed during the Greco-Roman period. Perhaps it is unfair to ask these questions of him; his use of the *translatio studii* seems only to have been intended to attribute to his university, without any further specification, the aura of antiquity and tradition.

From what has been said thus far, it is clear that for Gerson there is but one theological center for France and all Christendom and that center is Paris. Gerson urged bishops and rectors to send their most prominent students to Paris for their education. He indeed saw Paris as the intellectual capital of the world from which young doctors would go forth as the teachers of Christendom. He warns the rulers of Christendom that they are to show special concern for the proper cultivation and preservation of theological truth and the best way to fulfill that obligation is to have one intellectual center in Christendom which would be the source of all theological learning. Heresy, moreover, which is frequently engendered by the multiplicity of peoples, passions, and judgments would soon overrun all Christendom unless there is some recourse to a group of theologians who are of upright moral character and whose judgments are not affected by their personal passions and prejudices.[14] Gerson maintains that the University of Paris should and does contain such a body of theologians. To this body of theologians and to this university all theological disputes should be referred for resolution.

Some may contend that the papal curia should be such a tribunal and Gerson does not reject this suggestion outright. He admits it as a possibility but he has sincere doubts that theologians of outstanding character and integrity will ever be found in the curia. He characterizes theologians of the papal court as partial, seductive, proud, greedy and envious. These are hardly characteristics that will contribute to the formulation of an integral and balanced theology nor would such qualities guarantee the impartial settlement of theological disputes. He especially criticizes the papal theologians for their partiality towards secular powers and their overconcern for the

---

[14] *De examinatione doctrinarum*, P, 1, 18 B-C. "Providendum est sedulo per rectores Christianitatis ne studium theologicae veritatis depereat, sed alicubi resideat velut in fonte."

protection and preservation of papal prerogatives. They have, in brief, dedicated themselves to the service of vested interests rather than to the cause of truth.[15]

Gerson, therefore, considers Paris as the seat of all meaningful theological endeavor. He even asserts that theology is more abundantly and more truly found at the University of Paris than at any other university in Christendom.[16] He calls Paris the throne of divine wisdom. The University of Paris, moreover, sustains the Christian faith through its theological endeavors. Without the theological investigations of the University of Paris, the Christian faith would be less known and defended. The final result of such a situation would be the destruction and disappearance of belief. In Gerson's mind, love of the university and love of the Christian faith are identical.[17]

Despite Gerson's glorification, the University of Paris in the fourteenth and fifteenth centuries was in a period of transformation. The division caused by the schism had resulted in the loss of many leading theologians who were unsympathetic to Avignon. Among these were Henry of Langenstein, who moved to the University of Vienna, and Marsilius of Inghen († 1396), who took up residence at the University of Heidelberg. Many professors were frequently absent from the university on missions to various royal and papal courts on matters relating to the schism. Gerson himself was part of such embassies in 1403 and 1407. Requirements for university degrees and examinations were lowered and an increasing number of degrees were granted by papal indult and not through normal academic procedure. The papacy, indeed once its greatest supporter, came to regard the university principally as a political instrument for the advancement of its cause in the schism. The withdrawal of many students and professors belonging to the Roman obedience also lessened the European character of the university and caused it to become more French in its outlook and more narrowly involved in French politics. Benefices were increasingly reserved for French students. Instead of being primarily the teacher of Christendom, the university became

---

[15] *De examinatione doctrinarum*, P, 1, 18 C-D. "Si dixerit aliquis, fiet recursus ad sedem et curiam summi pontificis. Non negamus hoc, si theologia illic habuerit suos doctores non partiales, non seductos, non fastuosos, quaestuosos, aut invidos, non potestati seculari, non spirituali, plus quam veritati faventes; alioquin tolerabilius esset nullos habere quam tales pati."

[16] *Adorabunt eum omnes reges*, G, 7, 530.

[17] *Adorabunt eum omnes reges*, G, 7, 530.

increasingly the counsellor of the French crown. This nationalistic tendency in the university's orientation is indicated by Gerson himself in his frequent designation of the university as *filia regis*. The result of such involvement could only be a loss of prestige and independence on the part of the university.[18]

The function of the university most closely associated with Gerson's concept of reform is its quest for the peace and union of the church which had been considerably disrupted by the many years of schism which the church had experienced both in the East and the West. Gerson regards the University of Paris as a major instrument for the attainment of ecclesiastical peace and union. He gives several reasons for his position. He argues first from the analogy between natural bodies and the church as the mystical body of Christ. All natural bodies seek first and foremost their own internal peace and unity, which means in effect the peace and unity of all their members.[19] The quest for peace and unity, moreover, is the obligation of all members of the body and each member in his own way contributes towards that end. The analogy with the church as the mystical body is obvious. The mystical body too seeks to preserve its own union and peace and all its members are in varying degrees obliged to contribute towards the attainment of that goal. Since the university contains members of the mystical body drawn from all parts of the world, she will naturally be expected to play an important role in the search for peace and union.[20]

The university's obligation to secure the peace and unity of the church is much more, however, than the cumulative obligation of her members as individuals of the mystical body. The importance of the University of Paris within the mystical body is second only to that of the church's hierarchy. After the ecclesiastical hierarchy, the obligation to promote the church's peace and unity falls most heavily upon the University of Paris.[21] Gerson even attributes to the

---

[18] The state of the University of Paris in the late middle ages is discussed with pertinent bibliography in Delaruelle, *L'Église au temps du Grand Schisme*, 2, 468-473.

[19] *Pax hominibus bonae voluntatis*, G, 7, 766. "...disons que les hommes sont ordonnés de Dieu comme un corps mistique a l'exemple du corps naturel qui doibt avoir paix et union entre ses membres."

[20] *Pax hominibus bonae voluntatis*, G, 7, 767.

[21] *Tractatus pro unione Ecclesiae*, G, 6, 14. "Quantum ad quintum articulum in quo restat videre quomodo specialiter spectat ad Universitatem Parisiensium prosequi unionem Ecclesiae, sit prima conclusio: ad Universitatem Parisiensem post coetum praelatorum, maxime spectat hujusmodi negotium tractare."

university an important role in determining the government of the church.[22] The major reason given by Gerson for the prominence of the University of Paris in the life and activity of the church is that within the university there reside the *doctores solemnissimi*. No other university can boast of such a gathering of men learned in matters that so intimately pertain to the peace and unity of the church. In addition to the *doctores* actually living and teaching at the university, there are many others whom the university can summon whenever she has need of consultation on important matters.[23]

The skillful mastery and interpretation of divine, natural, and positive law, so necessary for the reformation of the church, is found, according to Gerson, among the *doctores* of the various faculties of the University of Paris. The faculties of arts and law contain specialists in the area of natural and positive law respectively. The theological faculty holds the most prominent position in the university because it is primarily concerned with the *lex divina*. The function of the theological faculty is to discern the principles of divine law and to separate them from the maze of positive ecclesiastical law. In this activity lies the reform, peace, and unity of the church.

2. THE THEOLOGIAN AND CHURCH REFORM

As a result of the preceding analysis, the theologian emerges as a most important figure in ecclesiastical society. Along with other university professors, he belonged to a distinct *ordo* in medieval society and enjoyed corresponding rights and privileges.[24] The theologian, moreover, occupies the highest rank within the university and his primary task is to promote the peace, union, and reform of the church. The exalted position of the theologian is further

---

[22] *Quomodo stabit regnum*, G, 7, 980. "Appert que a la fille du roy appartient selon doctrine jugier du gouvernement de saincte eglise, particulierement quant a la faculte de theologie, et quant aux autres en diverses matieres. . . ."

[23] *Tractatus pro unione Ecclesiae*, G, 6, 14-16. A high percentage of the leading theologians active at Paris during Gerson's time were associated in varying degrees with the College of Navarre. In addition to Gerson, these included Pierre d'Ailly, Nicholas of Clémanges, Jean Courtecuisse, Gilles Deschamps, and Gerard Machet. Cf. Feret, *La faculté de théologie de Paris*, 4, 169-304.

[24] See R. Guelluy, "La place des théologiens dans l'Église et la société médiévale," in *Miscellanea historica in honorem Alberti de Meyer*, 1 (Louvain, 1946), 571-589, and Gabriel Le Bras, "Velut Splendor Firmamenti: Le docteur dans le droit de l'Église médiévale," in *Mélanges offerts à Etienne Gilson*, pp. 373-388.

illustrated by the fact that Gerson lists his way of life as among the highest and most noble manner of serving God. The study of theology is considered on a par with the ecclesiastical states of virginity, widowhood, and the religious life.[25] Another indication of the high esteem accorded the theologian is seen in Gerson's assertion that, all factors being equal, the theologian's prayer is more effective than that of the simple laity. He gives two reasons for his position. He argues first that the theologian has a clearer and purer understanding of the divine goodness. As his second reason, he asserts that the theologian's prayer is more spiritual because it is freer from material phantasms. Gerson does not maintain that all theologians have attained this mode of prayer. Such a level of prayer is only attained with great effort and difficulty. Once attained, however, Gerson would attribute to it extraordinary efficacy in the life of the church.[26]

The importance of the theologian in Christian society is especially seen in the fact that Gerson frequently describes him in his teaching and preaching capacities as the successor to St. Paul. As such the theologian is contrasted with the sovereign pontiff, who is the successor to St. Peter. The theologian, moreover, follows directly in the tradition of the church's theologians just as the pope follows in the direct line of his predecessors. The theologian's knowledge, thus, represents not merely his own achievements but the entire theological inheritance of the church's *doctores*. Gerson further maintains that the same relationship which existed between Peter and Paul in the *ecclesia primitiva* exists in the church of his day between pope and theologian. As successor to Paul, the theologian has the right and duty to correct the pope not only on doctrinal matters but also on any occasion when the needs of the church merit such correction. Gerson justifies this right by the fact that Paul rebuked Peter at Antioch for the duplicity of his attitude towards the Gentiles. St. Paul narrates in Gal 2: 11-14 that he openly criticized Peter when, under pressure from Jewish circles in Jerusalem, he ceased taking his meals with the Gentiles. Paul attacks Peter's activity because it was

---

[25] *Gloyre soit a Dieu*, G, 7, 196. "Et pis font ceulx qui mocquent les personnes qui sont en estat plus hault et digne de Dieu servir comme est l'estat de uirginité ou de viduité ou de religion, ou d'estude de theologie. . . ."

[26] *Obsecro vos*, G, 5, 401. "Efficacior est ceteris paribus, theologorum oratio qui supra fidem simplicium clariorem et puriorem habent de divina bonitate cognitionem. Est enim talis oratio spiritualior et a phantasmatibus corporeis alienatior. Haec oratio conquiritur cum summa difficultate et pascit animam."

not in accord with the principles of the Gospel that all the apostles were commissioned to preach. Theologians follow in the same Pauline tradition whenever they ask of the pope: *Cur ita facis?* Gerson, furthermore, sees no contradiction between the theologian's corrective power and the fact that the *licentia docendi*, which grants him the authority to teach, rests upon papal authority. The corrective power of the theologian is a valid and, at times, necessary exercise of his office.

In addition to the precedent set by St. Paul, Gerson also maintains that the corrective power of the theologian is rooted in divine law as contained in Mt 18: 15-17. This is the law of fraternal correction which was advocated by Christ before any particular matter is brought to the whole assembly of the church. Gerson asserts that this procedure was widely advocated in all circles at the Council of Constance.[27] This corrective power, however, is not restricted in its application to the sovereign pontiff but extends as well to members of the ecclesiastical hierarchy. An example of this power is seen in the case of positive law. Gerson contends that, of itself, no positive law is capable of binding under pain of mortal sin. Laws of this category have the power to bind under serious sin only insofar as they embody elements of the divine law. No ecclesiastical prelate, therefore, is capable of making a purely positive law with the same binding force as divine law. Were he to attempt such an action, the theologian would be justified in resisting him and reminding him in the words of Paul that he is not conducting himself according to the truth of the Gospel.[28]

The activity of a theologian, according to Gerson, is primarily related to the Sacred Scriptures. Following faithfully in the medieval tradition, he defines the theologian in terms of the Scriptures.

---

[27] *An liceat in causis fidei a papa appellare*, G, 6, 284. "Ex quibus palam elicitur quod Summus Pontifex qui succedit Petro in apostolatu reprehendi potest publice per doctorem theologum qui in officio praedicationis succedit Paulo, etiam ubi non haereticaret vel erraret in fide. Et hoc similiter elicitur generalius et inconvincibilius ex auctoritate proxime allegata: si peccaverit in te frater tuus, quemadmodum pluries in sacro Constantiensi concilio latissime deductum est in sermonibus publicis et multiplicibus scripturis quorum copiae sunt apud multos." Cf. *Nimis honorati sunt*, G, 7, 722. For the relationship between the *licentia docendi* and papal authority see *De vita spirituali animae*, G, 3, 201-202.

[28] *De vita spirituali*, G, 3, 162. "Quod si quis praelatorum vellet hujusmodi legem aut diceret habere robur legis divinae, sibi fas esset per theologos aut alios hoc cognoscentes resistere in facie et dicere quod non recte ambulat ad veritatem Evangelii." Cf. Gal 2:14.

Theologian and scriptural exegete are therefore synonymous.[29] More specifically, the theologian is principally concerned with the divine law which is to be found in the Scriptures. His major task, consequently, is to elucidate, defend and strengthen the divine law through his study and teaching.[30]

The theologian, however, is more than mere interpreter and custodian of the *lex divina*. Since the early years of the church's endowment there has resulted a growing confusion between the various elements of divine, canon and civil law. This confusion has generated and prolonged the schism in the church and has been the major obstacle to its unification and reformation. The function of the theologian is to reduce this confusion and to redefine the proper domain of the various types of law. The theologian's task is to discern amid all the laws by which the church is governed those elements which pertain to divine law and those which belong to the domain of positive ecclesiastical legislation. The theologian exercises this discernment through the proper use of *recta ratio*. He is, as it were, the skilled goldsmith who knows how to distinguish gold from copper ore, and silver from lead.[31]

Discernment is especially needed in the area of canon law, for it is here that the greatest confusion reigns. Too much of what is purely positive ecclesiastical law passes for divine law; divine law is consequently submerged under a mass of positive legislation and the

---

[29] *Diligite justitiam*, G, 7, 608. "La police espirituelle, que nous nommons ecclesiastique ou evangelique, se gouverne principaument par l'evangile et par ceulx qui le scevent, que nous appellons theologiens." Throughout the Middle Ages, *theologia, sacra pagina,* and *scriptura* were used interchangeably. Aquinas, Bonaventure, and Ockham all exemplify this tradition. Cf. Henri de Lubac, *Exégèse médiévale* 1, 1, 59-61. and J. de Ghellinck, "'Pagina' et 'Sacra Pagina.' Histoire d'un mot et transformation de l'objet primitivement désigné," in *Mélanges August Pelzer* (Louvain, 1947), pp. 23-59. For the intimate relationship between scripture and tradition in the Middle Ages as well as the growing separation of the two in the late Middle Ages see Paul de Vooght, *Les sources de la doctrine chrétienne d'après les théologiens du xiv⁰ siècle et du début du xv⁰* (Paris, 1954), pp. 254-264. An excellent treatment of Gerson's teaching on scripture and tradition can be found in Meyjes, *Jean Gerson*, pp. 252-274.

[30] *Dominus his opus habet*, G, 5, 224. "...theologi proprio nomine dicuntur hi qui notitiam profitentur et habent eorum quae proprie dicuntur esse de theologia hoc est de jure divino, seu evangelico quod idem est, et qui illud sciunt elucidare, defendere, roborare."

[31] *De vita spirituali animae*, G, 3, 161. "Quamobrem decernere de legibus omnibus manifestum est spectare principaliter ad theologiam velut ad scientiam superiorem architectonicam, quatenus recta ratio separat illud quod juris divini est in eis ab illo quod humanum est sive positivum, tamquam si aurifaber peritissimus secernat aurum ab aurichalco et argentum a plumbo."

resulting confusion has effected considerable damage upon the church. Since its primary function is to make applicable in a practical manner the principles of the divine law, canon law always runs the risk of confusing the more practical aspects of ecclesiastical legislation with the very principles of divine law. When such confusion arises, it is to the theologian to whom recourse must be had, since he alone is most capable of distinguishing the principles of divine law from their practical application in time and circumstances.[32]

This prerogative of the theologian does not mean that he can blithely intrude in other disciplines. He must know and respect the principles and traditions that govern those disciplines. His is the duty, moreover, to carefully examine and interpret the principles upon which all disciplines are built. The theologian should have a better understanding of the methodology of the various sciences than many of those actually involved in those disciplines. Many canonists merely have a memorized knowledge of their field without truly understanding the principles which govern its methodology. The theologian should have such a knowledge of the methodology of canon law that he can readily become a canon lawyer. Gerson maintains, moreover, that it is considerably easier for a theologian to become a qualified canon lawyer than it is for a canonist to become a theologian.[33] It is easier, he argues, to deduce conclusions from principles than to argue from conclusions back to principles. Thus a theologian will more readily comprehend the process by which canon law draws its conclusions from divine law than a canonist will understand the ultimate theological principles upon which his legislation rests.

Ideally, Gerson would prefer to have each theologian become a canonist and each canonist a theologian. As *ambidextri*, they would know the methodology and principles upon which both theology and canon law operate and would be much more likely to respect the proper domain of each science. As theologians they would be able to discern the principles of divine law operative in the sacred canons

---

[32] *Conversi estis nunc ad pastorem*, G, 5, 175. "Subinde deducimus quod dubiis emergentibus circa partem hanc juris divini in corpore canonum repositam vel immixtam, finalis et certa decisio spectat ad originale principium unde haec sumpta cognovimus, hoc est ad theologicam disciplinam ad quam debet retrorsum fieri conversio. . . ."

[33] *Conversi estis nunc ad pastorem*, G, 5, 176.

and as canonists they would strive with greater exactitude to make sure that canonical legislation is firmly constructed upon the foundation of divine law. With such men the confusion between divine and canon law would be considerably mitigated, since they would know the proper limits of their respective sciences.[34]

Gerson realizes, however, that the chance of finding men who are truly *ambidextri* is relatively rare. Such a person would truly be deserving of the words of Sir 31:9: *"quis est hic et laudabimus eum?"* Since it is so difficult to find men who are truly *ambidextri* in both the theological and canonical disciplines, Gerson recommends that the canonists at least recognize the limits of their discipline. They should know the exact nature of their profession. When canonists observe due restraint and remain within the proper limits of their science, they are deserving of praise and honor. Praise and honor should not be accorded to any canonist who has transcended the boundaries of his discipline. Such a person is only capable of producing confusion and falsity and is hardly worthy of acclaim.[35]

A particular area of confusion that Gerson notes between theologians and canonists is that of terminology. Since he considers canon law as subordinate to theology and dependent upon that discipline for its principles, he is rather insistent that canonists respect the exact meaning of the terms used by the theologians. If both theologians and jurists understand the same terms in a different manner, the result can only be confusion within the two disciplines; neither the theologian nor the jurist will understand one another. For Gerson, whenever there is confusion of terminology between the two disciplines, the theological use and understanding of the term is always to be taken as normative.[36]

Closely related to the theologian's obligation to interpret and clarify divine law is his power in the area of *epikeia*. His is the obligation to determine when a situation exists in the church's life which necessitates the employment of the principle of *epikeia*. Theologians are thus empowered to determine when circumstances are such as to necessitate an exception to the law. This generally occurs whenever the strict interpretation of the law would go contrary to the expressed purpose of the legislator. In such cases the letter of the law is in contradiction with its spirit. Gerson felt that such a

---

[34] *Dominus his opus habet*, G, 5, 227.
[35] *Conversi estis nunc ad pastorem*, G, 5, 176.
[36] *Dominus his opus habet*, G, 5, 228.

situation prevailed in the church during the period of the schism. The literal interpretation of canon law had prevented the summoning of an ecumenical council and had thereby prolonged the schism and delayed reform. Gerson's proposed solution to the schism and the reformation of the church involved recourse to divine law and the application of the principle of *epikeia* to those positive laws that were impeding the convocation of the council. The determination of the positive ecclesiastical laws to which *epikeia* should be applied rests, for Gerson, principally with the theologian.[37]

One might object that since *epikeia* is applied to positive ecclesiastical legislation, its use should fall principally within the competence of the canon lawyer. Gerson, however, is not of this opinion. He maintains that application of the principle of *epikeia* rests primarily with the theologian. This is not to say that canon lawyers have no part in such a decision; they do play a role but one which is subordinate to that of the theologian.[38] The predominance of the theologian in the exercise of *epikeia* is based upon the fact that the principle of *epikeia* seeks to restore law to its proper finality which is essentially charity. Since the finality of law is basically a datum of the divine law, the implementation of *epikeia* falls more precisely within the competence of the theologian.

The important role attributed to the theologian in the interpretation of the divine law and in the application of the principle of *epikeia* naturally raises the question of the relationship of the theologian to the bishop. Gerson certainly does not propose that the church be run simply by theologians. His concept of the church is essentially hierarchical and in this hierarchy bishops hold a most important position. The roles of the theologian and the prelate, therefore, are not in opposition but complementary.[39]

Both bishop and theologian are intimately involved with matters of

---

[37] *Propositio facta coram Anglicis*, G, 6, 130. "Et haec est non parva congratulationis materia quod in unam conventum est sententiam per duas Universitates toto orbe celeberrimas. Et ipsis nonne fides dari debet cum illic sint viri spirituales et sapientes, secundum qualium judicia medium virtutis accipere jubet Philosophus? Illic praeterea sunt ideonei conditores legum doctrinaliter et instructive, quibus similis interpretatio per epikeiam debita est."

[38] *Tractatus de unitate Ecclesiae*, G, 6, 138. "Auctoritas vero doctrinaliter utendi epikeia residet principaliter apud peritos in theologia, quae est architectoria respectu aliarum, et consequenter apud peritos in scientia juris canonici et civilis prout ex principiis juris divini et naturalis habet accipere fundamenta."

[39] *Tractatus pro unione Ecclesiae*, G, 6, 7. "Post praelatos maxime obligantur doctores Ecclesiae ad procurandam unionem Ecclesiae."

faith but each according to the specific nature of their respective offices. The function of the theologian is primarily scholastic in nature. His is the task to speculate upon the various elements of belief and through the normal academic procedures of investigation, reflection, discussion, and disputation arrive at a better understanding of the faith, especially those matters directly related to divine law. In these scholastic endeavors the Scriptures are always the primary object of the theologian's investigation. Gerson describes the function of the theologian by the phrase, *doctrinaliter* or *scholastice determinare*.[40] The role of the bishop is summed up in the expression, *judicialiter determinare*. His is the task of giving authoritative force to the teachings of the theologians through his powers of jurisdiction. He does this by punishing those who act contrary to his decisions in matters of faith. Gerson advises the bishop not to define any article of faith as binding upon the conscience of the faithful unless it has been previously discussed and scholastically determined by theologians. Unless the bishop respects the work of the theologian, he renders useless an important segment of the church's life. He frustrates the mission assigned to the theologian by the church when it grants him the *licentia docendi*. This licentiate specifically entails the power to interpret the Sacred Scriptures. The bishop, therefore, is to be guided in the formation of his theological decisions by the deliberations of the theologians.[41]

Gerson illustrates the relationship that should prevail between theologians and bishops by an analogy. The activity of theologians and bishops in the mystical body is analogous to that of the human intellect and will. Nothing is chosen by the will unless right reason first indicates the propriety of such action. Right reason is the faculty that determines a course of action by designating it as good or bad. The will then carries into execution the dictates of right reason. A similar relation exists between theologians and bishops. The theologians are, as it were, the *recta ratio* of the mystical body with the bishops playing more or less the role of the *voluntas*. The

---

[40] *Ad justificationem condemnationis*, G, 6, 176. Cf. *De vita spirituali animae*, G, 3, 201.

[41] *Tractatus pro unione Ecclesiae*, G, 6, 14-15. "Primo quod Ecclesiae praelati nihil debent, in fide scilicet, auctoritative definire nisi prius fuerit discussum et scholastice determinatum a doctoribus Ecclesiae. Patet quia ad hoc sunt ordinati doctores Ecclesiae; frustra enim essent in Ecclesia sancta Dei nisi illos actus exercerent qui sunt proprii actus ipsorum, scilicet scholastice determinare et disputare ea quae sunt fidei." On the theologians and the *licentia docendi* see G, 6, 7, 12.

bishops, therefore, put into effect the counsels and decisions of the theologians.[42]

Gerson realizes that his position on the relationship between theologians and bishops might give the impression of relegating the episcopal body to a merely executive role in the functioning of the mystical body. He entertains the objection that bishops possess the power to *scholastice determinare* as well as *judicialiter determinare*. This objection has a twofold basis. First it is argued that bishops have a higher degree of authority than theologians. As such their authority would formally include all lower forms of authority and, therefore, that of theologians. The second argument is that the teaching authority of theologians comes from the the church. The *licentia docendi* has been granted to the theologians by the church. On the basis of the above reasoning, it is concluded that the bishop formally possesses the authority to *scholastice determinare*.[43]

When pushed on the question of the respective competence of bishops and theologians in the area of theological speculation, Gerson readily admits that there is no easy solution to the problem; at times the problem appeared to him as insoluble. On occasions he admits that the bishops have this power but since they have many other important activities to perform within the church they must necessarily relinquish it to the theologians. The theologians, therefore, are to be more or less exclusively concerned with theological speculation. Gerson argues, in effect, that the efficient distribution of labor concedes the major portion of theological activity to the theologians. At other times, Gerson formally excludes the power to *scholastice determinare* from the number of episcopal prerogatives. Such activity is exclusively the function and mission of the *doctores*. But even here Gerson is not certain of his position. He realizes that the bishops must possess that power in some degree if they are effectively to fulfill the pastoral office of educating their subjects in the area of faith and morals.[44] In general, Gerson feels that the activities of theologians and bishops can be more readily distinguished in theory than in practice.[45]

From what has been said thus far about the theologian, it may seem that Gerson describes him solely in terms of his intellectual

---

[42] *Tractatus pro unione Ecclesiae*, G, 6, 15.
[43] *Tractatus pro unione Ecclesiae*, G, 6, 15.
[44] *Tractatus pro unione Ecclesiae*, G, 6, 15.
[45] *Voluimus propter elucidationem*, G, 6, 150.

activities. Such an impression would be misleading and would reveal only a partial aspect of Gerson's thought. While placing high priority on genuine intellectual ability and dedication to a life of study, Gerson also requires that a theologian possess more than the intellectual virtues. The theologian must be morally virtuous as well as, intellectually competent. The theologian must be humble, especially in the formulation and expression of his judgments. His life moreover, should be as free as possible from all moral defects. Moral weaknesses have a detrimental effect upon intellectual activity, for they minimize the theologian's ability to arrive at truth. They distort his intellectual activity and exercise a negative influence upon his judgment. Any person who lacks both intellectual ability and moral integrity is unfit for the study of the Sacred Scriptures. Such a person will never arrive at a true understanding of God's Word.[46] Gerson thus sees the ideal theologian as a morally good man who is learned in the Sacred Scriptures. His erudition, however, must have its source, not only in his intellectual activities, but also in his affective experiences. What he has learned intellectually must be transformed by the affections of the heart and then carried into execution.[47]

From what has preceded, it is clear that the theologian is a most important agent in the reform of the church. His importance rests on his close association with divine law. Since the prolongation of the schism has its roots in the confusion of divine and positive law, the settlement of the schism and the reform of the church can only be achieved by a conversion to the principles of divine law and the application of *epikeia* to the existing maze of positive ecclesiastical law. The convocation of a general council, therefore, to heal the schism and plan for the reform of the church is possible only through recourse to divine law and the principle of *epikeia*. Herein lies both the *reformatio pacis* and the *reformatio in capite et membris*.

The resort to divine law and *epikeia* remains abstract and meaningless unless seen in the context of the human agents with whom law and *epikeia* are identified. The theologian is clearly among

---

[46] *Contra haeresim de communione laicorum sub utraque specie*, P, 1, 458 B.

[47] *De consolatione theologiae*, P, 1, 177 B. "... ita theologum nominamus bonum virum in sacris litteris eruditum; non quidem eruditione solius intellectus; sed multo magis affectus; ut ea quae per theologiam intelligit, traducat per jugem ruminationem in affectum cordis, et executionem operis. ..."

the more important agents in the church entrusted with the interpretation of divine law and the application of *epikeia*. He above everyone else dedicates himself to the study of the sacred Scriptures wherein the divine law is contained. Through his study of the Scriptures, he is capable of clearly discerning the various principles of divine law. This power of discernment allows him to separate those aspects of canon law which are solidly founded upon divine law from those which are purely of human and ecclesiastical origin. The recourse to *epikeia* also rests primarily within the power of the theologian. Since the conversion to divine law and the application of *epikeia* are his major prerogatives, the theologian naturally emerges as a personality of supreme importance in the reformation of the church.

3. THEOLOGICAL REFORM

a) *Curiositas* and *Singularitas*

In addition to his work for the reform of the church, the theologian must, himself, undergo a professional reformation. Gerson, it is well known, was not content with the theological education of his day. In April 1400, in a letter to Pierre d'Ailly, and in two university lectures delivered in November 1402, Gerson called for a *reformatio* of theology.[48] He condemned the theologians of his day on two counts. They were guilty of *curiositas* and *singularitas*. *Curiositas* in a theologian is a fault by which he turns from more useful fields of theological endeavor and directs his scholarly interest towards areas that are either less beneficial, unattainable, or even harmful. Gerson realizes that the norm for determining what is useful will vary according to time, place, person, age, professional status, and even according to one's country. *Singularitas* is a fault by which a theologian bypasses more useful fields of theological activity and devotes his attention to teachings that are alien and unusual. Gerson does not consider *curiositas* and *singularitas* as totally distinct realities, for they have much in common. He views them as related concepts. Both are guilty of abandoning useful areas of theological endeavor. Each does so, furthermore, in order to enhance self-esteem.

---

[48] *Dum mentis aciem*, G. 2, 26-28. The two university lectures comprise the treatise *Contra curiositatem studentium*, G, 3, 224-249. Gerson's *De theologia mystica*, G, 3, 250-292, should also be considered as an essential part of his program for theological reform.

Curiosity, however, acts from a motive to know what is improper whereas singularity desires novelty.[49]

Gerson finds that the notions of *curiositas* and *singularitas* have their root both in the classical as well as in the biblical tradition. He frequently quotes Seneca as stating: *"necessaria nesciunt quia supervacua didicerunt."*[50] He discovers adumbrations of *curiositas* and *singularitas* in Ps 63:7 where the Psalmist accuses his enemies of having wasted themselves away in the complexity of their own thought. St. Paul in Rom 1:21 also criticized the philosophers of his day because "they became futile in their thinking and their senseless minds were darkened."[51] According to Gerson, the principle of *curiositas* is also behind St. Paul's admonition to the Romans that they should not strive to know more than is necessary; they should, rather, keep their knowledge within the bounds of sobriety.[52] The clearest scriptural injunction against *curiositas* and *singularitas* is contained in Sir 3:22. There the reader is enjoined not to seek what is too difficult to understand nor investigate what is beyond his power. He is told to reflect upon what has been assigned to him, for he does not need to know what is hidden.[53]

Gerson designates seven aspects of theological activity in his day which he considers as clear indications of *curiositas* and *singularitas*. The first sign is a disdain for teachings which have been fully formulated and an enthusiasm for those which are unknown and unexamined. This form of *curiositas* is always in search of new doctrines; its quest is always for subtleness and novelty. To restrict one's study to the teaching of accepted theologians and never to set out upon new intellectual endeavors is considered an indication of limited intelligence. Gerson's censure of such an attitude is not an attack against theological progress; it is more a criticism of those who turn their back completely on tradition. What he is saying is that without a proper appreciation of tradition within which to

[49] *Contra curiositatem studentium*, G, 3, 230. "Curiositas est vitium quo dimissis utilioribus homo convertit studium suum ad minus utilia vel inattingibilia sibi vel noxia." "Singularitas est vitium quo dimissis utilioribus homo convertit studium suum ad doctrinas peregrinas et insolitas." Cf. *A Deo exivit*, G, 5, 23-24.

[50] *Jucundum est*, G, 2, 31. Cf. Seneca, *De ira*, 2, 11, 2, *Ad Marciam de consolatione*, 1, 6, ed. Emil Hermes, *Dialogorum libri XII* (Leipzig, 1923), pp. 82, 153, and *Ep.*, 70, 15, ed. Otto Hense, *Ad Lucilium epistolae morales* (Leipzig, 1915), p. 239.

[51] *Contra curiositatem studentium*, G, 3, 231.

[52] *Regnum coelorum*, G, 7, 1000. Cf. Rom 12:3.

[53] *De vita spirituali animae*, G, 3, 164.

incorporate new theological developments those advancements cannot be fully comprehended.[54]

The second indication of *curiositas* is an exaggerated adherence to one theological school of thought. He argues that the students of his day are excessively prone to identify themselves with a single theologian. They become so identified with their theological idol that they prefer his school of thought above all others. Every element of his teaching is defended with equal vigor and never is there manifested the slightest doubt that the different aspects of his thought might admit of varying degrees of truth. Gerson, therefore, is not attacking adherence to one school of thought as such; that is to be commonly expected. What he is attacking is the excessive partiality to one theological school which blinds the theologian to its weaknesses and errors and thus prevents him from attaining truth. Allegiance of this type is hardly conducive to the impartial quest for truth. Such an attitude leads to excessive theological contention, errors of faith, and eventually to schism.[55]

Gerson next censures the theologians of his day for their excessive concern with logic, mathematics, physics and other sciences. These sciences are no longer considered as ancillary to theology but have almost become ends in themselves. Gerson maintains that theological methodology should be drawn primarily from theological principles and not from other sciences. To be a theologian one must adhere to theological method; the methodologies of other sciences will serve to no advantage. If a student feels that he cannot understand theological methodology unless he has first specialized in logic, philosophy, and the other sciences then he should, temporarily, leave the school of theology and matriculate in the arts faculty. He is not yet ready for theological speculation.[56]

The fourth manifestation of *curiositas* is somewhat similar to the second and consists in an excessive desire to attack some theologians while defending pertinaciously the teachings of others. Such a student of theology is always more prone to accentuate the differences that exist between theologians than to search out their areas of agreement and harmony. What appears as contrary and opposing will often, if approached in a spirit of concordance, turn out to be relatively similar although expressed in a different manner.

---

[54] *Contra curiositatem studentium*, G, 3, 238.
[55] *Contra curiositatem studentium*, G, 3, 239.
[56] *Contra curiositatem studentium*, G, 3, 239-240.

Curiositas leads to continual conflict and dissension; *concordantia* alone will lead to theological peace.[57]

The desire to create new theological terminology is also a complaint of Gerson and he considers this a fifth indication of *curiositas* in the theologians of his day. Gerson is especially concerned about the use of unconventional terminology in trinitarian speculations. Whenever he is concerned with the problem of terminology in theological studies, Gerson has recourse to a rule of St. Augustine on the subject. Augustine states that while philosophers have a wide range of terminology which they do not hesitate to use even when treating of the most difficult matters, thereby creating confusion in the minds of their listeners, the theologian must always speak according to fixed rules. Gerson understands Augustine's statement as referring to fixed and established terminology. The need for adherence to an exact terminology is especially evident in the history of the councils. If there is anything that emerges clearly from conciliar deliberations, it is the need for an accurate and scientifically formulated terminology. Gerson would have the theologians of his day adhere to the traditionally accepted terminology in matters theological. When unconventional terminology must be used, Gerson advises that the theologian indicate exactly the manner in which he, or the source he is using, understands that term.[58]

A sixth area of concern for Gerson in the matter of *curiositas* and *singularitas* is the tendency of many theologians to employ philosophical principles drawn from pagan philosophers such as Plato, Aristotle, Avicenna, and Algazel. He feels that such principles, if used uncritically in theological speculation, will necessarily lead to conclusions contrary to revealed matters of faith. The seventh and last sign of *curiositas* and *singularitas* for Gerson is relatively similar to the first. He condemns those who would neglect clear and established teachings of the schools and dedicate themselves to the investigation and study of more obscure theological problems. Such persons tend to look upon the traditional areas of theological investigation as unchallenging. Theological profundity, according to such theologians, must always be involved with what is difficult to comprehend or even with what is incomprehensible. They fail to recognize that profundity and simplicity are often identical.[59]

---

[57] *Contra curiositatem studentium*, G, 3, 240-241.
[58] *Contra curiositatem studentium*, G, 3, 244.
[59] *Contra curiositatem studentium*, G, 3, 245-248.

The general objection that Gerson has against all theologians guilty of *curiositas* and *singularitas* is that they have transcended the limits of theological investigation. Each discipline has, according to Gerson, a distinct area of operation. This area of operation can be termed its material and formal object. As long as students remain within the limits of the material and formal object of their discipline, their research can yield true and profitable results. Deception and error comes primarily when these boundaries are transcended. The desire to transcend the natural limits of theological investigation is generally the work of *curiositas* and *singularitas*.

Gerson asserts that the ancient philosophers succumbed to the temptation of *curiositas* and *singularitas*, especially in their speculations about God. They failed to realize that philosophical reasoning cannot advance indefinitely; as with any science, there are limits to its scope of investigation. Philosophy can learn that God is one and that he exercises divine providence over all creation. The philosopher, moreover, can understand God as that than which nothing greater can be conceived. As long as pagan philosophers had remained within these limits all was well. Spurred on by *curiositas*, they attempted to go beyond the boundaries of their discipline, and, as a result, they have stumbled over the stone of error.[60]

Under the driving force of *curiositas* and *singularitas*, the theologian can succumb to the same temptation. There is no doubt that theology transcends philosophy but this should not be interpreted to mean that theology's scope of investigation has no limits. Theology has its predetermined boundaries set by the Sacred Scriptures. If any theologian in his investigation seeks to transcend the limits of knowledge set by the Scriptures, he too will stumble upon the rock of error as did the pagan philosophers in their speculations about God. Gerson finds strong support for his position in the first chapter of the *De divinis nominibus* where Dionysius lays down as a universal rule that nothing should be said either in word or in writing about the transcendent and hidden nature of God except those things which have been revealed to man by the Sacred Scriptures.[61]

Any theologian who would dare to delve deeper into the knowledge of God than Scripture allows inevitably leads astray both

---

[60] *Contra curiositatem studentium*, G, 3, 230-231.

[61] *Contra curiositatem studentium*, G, 3, 233. Cf. Dionysius, *De divinis nominibus*, 1, *MPG*, 2, 368 B-369 A.

himself and all those who would follow him. Gerson brings his point home by the use of an example. He imagines a person born blind receiving instructions about colors; he cannot understand these truths on his own experience but must accept them from others on faith. He might be told that whiteness deflects and blackness attracts light. If the blind person decides to extend his knowledge on this point beyond the limits of the information given him by others, he can easily fall into error. He may conclude on his own initiative that the experience of deflection is similar to the manner in which he experiences objects as scattered and divided through his sense of touch. Obviously, Gerson concludes, such reasoning is erroneous. The theologian who attempts to transcend the limits of the Scriptures is comparable to the blind man. He has attempted to understand divine truths which have not been revealed and is, therefore, more blind than the man in the example.[62]

Theologians often fall prey to *curiositas* through presumption or through a sense of shame in not having ready answers to questions asked of them. In matters that transcend the Scriptures, Gerson would have the theologian take refuge in the virtue of humility and admit that he does not know the answer. By giving such advice Gerson does not intend to discourage theological endeavor. All indolence in expounding the Scriptures is to be condemned with the same vehemence as excessive *curiositas*. Gerson would define the goal of theological investigation as the humble elucidation of the Scriptures within the limits possible to man. To theologians who adhere to this goal has been made the promise in Sir 24:31: "Those who make me more understandable to men will have eternal life." [63]

b) Repentance and Belief

To counteract the influence of *curiositas* and *singularitas*, which had so strongly infiltrated theological circles, Gerson issued a call for theological reform. The rejection of *curiositas* and *singularitas* and the return to the Scriptures in a spirit of *poenitentia* constitute the essential aspects of his proposal for the reformation of theological studies. Gerson understands *poenitentia* primarily in terms of justice; it is a species of justice which strives to render God his due. The sinner has deprived God of the honor that is his as creator and

---

[62] *Contra curiositatem studentium*, G, 3, 233.
[63] *Contra curiositatem studentium*, G, 3, 233.

redeemer and he is guilty of *lèse majesté* toward the divinity. He has, moreover, put himself in opposition to the divine love and, consequently, must submit himself to punishment according to God's law. *Poenitentia*, therefore, is that spirit of soul which enables man freely to detest and punish in himself sins against God. Detestation arises when one realizes the injustice of sin and its offensiveness to the divine majesty. The realization of this injustice should give rise to interior sorrow and herein is verified the notion of punishment. *Poenitentia*, finally, has for its aim full reconciliation with God, which produces in the soul a spirit of joy and contentment.[64] Although he has described *poenitentia* primarily in scholastic terminology, Gerson affirms that his definition is essentially that of Gregory the Great.[65]

One of the more immediate effects of *poenitentia*, is its conduciveness to belief in the Gospel. This relationship between repentance and belief is clearly exemplified in Mk 1:15 where Christ asks the people of Galilee to repent and believe in the Gospel. Penitence here precedes the command to believe in the Gospel: *Poenitemini et credite Evangelio*. For Gerson, repentance and belief in the Gospel are not two realities merely juxtaposed by Christ but are intimately related. *Poenitentia* is related to belief in the Gospel as cause to effect. He informs the theological students of Paris that the light of faith will clearly shine in their souls through the mediation of *poenitentia*[66].

Belief in the Gospel effected by *poenitentia* occurs through a gradual purgation of man's intellectual and volitional faculties. Gerson regards the human soul as essentially containing two sets of powers. The cognitive powers of the soul consist of *sensualitas, ratio,*

---

[64] *Contra curiositatem studentium*, G, 3, 234. "Poenitentia est habitus virtuosus inclinans liberum arbitrium detestari et punire in seipso peccatum contra Dei legem commissum vel omissum, et hoc ad finem beatitudinis consequendum. Vel sic: Poenitentia est habitus justitiae inclinans liberum arbitrium detestari et punire peccatum in seipso immediate vel mediate, pro sui reconciliatione ad Deum." Cf. *Memento finis*, G, 7, 694.

[65] *Poenitimini...Je voudroie bien savoir*, G, 7, 795. "Et pour entendre ce cry, saint Gregoire, l'un des quatre principaulx heraulx de sainte eglise, nous expose qu'il veut dire. Penitancia est preterita mala plangere, etc. Autant vault dire: repentez vous, comme dire: tous les pechiez passez plorez, et des advenir vous gardez." Cf. Gregory, *Homiliae in Evangelia*, 2, 24, 15, MPL, 76, 1256 B, and *Moralia in Job*, 16, 20, MPL, 75, 1133 A-B.

[66] *Contra curiositatem studentium*, G, 3, 225. "...qua (poenitentia) mediante potest lumen fidei ad animam clarius radiare. Propterea vero ad istud: credite Evangelio, praemittitur: poenitemini."

and *intelligentia simplex*; the appetitive powers are *appetitus sensualis, appetitus rationalis* and *synderesis.*[67] Both the cognitive and the affective powers, moreover, are mutually related. Their relationship is such that neither operates without the concurrence of the other. The affections play an important role in every cognitive activity and there is no affective activity which is not in some manner a form of experiental knowledge. The affective powers participate in the cognitive process to the same degree that cognition concurs in the generation of an affection.[68] Gerson uses the examples of light and heat to illustrate the reciprocal activity of the cognitive and affective powers. Human experience shows that there is never any form of light without the accompaniment of some form of heat. Likewise, heat always generates some form of light. Similar to the activity of light and heat, the cognitive and affective processes mutually fortify each other, thereby increasing the quality and perfection of their activity.[69]

The harmonious relationship between the cognitive and affective powers of the soul, however, is considerably lessened by original and personal sin. Experience is witness to the foul and sordid phantasms that make their way into man's cognitive powers. Concupiscence too has impeded the proper functioning of his affective powers. The overall result is that man has become immersed in the darkness of sin; his purity has become tarnished. His celestial orientation has been distorted and his interest is now more centered upon worldly matters. Man has gone from the realm of intelligibility to that of brutality.[70]

The reformation of the cognitive and affective powers of the soul is attained through *poenitentia*[71]. *Poenitentia* rescues man from the

---

[67] A more detailed discussion of these faculties and their operations can be found in Steven Ozment, *Homo Spiritualis, A Comparative Study of the Anthropology of Johannes Tauler, Jean Gerson, and Martin Luther (1509-1516) in the Context of Their Theological Thought*, Studies in Medieval and Reformation Thought, 6 (Leiden, 1969), pp. 59-71.

[68] *De theologia mystica*, G, 3, 262. "Omnis praeterea effectus, praesertim immanens, productus a tali natura rationali, dici meretur lumen aliquod, aut ratione claritatis in cognitiva aut caliditatis in affectiva aut simul utriusque; non enim forte contingit reperire cognitionem quae non sit formaliter aut virtualiter quaedam affectio, sicut affectio non videtur posse secerni quin sit quaedam experimentalis cognitio; quippe neutra potentia effectum suum causat sine altera; quoniam ad cognitionis causationem affectiva potentia sicut ad affectionem generandam cognitiva concurrit."

[69] *De theologia mystica*, G, 3, 262.

[70] *De theologia mystica*, G, 3, 266.

[71] *De theologia mystica*, G, 3, 266.

shadowy and distorted world of sin. *Poenitentia*, moreover, breaks the iron chains formed by the passions and shatters the bonds of sin that hold the soul captive. Man, therefore, is rescued from the darkness of sin through the purifying activity of *poenitentia* upon his cognitive and affective powers. Repentance cleanses, heals, and enlightens the eyes of reason.[72] Because of the reciprocal relationship between man's cognitive and affective powers, the purification and enlightenment of his cognitive powers will naturally result in the increased purity of the affective powers. As man's affective powers are restored to greater integrity, his intellectual faculties will be allowed to function more effectively. The soul's cognitive and affective powers are thus elevated and reformed until they reach the point where they are fully open to the workings of divine grace.

With the elevation and reformation of his cognitive and affective powers, man is more effectively disposed for the reception of the divine grace of faith. The faith for which *poenitentia* disposes reformed man is not some abstract notion; it is a living faith in the Gospel. The penitential theologian is thus summoned to a deepened belief in the Scriptures. This call to a greater faith in the Gospel is essentially the call to mystical theology. Gerson employs several definitions of mystical theology but his most interesting definition is that in which he describes mystical theology as the clear and savory intelligence of everything that is believed in the Gospels. The experience of scriptural truth is attained, according to Gerson, more through penitential affection than through the intellectual investigation of God characteristic of speculative theology.[73] Gerson thus counters the prevailing tendency towards *curiositas* and *singularitas* among the theologians of his day by a call to mystical theology which is achieved through *poenitentia* and terminates in an experience of the Gospel. His reform aims to correct the penchant of speculative theology towards *curiositas* and *singularitas* by a return to a more penitential and affective approach to the Scriptures.[74]

Gerson's call for theological reform through mystical theology should not be interpreted to mean that he sought to replace speculative theology completely. The penitential humility char-

---

[72] *Contra curiositatem studentium*, G, 3, 226.

[73] *Contra curiositatem studentium*, G, 3, 249. "Intelligentia clara et sapida eorum quae creduntur ex Evangelio, quae vocatur theologia mystica, conquirenda est per poenitentiam magis quam per solam humanam investigationem."

[74] *Contra curiositatem studentium*, G, 3, 249.

acteristic of mystical theology is not intended to destroy theological inquiry but rather to curb the excessive tendencies of speculative theology and to bring theological investigation of the Scriptures back to its proper limits. The penitential approach of mystical theology not only establishes the proper limits of theological investigation, but also effectively guarantees that theological investigation will attain its proper goal. Penitence, therefore, redirects the intellectual powers of the theologian and enables them to surmount their inherent limitations and attain to a higher degree of theological investigation.[75]

This elevating effect of mystical theology is possible because of the reciprocal relationship that exists between man's cognitive and affective powers. Just as *poenitentia*, through the purgation and illumination of man's cognitive powers, results in the greater purity of man's affective faculties, so also do the purified affective powers contribute towards the further illumination of the cognitive powers. Through *poenitentia*, then, the affective powers of the soul result in a deepening of the cognitive experience. The penitential approach of mystical theology not only reorientates the theologian in his study of the Scriptures but also gives him an intellectual experience of the Scriptures unattainable through mere speculation.[76]

Gerson's proposal for theological reform through the implementation of mystical theology has far-reaching consequences for the reform of the church. As seen earlier, Gerson defines the theologian primarily in terms of divine law. Upon divine law rests the convocation of the council which is to achieve both the *reformatio pacis* as well as the *reformatio generalis in capite et membris*. The theologian, therefore, plays a most important role in the reform of the church because of his close affiliation with the *lex divina*. His is the function of clarifying the extensive legal confusion within the church which has perpetuated the schism and has delayed the church's ultimate reformation. The theologian resolves that confusion by delineating the respective domains of divine, natural, and positive law, thereby allowing the church to gather in council.

---

[75] Ozment, "The University and the Church," p. 114.

[76] *Ad Deum vadit*, G, 5, 7. "Pes amoris in via hac Dei saepe intrat ubi cognitionis pes foris stat; quamvis itaque ambulando in via Dei modo praetacto dum pede fidei praeposito subsequitur pes dilectionis, trahi possit consequenter pes cognitionis ad ulteriora, propinquiori luce cognoscenda, eundo sic pede post pedem; attamen pes amoris dexter sublimius semper extendi potest pro hac via quam sinister. Haec est theologia mystica, id est occulta."

The reform of theology proposed by Gerson early in his career as chancellor of the University of Paris has as its goal the education of a theologian such as is necessary for the true reform of the church. This goal is achieved by freeing the theologian from vain and curious speculation and directing him to the true content of the Scriptures. Mystical theology delineates the proper perimeters of theological investigation and allows the theologian to understand the Scriptures with a degree of knowledge heretofore unattainable through the efforts of pure speculative investigation. If mystical theology results in a deeper knowledge of the Scriptures then it must also give the theologian a better comprehension of the *lex divina*.

Gerson's program of theological reform results, therefore, in the education of a theologian with a deep experiential knowledge of the divine law. The truly penitent theologian will thus be one whose life is lived in full harmony with divine law. This personal experience of the divine law not only makes the theologian a more genuine interpreter of that law, but also a more effective instrument in its utilization for the reformation of the church. If the reform of the church rests upon law then a penitent theologian versed in the riches of mystical theology is the best guarantor of that reformation.

CHAPTER FOUR

EPISCOPAL REFORM

Gerson's interest in reform extended not only to the church universal but to the local churches as well. The problems of schism, heresy, and moral decay that beset the church in general also manifested themselves in individual dioceses. Gerson, consequently, developed a detailed program for diocesan reform. This program of reform is essentially hierarchical in its orientation with the bishop as the central figure. Gerson indeed, saw the church primarily as a church of prelates. He uses the term *praelati*, however, in a much wider sense than is common today. For Gerson, the *praelati* constitute the entire hierarchical state of the church. This hierarchical state is comprised of *praelati majores* and *praelati minores*. The *praelati majores* include bishops, archbishops, and cardinals while the *praelati minores* comprise primarily the parish clergy. Bishops, archbishops, and cardinals thus occupy the upper echelon of the church's hierarchy with the parish clergy occupying the lower. The members of the parish clergy are frequently identified as *praelati secundi ordinis*.[1] The present chapter will center around the bishops as agents in the reform of the church.

Granted the hierarchical orientation of Gerson's ideas on diocesan reform, it is not surprising to find that the bishop's reforming activities are conceived within the context of the hierarchical activities of purgation, illumination, and perfection. These activities, moreover, are explained in terms of the image of God. The bishop is not only a member of the ecclesiastical hierarchy; he is also made in the image and likeness of God. The image thus becomes intrinsically related to the notions of hierarchy and hierarchical activities. Gerson's concept of episcopal reform, therefore, centers around the notions of hierarchy, hierarchical activity, and image.

---

[1] *De potestate ecclesiastica*, G, 6, 240-241. "... de statu hierarchico Ecclesiae non sunt proprie nisi duo status: praelatorum majorum videlicet qui succedunt Apostolis et sunt episcopi, archiepiscopi, et ita sursum; et minorum qui successores sunt septuaginta duorum discipulorum. Et dicuntur praelati secundi ordinis, dignitatis, vel honoris, quales sunt curati...."

1. IMAGE AND REFORM

The bishop, like all men, is made in the image and likeness of God. Scripture testifies to this fact in Gn 1:26; there we find that God made man according to his image and likeness. While Gerson at times varies his interpretation of the image of God in man, especially when treating of individual reform, his understanding of the image remains fairly constant in his writings on episcopal reform. The divine image in man, and, therefore, in the bishop consists of the triple powers of the soul, which Gerson designates as *vis rationalis, vis irascibilis,* and *vis concupiscibilis.*[2]

This triple division of the soul's powers reflects the influence of Dionysius and the Platonic tradition. While utilizing that tradition, Gerson develops his own interpretation of the nature and function of these powers in a trinitarian context.[3] The *vis rationalis* is the soul's power to strive toward truth. In the possession of truth, the soul reflects the Son, for within the Trinity truth is appropriated to the

---

[2] *Bonus pastor,* G, 5, 124. "Habet itaque anima tua, sicut et reliquae de humana specie, vim triplicem: habet vim rationalem respectu veri, vim irascibilem respectu ardui, vim concupiscibilem respectu boni."

[3] The division of the soul's powers as described by Gerson is similar, at least in name, to the tripartite description used by Plato. Plato enumerates the powers of the soul as τὸ λογιστικόν, τὸ θυμοειδές and τὸ ἐπιθυμητικόν. Cf. *The Republic,* 4, 434d, 1-441e, 7; *Timaeus,* 69b, 8-72d, 8, ed. J. Burnet, *Platonis opera,* 4 (Oxford, 1902). For Plato, the rational part of the soul alone is divine and immortal; the spirited and appetitive parts are specifically related to the senses and perish with death. Cf. A. E. Taylor, *A Commentary on Plato's Timaeus* (Oxford, 1928), pp. 496-499. As will be seen, Gerson assigns a more noble role to the second and third powers of the soul. He considers all the *vires* as essential parts of the divine image in man. He also identifies the *vires* with the rational appetites of the soul. Cf. *De mystica theologia,* G, 3, 261. The Platonic tradition of the tripartite nature of the soul continued into the patristic and medieval periods. Jerome's use of the triple *vires* is illustrative of the transformation of Plato's thought by patristic authors. In Jerome, the *vis concupiscibilis* is clearly associated with the love of virtue. Cf. *In Matthaeum,* 1, 2, super 13, 33, *MPL,* 26, 91 C. Jerome's view was incorporated in the *Glossa ordinaria, In Mattheum,* 13, *MPL,* 114, 133 B. For Dionysius' use of the triple *vires* see *De coelesti hierarchia,* 15, 8; *MPG,* 3, 364 A-B, and *Ep. 8, MPG,* 1093 A-C. Ambrose, Macrobius, Isidore of Seville, Alcuin, and Honorius of Autun all adopted the Platonic division of the soul. Cf. M.-T. Alverny, "Le cosmos symbolique du xiiᵉ siècle," *AHDL,* 29 (1953), 73-74. Thomas Aquinas remained closer to the Platonic interpretation of the *vires,* for he considered the *passiones irascibiles* and *concupiscibles* as parts of the sense appetites. See *Summa Theologiae,* 1, q. 81, a. 2, Marietti, pp. 396-397. Aquinas cites as his authorities Gregory of Nyssa and John Damascene. The writings of Bonaventure also contain references to the triple *vires.* Cf. *Commentarium in Evangelium Lucae,* 22, 58, Quaracchi, 7, 558 b. For the trinitarian context of the *vires* in Gerson's thought see *Bonus pastor,* G, 5, 125, and *De mystica theologia,* G, 3, 288. "Sic anima per has vires habet tendentiam ad benedictam Trinitatem, nimirum quia ad eam et ad ejus similitudinem facta est, ejus quoque imago constituta."

Son. The *vis irascibilis* represents the soul's power to encounter the difficult and the arduous. In Plato, the *vis irascibilis* is the courageous or spirited part of the soul. Dionysius describes the *vis irascibilis* as the soul driven by the virtue of fortitude. Gerson also conceives of the *vis irascibilis* as the courageous power of the soul in the face of the difficult; he sees this activity of the soul as a reflection of the Father, since power is appropriated to the first person of the Trinity. The *vis concupiscibilis*, finally, is the desire of the soul for good. Since good is appropriated to the Spirit, the soul through its possession of the good images the third person of the Trinity.[4]

The image of God has been described thus far primarily in terms of natural faculties; these faculties also operate in conjunction with divine grace. The triple powers of the soul are directly related to the theological virtues of faith, hope, and charity. The truth sought by the *vis rationalis* is the truth of faith; the fortitude exercised by the *vis irascibilis* is the fortitude which comes with the theological virtue of hope and the love exercised by the *vis concupiscibilis* is the virtue of charity. Together the theological virtues orientate man's triple powers towards the knowledge, hope and love of God.[5]

When Gerson treats of the three *vires* in relationship to episcopal reform, he is not concerned with the triple *vires* insofar as they lead to the personal reform of the bishop. He presupposes personal and internal reform as an ongoing phenomenon in every bishop; in this respect the bishop's activities do not differ radically from those of any individual Christian who is striving for interior renewal. The bishop, however, is more than just a mere individual; he is a member of the hierarchical order of the church and as such must work for the sanctification and reformation of all those entrusted to his care. Just as he achieves his own internal reformation through the proper orientation of the *vires* of his soul, so through these same *vires* he fosters the reformation of the image in others. The bishop, consequently, utilizes the triple powers of his soul for the pastoral care of the faithful in his diocese.

---

[4] *Bonus pastor*, G, 5, 125. "Relucet nimirum in suavi rationali sapientia seu veritas quae appropriatur Filio. Relucet in irascibili potentia seu strenuitas quae appropriatur Patri. Relucet in concupiscibili benevolentia seu bonitas quae appropriatur Spiritui Sancto."

[5] *Apparuit gratia*, G, 5, 69. "Sit in nobis fides vera et viva secundum vim rationalem ex recognitione immensae sapientiae; sit spes certa secundum vim irascibilem ex professione ejus summae potentiae; sit caritas fervida ex consideratione summae benevolentiae et gratiae quae apparuit nobis hodie in circumcisionis humilitate."

In a sermon given at the Synod of Rheims in 1408 Gerson finds the scriptural roots for his program of episcopal reform in Jn 10:11 where Christ describes the qualities characteristic of a good shepherd: "*Bonus pastor animam suam dat pro ovibus.*" According to the literal meaning of the text, the good shepherd is one who is willing to sacrifice his life for his sheep. Gerson, however, understands the phrase "*animam dat*" in another sense, namely, that the good shepherd utilizes the triple powers of his soul for the pastoral care of the faithful. Upon this interpretation he constructs his entire program of episcopal reform.[6] By the exercise of his triple *vires* on behalf of the pastoral needs of the laity, the bishop truly fulfills Christ's triple command to feed his flock.[7]

On the part of the faithful, moreover, there exists a triple pastoral need, which is rooted in the fact that they too are made in the image of God according to the same *vires*. By acting according to the image of God within himself, the bishop helps to restore that same image in the souls of those under his care. By the pastoral exercise of his *vis rationalis, irascibilis* and *concupiscibilis*, the bishop helps to restore the same *vires* in the faithful. Through his activity of preaching and teaching he disposes their *vis rationalis* for an increase in faith. The example of his life inspires hope in the *vis irascibilis* of the laity and by the administration of the sacraments, their *vis concupiscibilis* expands into the fullness of charity. The final result of such episcopal activity is the renewal and reformation of the image of God within the souls of the faithful.[8]

The bishop's exercise of the *vis rationalis, irascibilis* and *concupiscibilis* for the pastoral needs of the laity is identical with the hierarchical activities of purgation, illumination, and perfection which he enjoys as a member of the ecclesiastical hierarchy. By acting according to the trinitarian-like image of God within himself, therefore, the bishop exercises the hierarchical activities of purgation, illumination, and perfection. Gerson regards these hierarchical

---

[6] *Bonus pastor*, G, 5, 125. "Fiat igitur ab unoquoque pastore quod proponit Dominus: det animam suam pro ovibus suis; utique animam quae imago est beatae Trinitatis secundum triplicem vim praenominatam."

[7] *Bonus pastor*, G, 5, 125. "Hanc, o bone pastor, totam animam non unicam suae virtutis portionem, curaveris dare pro ovibus tuis triplici sedulitate pascendis."

[8] *Bonus pastor*, G, 5, 125. "Neque enim aestimo te latere quemadmodum olim primo pastori Petro ter interrogato terque respondenti, bonus pastor Christus ter subintulit dicens: pasce oves meos, pasce agnos meos; et rursum si diligis me pasce oves meas; pasce verbo, pasce exemplo, pasce subsidio; pasce verbo praeedicationis doctae, pasce exemplo conversationis sanctae, pasce subsidio caritatis piae."

powers as deeply rooted in Scripture. The hierarchical activity of purgation is described by St. Paul in 2 Tim 4:2 where he orders Timothy to refute and correct the errors of the Christians under his care. In this passage Gerson sees the scriptural source for the bishop's powers of fraternal admonition, interdict and excommunication. The best method of correction, Gerson asserts, is the example given by the bishop's own life. The activity of illumination is manifested in preaching and teaching. Gerson again employs a Pauline source to make his meaning explicit. In Ti 1:9, Paul portrays the ideal bishop. He states that a bishop should hold firm to the word of God in order to give sound doctrinal instruction and refute those who contradict his teaching. The hierarchical activity of perfection is achieved through sacrifices, prayers and especially through the administration of the sacraments, which Gerson sees as the main channels of sanctification and grace. He finds this activity described in Heb 5:1 where it is narrated that every high priest is taken from the ranks of men and appointed their representative before God. His function as high priest is to offer gifts and sacrifices for man's sins.[9] The final result of all hierarchical activity is essentially reformative in nature. The episcopal exercise of the activities of purgation, illumination, and perfection terminates in the reformation of the image of God within the laity. Hierarchical activity has been entrusted to the bishop primarily for this purpose.[10]

The hierarchical activity of the bishop according to his triple *vires* is closely identified with Gerson's conception of the episcopacy as a state of perfection. More specifically, the episcopacy is a *status perfectionis exercendae*. As such, the episcopacy is primarily concerned with fostering the growth of Christian perfection in the souls of those committed to their care; it is for this purpose that the hierarchical powers of purgation, illumination, and perfection have been entrusted to them. The bishop's state of perfection differs from that of religious orders which Gerson describes as a *status perfectionis acquirendae*.[11] Religious are primarily concerned with the growth of Christian perfection within their own souls.

Although the bishop's primary function is to cultivate and bring to

---

[9] *De consiliis evangelicis et statu perfectionis*, P, 2, 679 A.

[10] *Domine si in tempore hoc*, G, 5, 212. "... vestrum est officium ut ceteros purgetis, illuminetis, perficiatis, quatenus coelestem portent imaginem...."

[11] The distinction between *status perfectionis exercendae* and *acquirendae* was essentially developed by St. Thomas' time. Cf. *Summa Theologiae*, 2, 2, q. 186, a. 3, ad 5, Marietti, p. 820.

fulfillment the perfection of the Christian life in others, his state in life, nonetheless, requires the attainment of a very high degree of personal perfection. This does not mean that the bishop is already perfectly united to God but that the unitive process is an ongoing phenomenon in his personal life. St. Paul expressed this state most clearly in Phil 3:12, where he professed that he had not yet attained the fullness of perfection but that he expended himself daily in the quest for a greater degree of perfection. The *status perfectionis exercendae*, therefore, requires and presupposes that the bishop himself has attained a high degree of union with God and that he is constantly striving to increase that union.[12]

Christian perfection can be a very misleading term and for this reason it is most important to arrive at a clear understanding of Gerson's use of the term. For him, perfection is essentially identical with union. He illustrates this by drawing an example from natural life. The human body receives life through its union with the soul which is the principle of life and, in philosophical terminology, the substantial act of the physical and organic body. Therefore, the more closely united the soul is with the body, the more intimately the soul actuates, informs and vivifies the body. The perfection of the body's life, therefore, is in direct proportion to the degree of union with the soul, its vital principle.[13]

Gerson then applies the above analogy to man's spiritual life. Here the vital and perfective principle is God and the more intimately the soul is joined to God, the more perfect it becomes. This intimate union with God is the essence of the Christian life; in terms of this union the Christian life is measured according to varying degrees of perfection.[14] Union with God is achieved solely through grace and the theological virtues of faith, hope, and charity which are infused into the soul. Since the image of God reaches its fulfillment in the theological virtues, the more perfectly man possesses those virtues, the more perfect the image of God becomes in him. Of all the theological virtues, charity is the most preeminent. Charity is the highest of the theological virtues and the perfective principle of the

---

[12] *De consiliis evangelicis et statu perfectionis*, P, 2, 679 C.

[13] *De consiliis evangelicis et statu perfectionis*, P, 2, 669 A.

[14] *De consiliis evangelicis et statu perfectionis*, P, 2, 669 B—670 A. "Si igitur conformiter ad ista scire et investigare voluerimus, in quo stat et perficitur vita Christiana, sciemus istud, habito et cognito illo quod spiritum nostrum rationalem suo vitali et perfectivo principio, quod Deus est, perfectius et intimius unit, et intimat, et junget in ipso."

others. So much is this the case that it can be said that, in a formal
sense, charity is the vital, essential, intrinsic, and perfective principle
of the Christian life.[15]

Gerson gives several reasons for the preeminence of charity in the
life of the soul. First, charity is a perfective principle because it
unifies the soul to God. He finds the basis for this assertion in 1 Jn
4:16, where we read that God is love and he who abides in love
abides in God and God in him. In Col 3:14, Paul describes charity as
the bond of perfection and in 1 Cor 13:1-2 he states that prophetic
powers, understanding, and even faith are as nothing compared to
charity. The consummation of the soul's life in heaven, moreover,
takes place in charity. In heaven, faith and hope are no longer
operative; charity alone exists. The life of the blessed is essentially
loving union with God. The more charitable a person's life on earth
the more is he united to God and transformed into his likeness. His
life, therefore, reflects the life of the blessed in heaven. Finally,
charity is the most preeminent of the theological virtues because both
the Law and the Gospel terminate in charity. This finality he finds
substantiated in Rom 13:10 where Paul states that the whole law is
summed up in love.[16]

At times Gerson defines perfection in Aristotelian categories of
totality. Perfection, consequently, is predicated of that to which
nothing is lacking. Interpreted strictly, this definition would apply
only to God since he alone is totality. He alone of all beings lacks
nothing, for all existence is summed up in him. Gerson feels,
however, that there is a sense in which the term perfect applies to
created being. That creature can be said to be perfect which lacks
nothing which should belong to it according to its species, nature, or
spiritual condition. A man is said to be perfect in body when he lacks
none of the integral members that compose the human body.[17] He is
spiritually perfect when the Holy Spirit abides in him through
sanctifying grace. In this state such a person lacks nothing which is
necessary for his salvation. Gerson admits that the degree of
sanctifying grace will vary from person to person, but by the very fact

---

[15] *De consiliis evangelicis et statu perfectionis*, P, 2, 670 A. "Est igitur conclusio ista
fundamentalis hujusmodi: vitale, essentiale, intrinsecum, et perfectivum formaliter
principium vitae Christianae est charitas et ejus mandata." Cf. Thomas, *Summa
Theologiae*, 2, 2, q. 184, a. 1, Marietti, p. 796.

[16] *De consiliis evangelicis et statu perfectionis*, P, 2, 670 A-671 A.

[17] *De perfectione cordis*, P, 3, 436 B-C. Cf. Aristotle's *Metaphysics*, 5, 26, 1023b,
26-28; 12, 7, 1072a, 24-25, Jaeger, pp. 116, 252, and *Physics*, 3, 6, 207a, 13-14.

that he possesses divine grace man can be said to be in the state of Christian perfection.[18] In equating perfection with grace, Gerson returns to his basic notion of perfection as intimate union and love of God, for it is grace which brings charity and union with the divine.

Gerson regards the state of perfection characteristic of the bishop's office as of a higher nature than that of religious orders. He gives several reasons for this opinion. First, he asserts that the *status perfectionis exercendae* is more perfect than the *status perfectionis acquirendae* because it implies the attainment of an already high degree of personal union with God.[19] Secondly, the activity of promoting increased union with God among others is more perfect than the attainment of personal holiness. Gerson finds support for his reasoning in Aristotle's *Nicomachean Ethics*. In the fifth book of the *Ethics*, Aristotle states that a virtue is perfectly possessed when a person is able to use it on behalf of others.[20] There are many who are unable to impart the virtues they have attained to others. The function of the bishop, however, is to foster the life of virtue not only in himself but also in others. For this reason Dionysius calls the bishops *cooperatores Dei* and sees the episcopal order as the first and most sublime order within the church. Hugh of St. Victor († 1141), in commenting upon Dionysius, calls the bishop's office sublime and superior to all others. The bishop, more than other church figures, approaches the divinity itself.[21]

From what has been said thus far about the *status perfectionis exercendae*, the close relationship between this *status*, the triple *vires* and the *imago* should be clear. The bishop fosters union with God in the souls of those under his care by acting according to the image of God within him, i.e. by the exercise of the triple *vires* in purgation, illumination, and perfection. Through the pastoral exercise of the powers of his soul, therefore, the bishop contributes to the laity's

---

[18] *De perfectione cordis*, P, 3, 437 A.

[19] *De consiliis evangelicis et statu perfectionis*, P, 2, 679 B.

[20] *De consiliis evangelicis et statu perfectionis*, P, 2, 679 C. Cf. Aristotle, *Nicomachean Ethics*, 5, 1129a, 1-1130a, 13, Bywater, pp. 88-91.

[21] *De consiliis evangelicis et statu perfectionis*, P, 2, 679 B. Cf. *De coelesti hierarchia*, 12, 2-3, *MPG*, 3, 293 A-B, and *De ecclesiastica hierarchia*, 5, 5, *MPG*, 3, 505 A. For Hugh of St. Victor's comments see his *Expositio in hierarchiam coelestem*, 12, *MPL*, 175, 1110 C-1112 A. Thomas argues to the superiority of the episcopal state on the basis that the active factor is always superior to the passive. Cf. *Summa Theologiae*, 2, 2, q. 184, a. 7, Marietti, p. 803. He draws the general principle of his argumentation from Augustine, *De Genesi ad litteram*, 12, 16, *CSEL*, 28, pt. 1, p. 402, and Aristotle, *De Anima*, 3, 5, 430a, 17-19, ed. P. Siwek (Rome, 1965), p. 206.

growth in Christian perfection. This growth, moreover, leads to the renewal of the triple *vires* within the laity and results ultimately in the reformation of the image of God within them.

2. PREACHING AND EDUCATION

Our study has shown the manner in which the bishop reflects the divine image of the Trinity through the use of the triple *vires: rationalis, irascibilis,* and *concupiscibilis.* This activity, moreover, is identical with the hierarchical activities of purgation, illumination, and perfection and is directly related to the theological virtues. The *vires*, finally, are exercised respectively in preaching and teaching, the example of a good life, and the administration of the sacraments. Attention will now be directed towards developing Gerson's thought on these aspects of pastoral activity. First to be investigated will be that of preaching and teaching, which is a function of the bishop's *vis rationalis.*

In the second half of the fourteenth and the first part of the fifteenth centuries Europe experienced an intensification of popular preaching. Manuals for preaching and collections of sermons multiplied as well as the number of open-air pulpits associated with churches, cathedrals, and cemeteries. This age witnessed a new form of evangelization in the appearance of popular itinerant preachers such as St. Vincent Ferrer († 1419) and St. Bernardine of Siena († 1456). With the exception of Wyclif's "poor priests," most missionary preachers were members of the mendicant orders; mendicants indeed monopolized this form of popular preaching. The content of their preaching was more moral than dogmatic and centered around the basic themes of penitence and conversion. These missions, moreover, were directed not only towards individuals but also towards families and entire cities and sought to achieve civic as well as personal peace.[22]

---

[22] Delaruelle, *L'Église au temps du Grand Schisme*, 2, 629-656. A comprehensive history of preaching in the late middle ages has yet to be written. For Germany see R. Cruel, *Geschichte der deutschen Predigt im Mittelalter* (Detmold, 1879) and A. Linsenmayer, *Geschichte der Predigt in Deutschland von Karl dem Grossen bis zum Ausgang des vierzehnten Jahrhunderts* (Munich, 1886). For England there are the works of C. R. Owst, *Preaching in Medieval England* (Cambridge, 1926) and *Literature and Pulpit in Medieval England* (Cambridge, 1933). Gerson himself was one of the most outstanding popular preachers of the late middle ages, and his sermons have been studied by L. Mourin, *Jean Gerson, prédicateur français* (Bruges, 1952). The

Gerson reacts strongly against the monopolization of preaching by the mendicant orders; he accuses the ecclesiastical hierarchy of his day of excessive reliance upon substitutes to fulfill its pastoral obligations in the domain of preaching. The obligation to preach the Gospel is incumbent upon all members of the hierarchy and the seriousness of that obligation is measured according to one's hierarchical rank. The more closely one approaches the fullness of the pastoral office, the more is he required to apply himself to the office of preaching.[23] In the rite of consecration, the bishop-to-be is asked: *Scis utrumque Testamentum?* Gerson feels that many do not realize the importance of this question and reply without due reflection.[24] Too many bishops, moreover, neglect their duty to preach and entrust it to the care of mendicants. Other bishops feel that there is an excessive amount of preaching in the church and that they are, therefore, excused from this pastoral obligation.

Gerson is of the opinion that many bishops are more concerned with preserving their temporal jurisdiction than in providing for the spiritual needs of their diocese. They argue that their concern for temporalities is justified since the spiritual realm cannot long exist unless supported by temporal power and jurisdiction. Gerson does not deny the validity of this argument. He maintains, however, that it is more appropriate that such matters be entrusted to substitutes and that the bishops be concerned primarily with pastoral activities. In this manner, the proper balance between the temporal and the spiritual can be effectively maintained.[25]

Gerson also complains about the quality of the sermons delivered in his time. Many sermons are given, but few are really worthy of the title. Gerson maintains that many preachers adulterate the Word of God. Too often requests for money from the pulpit are considered equal in pastoral value to the preaching of solid piety. The Word of God is also frequently interspersed with frivolous anecdotes and even doctrinal error. Bishops are often more cautious in their choice of hired help for the care of their landed estates than they are in the selection of good preachers so necessary for the spiritual development

---

varying evaluations concerning the quality of late medieval popular preaching, especially in France, are discussed by Mourin, *Six sermons français inédits de Jean Gerson* (Paris, 1946), pp. 19-22.

[23] *Bonus pastor*, G, 5, 127.

[24] *Bonus pastor*, G, 5, 129.

[25] *Bonus pastor*, G, 5, 126-127.

of the laity. The bishops' concern, moreover, for temporal power and jurisdiction has so distorted their pastoral outlook that when they come to select men for the office of preaching they tend to prefer procurators and lawyers to those educated in sacred doctrine.[26]

He illustrates the need for preaching by comparing the ecclesiastical order with temporal society. Just as temporal society needs bodily food for sustenance, so does the church require the spiritual food which comes from preaching for the maintenance of its spiritual life. Christ, consequently, has renewed the saying of the Old Testament: "Not by bread alone shall man live, but by every word of God." [27] Gerson rebukes bishops who fail to realize that preaching is the highest episcopal function. He recalls Paul's saying that Christ did not send him to baptize but to preach the Gospel. The apostles, moreover, did not think it fitting that they should give up preaching the Word of God to serve table.[28]

Gerson realizes well the difficulties of preaching and the need for proper spiritual balance. Frequently it happens that what is condemned in a sermon gives rise to equal, if not more serious, violations of God's commandments. A preacher can so condemn the miserly for their sin of avarice that the spendthrift finds justification for his wasteful activities. If, on the other hand, he strongly censures the spendthrift, the avaricious may well become more convinced of the righteousness of their cause. Rare is the preacher who is able to maintain a prudent balance in his sermons. Some of the faithful, moreover, are so dull that nothing said in a sermon has any impression upon them. Others hear only what they want to hear. Whatever is preached from the pulpit they interpret in their favor and as a confirmation of the righteousness of their own lives. By so manipulating the Word of God, they blunt the force of its effectiveness.[29]

Gerson next proceeds to enumerate the qualities of a good preacher. He must be a man of quick intelligence, skilled, and extremely versatile. He must, moreover, be possessed of great eloquence and endowed with the power of persuasion. He needs, above all, a deep knowledge of the Sacred Scriptures as well as other areas of knowledge related to the problems of human morality. This

---

[26] *Bonus pastor*, G, 5, 127.
[27] *Bonus pastor*, G, 5, 126. Cf. Dt 8:3; Lk 4:4.
[28] *Bonus pastor*, G, 5, 126. Cf. 1 Cor. 1:17; Acts 6:2.
[29] *Bonus pastor*, G, 5, 128.

knowledge, furthermore, must be confirmed by an exemplary life, one which is free from any suspicion of wrong doing, especially avarice and lust which so easily destroy a preacher's reputation. Finally, the ideal preacher must have an experience of the spiritual through contemplation. Unless he has this experience, he will remain spiritually cold and, therefore, unable to enkindle in his audience the fire of heavenly desires. Gerson argues that any bishop who seriously meditates upon the qualities required of a preacher will not lightly convey this privilege upon others indiscriminately.[30]

Since preaching is a hierarchical function, it is not surprising to find Gerson insisting that preaching be strictly reserved to the members of the hierarchical order or to those explicitly commissioned by the hierarchy. This restriction finds its echo in St. Paul's admonition in Rom 10:15: "And how can men preach unless they are sent." Gerson also argues that the hierarchical order of the church would be considerably disrupted if everyone took upon himself the office of preaching. Gerson is here referring to Beguines and Beghards, known in French as Turlupins.[31] These and similar sects frequently justified their preaching on the principle of fraternal correction enunciated in Mt 18:15. Gerson argues that such reasoning is destructive of hierarchical order. He is willing, however, to admit that there are circumstances when a person may be empowered directly by God to preach and in these cases hierarchical authorization would not be required. Such persons, however, must prove their commission from God through miracles, prophecy or some other sign. The law of necessity may also empower one to preach if it is only through his preaching that truth in faith and

---

[30] *Bonus pastor*, G, 5, 129.

[31] Beguines were associations of pious women, virgins, and widows who led a communal form of life but without the traditional vows of religion. Their masculine counterparts were named Beghards. These associations originated in the twelfth century and flourished in the cities. They devoted themselves to spiritual exercises, fasting, manual labor, care of the sick, burial of the dead, and religious instruction of the young. By the middle of the thirteenth century the terms Beguine and Beghard were generically applied to anyone who followed a life of piety outside traditional religious communities and began to be used in a pejorative sense in view of the fact that many such figures had fallen under the suspicion of heresy. It is in this latter sense that Gerson is most likely utilizing the terms. Cf. E. W. MacDonnell, *Beguines and Beghards in Medieval Culture* (New Brunswick, 1954); J. Greven, *Die Anfänge der Beginen* (Münster, 1912); and H. Grundmann, "Zur Geschichte der Beginen im dreizehnten Jahrhundert," *AKG*, 21 (1931), 296-320. There are also many studies on the Beguines and Beghards in the various countries and cities of Europe.

morals can be preserved. In all other situations, the preacher must be directly authorized by the hierarchy.[32]

While he follows in the medieval tradition in insisting that all sermons aim at the moral renewal of the audience, Gerson also demands that sermons be built solidly upon basic beliefs of the Christian faith. In the first place, sermons should stress the ten commandments since there is an abysmal ignorance of these essential tenets of Christianity. He also cites the need to preach upon the more important articles of faith, the seven deadly sins and the works of charity. These elements constitute the solid core upon which all preaching should be based. Gerson advocates that such sermons be preached not only to the laity but to ecclesiastics as well.[33]

Gerson's understanding of the dignity of the preacher's office sheds considerable light upon his concept of reform. This dignity is found not so much in the mere preaching of the Word of God but more in its salvific effect upon the faithful. The preacher contributes to the personal conversion of the sinner and thus to the restoration of the image of God within him. He turns him from the way of error and death to that of salvation. In the conversion of the sinner, then, lies the prime dignity of the office of preaching and by the fulfillment of his office the preacher achieves his own salvation. Gerson draws support for his ideas from Jas 5:20 where the notion of conversion is prominent: "...if anyone among you wanders from the truth and some one brings him back, let him know that whoever brings back a sinner from the error of his way will save his soul from death and will cover a multitude of sins."[34]

The proposals advanced by Gerson for the reform of preaching may be categorized as immediate or long range. Among the more immediate proposals, Gerson recommends that bishops examine preachers in order to be sure that they possess sufficient knowledge of the basic elements of the faith, especially the commandments and moral teachings. Mere knowledge, however, is not sufficient; preachers should also know the techniques of their profession and the manner in which religious truths are to be presented. They are to be warned, moreover, that their sermons are to be restricted to matters of faith and morals and they are not to indulge in old wives' tales or trifles. Gerson also proposes that manuals be prepared for

---

[32] *Bonus pastor*, G, 5, 129.
[33] *Scriptum est melius*, G, 2, 111, 116.
[34] *Bonus Pastor*, G, 5, 128.

priests actively engaged in preaching which would explain the basic doctrines of faith, the commandments and the sacraments. In brief, they should contain those matters in which the clergy should be knowledgeable if it is to instruct the faithful. All members of the clergy should be obliged to purchase such handbooks but for poor clerics the bishops might, in their charity, provide these manuals free of charge.[35]

The long-range proposals made by Gerson for the reformation of preaching are concerned primarily with the education of the clergy. These proposals have as their ultimate goal the more effective preaching of the Word of God and rest upon the belief that by raising the level of theological learning among the clergy, the quality of preaching will necessarily be improved. Gerson calls first for the implementation of the decretal of Gregory IX (1227-1241) which provided for the establishment of a school of theology in every metropolitan church.[36] This decretal incorporated the legislation of the Fourth Lateran Council (1215) which demanded that each metropolitan church should have a theologian who was to instruct the clergy in the Sacred Scriptures and in all matters related to the *cura animarum*. Each metropolitan was called upon to designate one benefice for the temporal support of the cathedral theologian. This benefice was to be chosen from those traditionally assigned to the canons of the cathedral.[37] Gerson, moreover, would extend the existing legislation to include all cathedral and the more outstanding collegiate churches.[38] The far-reaching nature of this latter proposal is seen in the fact that the extension of theological lectureships to cathedral and collegiate churches was not realized until the fifth session of the Council of Trent in 1546.[39]

Gerson's interest in raising the educational level of the clergy is again seen in a treatise on the episcopal office written during the years 1406-1408 when the French hierarchy had partially withdrawn its obedience to Benedict XIII. In that treatise, he recommends that in the visitation of religious houses located within their dioceses, bishops should be on the lookout for promising young scholars.

---

[35] *Bonus pastor,* G, 5, 131-133.

[36] *Bonus Pastor,* G, 5, 131. Cf. *Decretales Gregorii Papae IX,* lib. 5, tit. 5, ch. 4, ed. Aemelius Friedberg, *Corpus Iuris Canonici,* 2 (Leipzig, 1881), 770.

[37] Alberigo, *Decreta,* p. 216.

[38] *Bonus pastor,* G, 5, 131.

[39] Alberigo, *Decreta,* p. 644. See also Louis B. Pascoe, "The Council of Trent and Bible Study: Humanism and Scripture," *CHR,* 42 (1966), 24-25.

Those religious orders with sufficient financial resources should send such students to the University of Paris for their theological formation.[40]

Mere attendance at the cathedral schools or university is not sufficient. Gerson calls upon the young clerics of his day to undergo a real *conversio ad studium*. This conversion can be considerably facilitated by the power of personal example. He recommends, consequently, that bishops have among their associates learned theologians and jurists with whom students can easily consult on matters concerning popular preaching, morals, and justice. The presence of such men will not only aid the bishops in the pastoral administration of their diocese but will also have great impact upon the young. As a result of their influence, the young, who under normal circumstances might follow the tendency of their age to seek ease and pleasure, would be converted to a life of study and solid virtue. The reformation of young scholars is thus conceived in the context of an intellectual and moral conversion. If the bishops do not seek to promote this *conversio ad studium* among their clerical students, they should realize that they are not fulfilling their pastoral obligations; there is nothing more dangerous and destructive than to expose one's flock to the care and direction of ignorant clerics. Gerson maintains that the whole reformation of the church rests upon the intellectual and moral conversion of its clergy.[41]

The bishop should, moreover, reflect upon the results of his consultation with theologians and jurists regarding pastoral problems and then draw up a program of pastoral renewal. After further reflection, he should revise, add, delete, and correct various parts of that program. Once sufficient reflection and revision have taken place, the bishop should strive with every effort to put his ideas into effect.[42] Such a program of episcopal action, once expressed in writing, would be of great aid to his successors. Gerson's letter of 1408 to Gilles Deschamps, newly elected bishop of Coutances, contains such a program of pastoral renewal and Gerson advises the bishop that he may forward that program to fellow bishops and even to the Roman Curia.[43]

---

[40] *Rememoratio agendorum durante subtractione*, G, 6, 112.

[41] *Scriptum est melius*, G, 2, 111. "In hoc autem, ut videtur, jacet tota Ecclesiae reformatio et scandalorum malorumque in dies pullulantium repressio."

[42] *Scriptum est melius*, G, 2, 112.

[43] *Scriptum est melius*, G, 2, 116.

The conversion of young clerics to a life of study and moral integrity is achieved not only through good example but also by providing necessary stimuli. Gerson argues that the church would have better clerics if there were more rigorous norms for promotion to benefices and university offices. Only when bishops make the requirements for such offices more rigorous will young clerics abandon their lives of ease and pleasure and apply themselves to study. Not until then will clerics put order into their lives, refrain from scandalous activity, and do something of value for themselves and for those who support them.[44]

Since the church flourished in its initial years primarily because of the virtuous lives of its early fathers, Gerson maintained that in his time the church can only be preserved through the learned and virtuous lives of its clergy.[45] In a sermon preached before Pope Benedict XIII in 1404 at Tarascon, Gerson strongly asserted that the reformation of the church hinges on the appointment of God-fearing men, conspicuous both in equity and merit, to positions of authority within the church. If a bishop wants the church under his guidance to be governed happily, then, he argues, let him appoint such men to serve in the administration of his diocese.[46]

Closely allied to Gerson's concept of clerical education are his ideas on the education of children. As chancellor, Gerson not only supervised the various faculties of the university but also six elementary schools.[47] The education of the young, consequently, was of major concern to him. His interest in the young was so great that he incurred the opposition of some persons who complained that he was compromising the dignity of his office as chancellor of the University of Paris by his work with the young. His opponents argued that the dignity of his office precluded such work on behalf of

---

[44] *Scriptum est melius*, G, 2, 114.

[45] *Scriptum est melius*, G, 2, 114. "In quo etiam, ut praemissum est, tota jacet Ecclesiae reformatio et fructus ab eadem expectati utilis reparatio, quae scilicet Ecclesia, prout ut ex virtutibus sanctorum patrum originem, bona et possessiones accepit, sic etiam per virtutes non aliter servanda est."

[46] *Apparuit gratia Dei*, G, 5, 77.

[47] The schools under the chancellor's supervision included those of Saints Séverin, Eustache, Paul, Gervais, Germain-l'Auxerrois, and Nicholas-des-Champs. Cf. Glorieux, "La vie et les oeuvres de Gerson," *AHDL*, 18 (1950-51), 168. For the contribution of Gerson to changing ideas on childhood and childhood education in the fifteenth century see Philippe Ariès, *Centuries of Childhood*, trans. Robert Baldick (New York, 1962), pp. 106-108, 168-169, 329-331. Because of his awareness of the distinctive psychological traits of childhood and his efforts to adopt educational methods to the psychology of the child, Ariès calls Gerson "one of the first modern educationalists".

children; his time would be better spent on the more important business of the university. Others maintained that by his work and interest in children Gerson had broken with the traditions of the chancellor's office.[48] Gerson retorted with the statement that each person is custom unto himself. If no innovation were allowed in the political life of the state, the state would not only be incapacitated but also on the verge of destruction. Gerson maintains that the same principle applies to the chancellor's office.[49] He regards his work for the education of children as a major instrument for reforming the church. For him, the reformation of the church must begin with the proper education of her children. The deformities which are all too prevalent in the church of his day have their origin in the improper education of children.[50]

Gerson stressed the education of children because he felt that in their early years students were still open to the formative influences of education. He strongly believed that a student's later life is considerably conditioned by his early education. Once fixed in his ways, the older student can be changed only with great difficulty. To support his position he quotes Prv 22:6, "*adolescentior juxta viam suam et cum senuerit non dimittet eam*."[51] In a treatise on the education of the young, Gerson described the flexibility of youth and the importance of proper intellectual and moral formation. He compares children to young plants which easily bend and turn under the guiding hand of a caretaker. Once a person grows in years, he is turned from his habitual way of life only with great difficulty. The *reformatio*, the *reparatio* and the *cultura* of the church, consequently, must begin with youth.[52]

In addition to his own work among children Gerson calls upon each parish to exercise due care in the education of its young, especially in the realm of morals. He establishes two norms for such pastoral activity. First, the education of the young is to be achieved according to the prescribed canonical legislation of the church.

---

[48] *De parvulis trahendis ad Christum*, P, 3, 285 D.

[49] *De parvulis trahendis ad Christum*, P, 3, 288 B.

[50] *Bonus pastor*, G, 5, 132. "Ecclesiae siquidem reformatio, sicut quidam ait, debet inchoari a parvulis quoniam ejus deformatio venit ab eis prave et nequiter institutis."

[51] *Rememoratio agendorum durante subtractione*, G, 6, 111-112.

[52] *De parvulis trahendis ad Christum*, P, 3, 280 A. "Quod si juxta deductionem hanc reparatio Ecclesiae et ejus cultura initianda esset a parvulis (sicut esset) ubi, precor, efficacius sanctissimum opus exercebitur, quam in celeberrima Civitate Pariensi?" Cf. *Rememoratio agendorum durante subtractione*, G, 6, 268.

Secondly, the content of this education should reflect what Gerson calls the rudiments of our primitive religion.[53] He requests that more promising youth be sent to continue their education in Paris since the capital city provides excellent educational opportunities. Those who receive their education in Paris will eventually be dispersed throughout the whole of Christendom. From their numbers will come the future teachers of Christendom.[54]

Considerable care is also shown by Gerson for those involved in the education of the young. He is especially concerned that teachers be preeminent in both knowledge and moral integrity. Even when instructing the young on such a rudimentary level as the alphabet, they should be of such character that they will not fail to inculcate a knowledge of Christ's law and the works of charity.[55] He is also most concerned about their material welfare and proposes means by which their temporal needs are to be provided. Teachers drawn from the secular clergy are to receive benefices while members of the mendicant orders should have their temporal needs provided directly by the bishop or local pastor. If procurators, advocates, and preachers receive fixed and substantial incomes why should not similar support be provided for those involved in the education and moral formation of the young? Such persons are, in effect, the bishop's main assistants in the exercise of his pastoral office.[56]

According to Gerson, the overall concern for the education of youth rests with the bishop. To those who complained that he was breaking the long-standing traditions of the chancellor's office by his work with children Gerson replied that he had secured permission for this work from his bishop, who is the lord of the harvest and can commission people for the apostolate as he sees fit.[57] Gerson, moreover, makes the education of the young a major item in episcopal visitations. In their visitations bishops are to investigate whether or not there are sufficient schools in their diocese. They are also to inquire into the quality of education provided by the schools. He is to visit all schools personally, whether they are associated with parishes or operated by religious orders. In giving his reasons for such vigilance on the part of the bishop, Gerson returns to his major

---

[53] *Bonus pastor*, G, 5, 132.
[54] *De parvulis trahendis ad Christum*, P, 3, 280 A.
[55] *Scriptum est melius*, G, 2, 111.
[56] *Bonus pastor*, G, 5, 132.
[57] *De parvulis trahendis ad Christum*, P, 3, 288 B.

theme that the reformation of the church must begin with the children.[58]

Gerson also reminds parents and teachers that they play a most important role in this process of reform since they have great influence upon the intellectual and moral formation of children. In the area of moral development, Gerson regarded confession as the most important way to lead a child to Christ. He advises teachers and parents to urge their charges not to conceal their sins but to confess them openly. He is unsympathetic towards those who feel that the young are incapable of committing serious sin. He reminds parents who hold this opinion to search their consciences to see whether or not this is really true.[59]

3. Curial Reform

The bishop's concern for the amelioration of preaching and teaching as well as the education of the clergy and the young are all manifestations of the pastoral exercise of his *vis rationalis*, which constitutes the first part of the image and is essentially identical with the hierarchical activity of illumination. The overall effect of the bishop's exercise of the *vis rationalis* is to promote an understanding of the faith among his people. If his efforts in the area of preaching and teaching are successful, then he will have considerably illumined the *vis rationalis* of those under his care and thereby contributed to the renewal and reformation of the image of God within them.

The second power of the soul made to the image and likeness of God is the *vis irascibilis*, which is associated with the hierarchical activity of purgation and the theological virtue of hope. The *vis irascibilis* is normally concerned with the fortitude required to encounter the difficulties that normally occur in any serious attempt to lead a Christian life. The bishop exercises his *vis irascibilis* in a pastoral manner primarily through the example of his own life. He must strive to remove from his life all signs of avarice, hypocrisy and material extravagance. The removal of these vices will require a deep hope and trust in God on the part of the bishop. Only when he has eradicated these vices from his life can the bishop, as the pastor of souls, be truly said to give his life for his flock.[60] By such activity,

---

[58] *De visitatione praelatorum*, P, 2, 560 D.
[59] *Notes sur la confession*, G, 7, 411-412.
[60] *Bonus pastor*, G, 5, 134.

moreover, he will inspire hope and confidence among his people. By the example of his life, then, the bishop provides for restoration of the *vis irascibilis* in the faithful and the renewal of the image of God within them.

When speaking of the eradication of avarice, Gerson holds up to his audience the Pauline ideal of a good bishop. The good bishop, says St. Paul in Ti 1:7-8, is one who is not greedy for gain but hospitable.[61] Gerson takes the Pauline admonition concerning hospitality seriously. The bishop's guests, however, are not the visitors passing through his diocese, but the patients in his hospitals. Gerson, moreover, calls upon the bishop to effect a reform of the hospitals. This reform is to extend to both the temporal and spiritual aspects of their administration.[62] He is especially insistent that the hospitals of the diocese provide for the spiritual care of the sick. The hospitals, indeed, owe their original foundation to the desire of benefactors to provide first and foremost for the spiritual care of the poor and the sick.

The hospitals of Paris can serve as an example in this reform. They have implemented the demands of the decretal which requires that spiritual doctors be summoned before the medical.[63] In Paris, the patient, upon entering the hospital, immediately confesses his sins and is given absolution; only afterwards is he placed under the care of medical doctors. Special vigilance should be taken that Extreme Unction be administered to the sick while they can fully and consciously benefit from the sacrament. Finally, patients who die without relatives or friends are to be buried with all due piety.[64] The reformation of the hospitals proposed by Gerson extends as well to religious associated with the work of the hospitals. The bishop is to see that they observe their vows of poverty, chastity and obedience.

---

[61] *Bonus pastor*, G, 5, 134.

[62] *Bonus pastor*, G, 5, 134. "Fiat, inquit, reformatio hospitalium. Hoc est enim de cura pastoris. Fiat haec reformatio tam in temporali quam in spirituali regimine. . . ."

[63] *Bonus pastor*, G, 5, 134. The decretal referred to by Gerson was promulgated in 1215 by the Fourth Lateran Council, Canon 22. Cf. Alberigo, *Decreta*, pp. 221-222. This decretal was incorporated in practically all the statutes of medieval hospitals. Cf. Jean Imbert, *Les hopitaux en droit canonique* (Paris, 1947), pp. 131-132. The directives of the decretal were based on several reasons. First it was argued that bodily infirmity was frequently a result of sin; by removing the latter, the patient could be helped along the road to recovery. Secondly, it was felt that if the patient were treated first by the doctor and then told that he should confess his sins, he might overestimate the seriousness of his illness and sink into a state of despondency which would considerably hinder the possibilities of recovery.

[64] *Bonus pastor*, G, 5, 142.

He indicates that there have been clear indications of infractions against the vow of poverty. He is also of the opinion that religious spend too much time visiting the homes of the laity.[65]

A bishop who strives to provide for those under his care, and, at the same time, amass wealth and possessions is a contradiction in terms. The bishop, moreover, must not only restrain his own desire for wealth but also prevent his officials from pursuing gain at the expense of the laity. Only then will the bishop be completely faithful to the Pauline conception of the episcopal office. Bishops, consequently, are to combat the avarice of diocesan officials whose greed constantly oppresses the poor. They will need courage and determination if they are to expel this evil from their diocese but they have a good example of these virtues in their fellow bishop, Ambrose of Milan.[66]

Gerson maintains that clerical avarice, in effect, deprives the poor of their patrimony. This deprivation occurs whenever ecclesiastics misuse the wealth of the church by living in a manner beyond their basic needs. Gerson admits that an ecclesiastic's level of living will vary according to his rank. He argues, however, that the resources of the church that remain after the maintenance of the clergy are, in reality, the possession of her poor. Consequently, whenever a cleric lives in a manner beyond his ecclesiastical rank, he is, in effect, depriving the poor of their patrimony. Gerson finds support for his position in the works of Jerome and Bernard who considered such extravagances as sacrilegious.[67]

---

[65] *Bonus pastor*, G, 5, 134.

[66] *Bonus pastor*, G, 5, 134-135.

[67] *Bonus pastor*, G, 5, 135. Gratian's *Decretum* incorporates a passage from a letter of Jerome to Pope Damasus I which accuses those clerics of sacrilege who deprive the poor of their share of church income. Cf. *Decretum*, 2, causa 1, q. 2, can. 6, Friedberg, 1, 409. I have been unable to locate this passage in the extant letters of Jerome to Damasus but an identical passage is found in the *Regula monachorum*, 4, *MPL*, 30, 344 B-C, where it is stated that the clergy is to give to the poor whatever income is left over from its necessary expenses in the area of food and clothing. Whoever retains more than is necessary for his basic sustenance is guilty of theft. For the fourfold division of ecclesiastical income according to bishop, clergy, the poor, and the maintenance of church edifices see *Decretum*, 2, causa 12, q. 2, can. 28, Friedberg, 1, 697. The *Decretum* also states generically that whatever the clergy possesses is essentially the property of the poor. Cf. *Decretum*, 2, causa 16, q. 2, can. 68, Friedberg, 1, 784-785. Bernard of Clairvaux portrays the poor as accusing bishops of depriving them of their patrimony by their luxurious style of living. Cf. *De moribus et officio episcoporum*, 2, 7, *MPL*, 182, 815 D-816 B. St. Thomas discusses whether bishops sin seriously who do not distribute ecclesiastical wealth to the poor. While defending the bishops' right to private property, he does affirm that those bishops sin seriously who

The use of the church's wealth for the poor is of particular importance in Gerson's conception of the episcopacy. The bishop, by the very nature of his office, has the duty of caring for orphans, widows, the needy, the sick and the afflicted. Gerson would also have the bishop show special concern for elderly and sickly farmers. Concern for these classes is to extend not merely to their spiritual welfare but also to their material well-being.[68] He calls upon the bishop to offer material aid to all classes of the needy. Such use of the church's wealth represents the proper use of her patrimony. Gerson agrees rather strongly with Gregory the Great who maintained that if the bishop is unwilling to provide for the poor from his material resources, he can never be expected to show true concern for their spiritual well-being.[69]

The impoverished state of the lower clergy should also elicit the bishop's immediate attention. Because of its impoverished condition, the clergy does not receive due reverence and obedience. The clergy, moreover, should be freed from the numerous taxes, dues, and other financial burdens which weigh more heavily upon it than upon the laity. Bishops, moreover, are to see that their curates receive a salary sufficient for their basic needs. Gerson felt strongly about the material state of the lower clergy and urged bishops to correct this injustice.[70]

The bishop's manner of life must be free not only of avarice but of hypocrisy as well. The removal of hypocrisy constitutes the second manner in which the bishop exercises his *vis irascibilis*. Hypocrisy as it relates to the bishop's office is concerned primarily with the administration of the episcopal curia. In 1 Tim 3:4 St. Paul states that a bishop must manage his own household well, for if he cannot manage his own household how can he rule the church committed to him.[71] Gerson equates the episcopal household with the episcopal curia and its officials. The bishop's curia should be noted for justice and zeal in the correction of abuses; it should build up and not corrupt the body of the faithful. The curia, moreover, should not be an instrument of extortion or incessant litigation but a mainstay of

---

appropriate or misuse that portion of ecclesiastical income designated for the poor. Cf. *Summa Theologiae*, 2, 2, q. 185, a. 7, Marietti, 813-814.

[68] *Scriptum est melius*, G, 2, 109.

[69] *De consiliis evangelicis et statu perfectionis*, P, 2, 679 B. Cf. Gregory, *Regula pastoralis*, 2, 7, MPL, 77, 41 A-B.

[70] *Bonus pastor*, G, 5, 135-136.

[71] *Bonus pastor*, G, 5, 136.

peace.[72] If the people hold the episcopal curia and its officials in high esteem, they will more freely and effectively heed the admonitions of the bishop in spiritual matters.[73]

To achieve these goals, Gerson calls for a complete reformation of the episcopal curia. Just as charity begins at home, so too should the reformation of the church begin with the reform of the bishop's curia.[74] He offers four specific proposals for the achievement of curial reform. He calls upon the bishops first to put an end to the tyranny of curial officials in levying excessive taxes and in issuing unjust warrants of arrest. In such arrests, the accused are usually freed once the grounds for their custody are shown to be insufficient. They are, however, required to pay the necessary expenses for legal procedures. Gerson is of the opinion that such procedures are, in reality, a form of extortion and are perpetrated by curial officials primarily for financial recompense. Injustices of this type could be effectively avoided if curial officials received sufficient salary for their work. Gerson concludes with a reminder from Is 10:1-2, where the prophet inveighs against those who issued iniquitous decrees, and deprived the needy of justice. Like Isaiah, Gerson bemoans the fact that the poor are denied their rights.[75]

Gerson's second proposal for the reformation of the episcopal curia demands the curtailment of excessive excommunications levied upon the faithful for insignificant matters or for purely secular reasons. Gerson cites the early church as a model for reform in this area. Christ recommended excommunication only for those who refused to obey the church in spiritual matters related to their eternal salvation. Present practice employs excommunication for the most trivial reasons, and is comparable to a man who uses an ax to remove a fly from the forehead of his neighbor and, consequently, ends up bashing out his brains.[76]

The third proposal for curial reform concerns simony. Gerson urges the observation of those decretals that regulate the payment of

---

[72] *Bonus pastor*, G, 5, 136.

[73] *Rememoratio agendorum durante subtractione*, G, 6, 108.

[74] *Bonus pastor*, G, 5, 136. "Sicut autem caritas incipit a se, sic et reformatio debet inchoari ut primum fiat judicium a domo praelati sicut fit in universo a domo Dei, ne praeterea contingat objici praelato: medice cura teipsum; et illud Apostoli: qui praedicas non furandum furaris, immo et sacrilegium facis." Cf. Lk 4:23; Rom 2:21.

[75] *Bonus pastor*, G, 5, 136. The disastrous consequences of excessive excommunications upon parochial life in late medieval France have been studied by Paul Adam, *La vie paroissiale en France au xiv͏ᵉ siècle* (Paris, 1964), pp. 179-206.

[76] *Bonus pastor*, G, 5, 136-137.

money for the administration of the sacraments. Due moderation should be especially displayed in the conferral of orders and benefices. In the execution of their duties, officials of the episcopal curia are so to act that they avoid the charge of simony.[77] In 1416, Gerson wrote a detailed treatise which called for the reformation of norms regulating financial recompense for the administration of the sacraments. He does not rule out recompense for the administration of the sacraments, or for the conferral of benefices provided that financial gain is not the primary motive in such transactions. Christ's words that the laborer is worthy of his hire justify some remuneration if the clergy is not to be reduced to a life of penury. Gerson also warned against using the reform movement as a pretext for depriving the church of her just inheritance.[78]

His fourth and last proposal for curial reform demands that the bishop's officials punish offenders according to the nature of their crime. He also asks that punishment be imposed primarily with the intent of aiding the accused. Too often the bishop's curia is concerned only with financial exactions. If financial payments are required as a form of punishment, such income should be applied to charity. Officials are also rebuked for demanding oaths from litigants and then refusing to accept testimony given under oath. This practice stands condemned in the words of Heb 6:16: "Men indeed swear by a greater than themselves, and in all their disputes an oath is final for confirmation."[79]

The third manner in which the bishop exercises his *vis irascibilis* is by removing from his life all traces of material extravagance. As before, Gerson resorts to the Pauline prototype of the bishop and finds that the notion of temperance is among the foremost qualities of a good bishop. St. Paul would have a bishop be master of himself, patient, upright, holy and self-controlled.[80] With St. Paul as his norm, Gerson now turns to the material aspects of the bishop's life that stand in need of reformation. The first area Gerson censures concerns the quality of food and clothing used in the episcopal household. He calls for a considerable reduction in the number of dishes served; the great variety of food is not only a waste but a scandal. Carelessly wasted food could well be used to fill the

---

[77] *Bonus pastor*, G, 5, 137.
[78] *Ad reformationem contra simoniam*, G, 6, 180-181. Cf. Lk 10:7.
[79] *Bonus pastor*, G, 5, 137.
[80] *Bonus pastor*, G, 5, 137. Cf. 1 Tim 3:2; Ti 1:7-8.

stomachs of the poor. Frequently dogs in ecclesiastical households eat much better than poor people. Gerson also inquires whether, in the light of modern attitudes, prelates should wear rich and exquisite clothing. Would it not be better to imitate the poverty of Christ and his apostles by wearing simple and coarse clothing? He especially recommends that ecclesiastical legislation with regard to fasting be restored among the rich, the powerful, and the clergy. At the present time, he argues, only the poor and the farmers fast, although they are scarcely able to get enough black bread to sustain life.[81]

Gerson next censures ecclesiastics for the pomp and splendor of their entourage. He criticizes the inordinate number of servants, horses, and mules that accompany ecclesiastics on their journeys. The dress, activities, and, indeed, the lives of his servants, should be beyond reproach.[82] People have a general tendency to judge the prelate's mores by those of his servants. The moral integrity of his servants, moreover, should be such that he can confidently entrust to them all the temporal cares of his household and devote himself fully to the spiritual duties of his office.[83]

With his call for a more apostolic style of episcopal living, Gerson completes his analysis of the manner in which the bishop exercises his *vis irascibilis*. The exercise of this power of the soul has been essentially purgative in nature and corresponds to the first of the hierarchical activities. In the application of this power, the bishop purges himself and his curia from all forms of avarice, hypocrisy and material extravagance. By so doing he frees himself of excessive dependence upon financial and material resources and places his hope and trust in God and in the reward that a good and holy life brings. In seeing the example set by the bishop, his people in turn are encouraged to place their hope and trust in God and in the rewards of virtuous living. By so doing, their *vis irascibilis* is renewed by the virtue of hope and the image of God within them is further reformed.

4. Sacramental Renewal

The third and final aspect of the image of God within the bishop's soul is the *vis concupiscibilis*, which by its very nature tends towards

---

[81] *Bonus pastor*, G, 5, 138.
[82] *Bonus pastor*, G, 5, 138.
[83] *Rememoratio agendorum durante subtractione*, G, 6, 108.

the good. In the pastoral context in which Gerson has placed the triple powers of the soul, the bishop's *vis concupiscibilis* is directed, not towards his own personal good, but towards the realization of the good in others. Pastorally speaking, then, by the application of this *vis concupiscibilis*, the bishop strives to foster charity in the souls of those committed to his care. He does this primarily through the administration of the sacraments. This aspect of episcopal activity, consequently, is identical with the hierarchical function of perfection.[84]

The sacraments are the primary source of grace and the theological virtues which effect such a radical change in man's orientation to God. Through sacramental grace and the infusion of the theological virtues, the image of God within man is restored to its pristine vigor. The sacramental context of renewal in Gerson's thought, moreover, necessarily implies the element of the hierarchical since it is the ecclesiastical hierarchy which administers the sacraments. The notions of hierarchy, sacrament, and renewal are so closely related in Gerson's thought that the unworthiness of the minister of the sacrament has no deterrent effect upon renewal. Gerson strongly insists that the value of the sacraments is not diminished when administered by a sinful priest. He opposes those who would lessen the value of any sacramental activity performed by an unworthy priest. Because of the unedifying lives of the clergy, many sects tended to neglect the sacraments as a source of sanctity and concentrated upon pious practices and devotions. Gerson considered it dangerous and scandalous to prefer the pious activities of the laity to the hierarchical activity of the priesthood.[85]

Since the bishop is primarily responsible for the administration of the sacraments within his diocese, Gerson proposes some general norms for a more effective ministry of the sacraments. These proposals were made in major addresses given by him at the Synods of Rheims in 1408 and Lyons in 1421 as well as in his treatise on the duties of bishops during the period of subtraction of obedience in 1408. He stipulates first that a thorough examination be made of all priests actively involved in the administration of the sacraments; they are to be questioned on the form, matter and proper intention required for the valid conferral of the sacraments. The clergy is also

---

[84] *De potestate ecclesiastica*, G, 6, 219, 241.
[85] *Responsio ad errores de orationibus privatis fidelium*, P, 2, 654 C-D.

to be acquainted with the various difficulties that can occur in the administration of the sacraments. A similar examination should be required of midwives and other members of the laity who administer the sacrament of baptism in cases of emergency.[86] Gerson also calls for a more reverential attitude in the administration and reception of the sacraments, especially on Sundays and other holy days of obligation.[87]

As his second proposition, Gerson stipulates that both priests and bishops should administer the sacraments without any financial remuneration, since in Mt 10:8 Christ said: "You received without pay, give without pay." Gerson admits that the subject of financial remuneration is a most controversial topic since Christ also said in Mt 10:10 that the laborer was worth his hire. He is no less aware that the income of many churches depends upon such fees. Despite all these factors, Gerson desires that, if at all possible, the sacraments be administered freely.[88]

His third general norm for sacramental renewal is that bishops and priests realize that they are obliged to administer the sacraments either by themselves or by suitable substitutes even during periods of plague and epidemics. This is indeed a most difficult obligation, but if done with the right intention, such action is as meritorious as martyrdom, especially if death follows. Because of such sacrifices, the laity should hold the parish clergy in great respect, even greater respect than that given members of religious orders, who have no such obligations.[89] Gerson's fourth proposal is that both priests and bishops realize that they are not obliged to offer the sacraments to all who seek them. At times, he contends, pastoral obligations require them to deny such requests. He cites several instances where this course of action is recommended. Denial of the sacraments should be made in cases where excommunicates are involved or incorrigible

---

[86] *Redde quod debes*, G, 5, 490. Cf. *Bonus pastor*, G, 5, 140. The Fourth Lateran Council (1215), canon 27, called upon the bishops either personally or through delegates to instruct candidates for the priesthood in the proper manner of administering the sacraments. The Third Lateran Council (1179), canon 3, and the Second Council of Lyons (1274), canon 13, stressed that the priest should have the moral and educational training necessary for his office. Cf. Alberigo, *Decreta*, pp. 224, 188, 297-298.

[87] *Bonus pastor*, G, 5, 140-141.

[88] *Redde quod debes*, G, 5, 490. Cf. Fourth Lateran Council, canon 66, Alberigo, *Decreta*, p. 241.

[89] *Redde quod debes*, G, 5, 490.

sinners or where there is sufficient reason to believe that the person has not been to confession.[90]

When he comments upon the individual sacraments, Gerson gives considerable attention to penance. Penance marks an important moment in the conversion of the soul to God, since through this sacrament begins the reformation and renewal of the image of God. The sacrament of penance results in a new mode of life; the spiritually sick and undernourished are cured and provided with sustenance. Because of the importance of this sacrament, the selection of confessors for a diocese should receive special priority. Those chosen should be upright, continent, learned, and zealous; they should know how to question penitents intelligently. Finally, they should not be given to drink or sudden anger since such men are more likely to break the seal of confession. Failure to provide competent confessors is tantamount to exposing Christ's flock to the attacks of ravenous wolves.[91]

Closely related to confessional procedure is the practice of reserved sins. Reservation of sins is the limitation by an ecclesiastical superior of an inferior's power of absolution in specific cases with the result that the latter cannot absolve because he lacks the necessary jurisdiction. In such cases the penitent must have recourse to the proper ecclesiastical superior or to a special confessor entrusted with the necessary jurisdiction. In the case of reserved sin, Gerson advocates considerable moderation, showing thereby his strong pastoral sympathies. Young persons under the age of fourteen should be freed of all forms of reservation since they do not yet have the full use of reason. Adolescents are also at an age when it is very hard to resist temptation. They find it difficult, moreover, to be open with confessors who are unknown to them, especially when matters of sex are involved. Women, furthermore, should not be sent to special confessors for reserved sins. When this happens too frequently, their husbands become suspicious. Gerson would have all cases involving reserved sins left to local pastors.[92] Gerson, in fact, questions the pastoral effectiveness of the entire system of reserved sins. Rather than reducing sin, reservation only serves as an occasion for further sin because it prevents many from coming to confession.[93]

---

[90] *Redde quod debes*, G, 5, 491.
[91] *Bonus pastor*, G, 5, 141.
[92] *Bonus pastor*, G, 5, 141.
[93] *Pontificali dignitati*, G, 2, 90.

Pastoral problems related to the sacraments of confirmation, orders, marriage and extreme unction are treated more briefly. Bishops are urged to administer the sacrament of confirmation more frequently throughout their diocese. Infrequent confirmation lowers the people's estimation of this sacrament.[94] With regard to holy orders, candidates should be carefully examined before being approved for ordination. The areas of special concern should be those of continence and learning. There should be no relaxation of ecclesiastical norms and ideals in these areas; it is better for the church to have fewer but more carefully chosen priests.[95] Failure to screen candidates for the priesthood will only result in continued problems for the church and considerably reduce her esteem among the people.[96] In the realm of matrimony, Gerson is especially concerned that the rite be performed in the more solemn atmosphere of a church. Marriages in private homes are to be shunned. Extreme Unction, finally, is to be ministered while the sick person has full control of his senses and is conscious of the sacramental action, since only then will he reap the full benefit of the sacrament.[97]

5. SYNODS, VISITATIONS, AND REFORM

Gerson gives considerable emphasis to provincial and diocesan synods as a major force for reform in the church. In a major address to the Council of Constance in 1415, he informed the assembled bishops that the regular convocation of councils and synods was the most efficacious means for church reform.[98] Writing in 1408 to Gilles Deschamps, bishop of Coutances, Gerson designates synods as a primary means for diocesan reform. In such synods the duties of deacons, curates, and other ecclesiastics can be clearly defined. Synods are especially helpful in eradicating the vices of both clergy and laity. They are also most instrumental in instructing clergy and laity in the basic elements of Christian belief. In brief, their purpose is to aid the faithful in their attempt to lead a more virtuous life.[99] In his address

---

[94] *Bonus pastor*, G, 5, 140.

[95] *Bonus pastor*, G, 5, 142.

[96] *Rememoratio agendorum durante subtractione*, G, 6, 109.

[97] *Bonus pastor*, G, 5, 142.

[98] *Ambulate dum lucem habetis*, G, 5, 45. "Ecclesia non habet efficacius medium ad generalem sui ipsius reformationem quam si statuatur generalium conciliorum continuatio, celebrationem provincialium non omittendo." Cf. *De potestate ecclesiastica*, G, 6, 225.

[99] *Scriptum est melius*, G, 2, 115-116.

before the Synod of Rheims in 1408, Gerson praised the custom of
holding annual provincial synods. Nothing is more conducive to the
growing lack of discipline in the church than the failure to hold
provincial synods. He attacks those who neglect canonical legislation
which requires the regular convocation of provincial synods.[100] Such
an attitude deprives the church of one of the most effective means at
her disposal for correcting the mores of ecclesiastics.[101] In an address
before the King of France in 1405, Gerson praised the ancient
canonical tradition of provincial synods since they can effectively
result in the reformation of the entire Gallican Church.[102]

The value of any synod rests, however, on the effectiveness of
episcopal visitations. Gerson does not explicitly analyze the
relationship between visitations and synods but from the manner
with which he develops his proposals regarding visitations it is safe to
conclude that only when prelates and administrative officials know
the exact conditions existing in their province or diocese will synods
be able to legislate wisely and effectively. Gerson implies this much
in his letter to Gilles Deschamps. The ideal bishop, he declares, is
one who is well informed about the spiritual welfare of all those
under his jurisdiction. Once sufficiently informed, he is to convoke a
diocesan or provincial synod which will aim to eradicate vice and to
foster virtue among the members of his flock.[103] The necessary
information required for a synod can only be obtained through
visitations.

Gerson's proposals for the renewal of episcopal visitations came at
a time when episcopal absenteeism in France was considerably high.
Many bishops resided at the papal curia in Avignon as well as at the
royal court of France. Absentee bishops, moreover, frequently failed

---

[100] The canonical legislation to which Gerson refers dates back to the Council of
Nicaea (325) which in its fifth canon called for provincial synods twice yearly. This
legislation was repeated in the nineteenth canon of the Council of Chalcedon (451). In
692 the Council in Trullo reduced the required synods to one yearly. The Second
Council of Nicaea (787) incorporated this legislation in its eighth canon. The Fourth
Lateran Council, canon 6, restored the canonical tradition of provincial synods. The
council also provided for the annual convocation of diocesan synods. Cf. Alberigo,
Decreta, pp. 7, 72, 119-120, 212-213.

[101] *Bonus pastor*, G, 5, 143. "Hoc praeterea respicit celebrationem annuam
conciliorum provincialium, quia secundum verba juris nihil pene sic mores
disciplinatos ab Ecclesia magis expellit quam negligentia sacerdotum qui contemptis
canonibus ad corrigendos ecclesiasticos mores synodum facere negligunt."

[102] *Vivat rex*, G, 7, 1185.

[103] *Scriptum est melius*, G, 2, 110.

in their obligation to conduct diocesan visitations. Episcopal visitations were further hampered by the lack of safety along travel routes, the disturbances of the Hundred Years War and the conflicts over episcopal jurisdiction resulting from varying allegiances in the Great Schism. Some dioceses, consequently, had several claimants to the episcopacy.[104] Despite these difficulties, however, Gerson called for the restoration of episcopal visitation. If the bishop himself is unwilling or unable to carry out the visitation then he should at least appoint learned men as deputies and give them full ecclesiastical power to promote the work of reform. Shortly after his address before the Synod of Rheims in 1408, Gerson composed his *De visitatione praelatorum* which is a synthesis in question form of many ideas developed at Rheims. This work is, in effect, a detailed checklist to aid bishops in their visitations. Gerson saw in the visitation the most profitable means at the bishop's disposal for the moral reformation of those under his care.[105]

Some might object that it is sufficient to promulgate laws already in existence rather than hold new visitations and synods. There is ample legislation, they maintain, to solve most of the problems in any diocese. The difficulty, however, according to Gerson, is that legislation of itself frequently becomes lifeless and ineffective. Laws which are repeatedly violated must be continually repromulgated just as plants which produce unhealthy offshoots must be regularly pruned. Episcopal visitations remain the most effective means to insure the vivification of dormant legislation.[106] The revitalization of law is achieved through the presence of the bishop among his people during visitations. The bishop is the *lex viva* who reforms the morals of his people.[107]

---

[104] Adam, *La vie paroissiale*, pp. 209-220.

[105] *De visitatione praelatorum*, P, 2, 558 B. "... saluberrimum videtur pro reformatione morum et subditorum emendatione, quod pastor juxta canonicas sanctiones visitet diligenter et crebro suum gregem aut per ipsum, aut per vicarios doctos, habentes plenariam ab eo potestatem. ..."

[106] *Bonus pastor*, G, 5, 143.

[107] *De visitatione praelatorum*, P, 2, 558 B. The notion of the bishop as *lex viva* recalls the idea of νόμος ἔμψυχος applied to kings by the neo-Pythagorean philosopher, Diotogenes. His principle of *lex animata* made the king foremost in virtue and the source of all law. If the king was law unto himself it also followed that he must be the embodiment of justice. Gerson develops a similar theme when, as will be seen, he relates the idea of the bishop as *lex viva* to the principle of *epikeia*. The notion of *lex animata* became part of the Roman legal tradition when Justinian incorporated it in his legislation. Cf. *Novellae*, 105, 2, 4. Although unknown in the West during the early Middle Ages, the idea of *lex animata* subsequently played an important role in

The conception of the bishop as *lex viva* means that by his presence the bishop not only renews and vivifies the law but also that he is the interpreter of the law according to the principle of *epikeia*. The bishop is, indeed, the embodiment of *epikeia*. No legislator can foresee all the circumstances in which his laws are to be operative. Frequently the implementation of law in unforeseen circumstances will militate against its very spirit and will go contrary to the specific intention of the legislator. Such circumstances can work considerable hardships upon those who are obliged to obey the law. The bishop, however, through his visitation, is able to see at first hand the concrete conditions under which the church's law must operate. If conditions are such as to militate against the spirit and intention of the law, he is capable of so modifying the law that it will be less burdensome for his subjects.[108] Frequently the situation will demand a complete legal revision. Such is the case when antiquated legislation remains on the books. Legislational revision would enable the bishop to conduct his visitation more effectively. Useless legislation hinders his pastoral work and should be deleted.[109]

The bishop's presence throughout his diocese not only vivifies and adapts the church's law to the circumstances of actual life but also lends authority and honor to the Word of God. Bishops have been most negligent in preaching, and, as a consequence, the Word of God has fallen into dishonor among the people. For many, Scripture has become a collection of storytales. The people, moreover, see only

---

medieval political theory with the revival of Roman Law. Godfrey of Viterbo († 1191) claimed that the famous four doctors of Bologna applied the title to Frederick Barbarossa at the Diet of Roncaglia in 1158. The *Glossa Ordinaria* of Accursius in the first half of the thirteenth century referred to the emperor as *lex animata*, and the Italian jurists in their gloss on the *Liber Augustalis* applied the term to the emperor. In 1232 Frederick II referred to himself as *lex animata*. This tradition was continued into the fourteenth century by Baldus (c. 1327-1400) and Andreas of Isernia († 1316). The idea of *lex animata* also had its impact in the ecclesiastical sphere, for at the beginning of the thirteenth century the English canonist Alanus transferred the title to the pope who thus became *lex vel canon vivus*. Johannes Andreae († 1348) explicitly called the pope *lex animata*. For the historical development of the term *lex animata* see Ernst H. Kantorowicz, *The King's Two Bodies: A Study in Medieval Political Theology* (Princeton, 1957), pp. 127-132. Gerson's application of *lex animata* to the bishop represents a new extension of the term's use within the church.

[108] *De contractibus*, P, 3, 172 A. "Est itaque legislator tamquam lex viva, director et epikeies; dum et ubi provenit circa leges difficultas ex circumstantiarum varietate, quae sunt innumerabiles, nec cadere possunt sub arte vel lege; quia per accidens sunt." Cf. *Gratia vobis et pax*, 2, 238, where Gerson applies the idea of *lex viva* to religious superiors.

[109] *Rememoratio agendorum durante subtractione*, G, 6, 113.

the members of the mendicant orders preaching the Word. There are also many poor and wandering preachers but these command little respect among the laity. If the bishop himself were to become actively involved in preaching, the people would have greater respect for God's Word; they would see bishops honoring the Word of God by their preaching and their belief would be correspondingly strengthened.[110]

The bishop is to be aided in his visitation by à group of assistants known as *reformatores* who are to determine the time, manner, and order of the visitation. Gerson advises that those geographical areas be bypassed wherever the clergy is so opposed to the visitation as to render its results doubtful. Any attempt to achieve reform in such areas is tantamount to throwing pearls before swine and exposing the sacred to ravaging dogs. If it becomes commonly known that the bishop's visitation was badly received in one part of the diocese, the effectiveness of the visitation would be considerably jeopardized throughout the whole diocese.[111]

The *reformatores* are to designate, moreover, the monasteries and parishes which the bishop is to visit and they are to send officials beforehand to notify the populace of the impending visitation. Announcements of this type will enable the people to abstain from their daily labors and prepare themselves for the bishop's arrival. Gerson even advises that a written proclamation be issued describing the manner in which everyone should prepare for the visitation. This decree would be read publicly in the churches. Men and women are

---

[110] *Bonus pastor*, G, 5, 143.

[111] *Rememoratio agendorum durante subtractione*, G, 6, 110. The origin of the *reformatores* deserves further research. They may well have their beginnings in the Fourth Lateran Council which in its sixth canon strove to make annual provincial synods more effective instruments of reform by requiring metropolitan and suffragan bishops to appoint officials who, during the year, would travel about the dioceses investigating those aspects of church life which required correction. These officials had no jurisdictional powers but were to report their findings to the provincial synods in order that reforms could be effectively implemented. Cf. Alberigo, *Decreta*, pp. 212-213. The Lateran decree, however, does not use the term *reformatores*. The *reformatores* as described by Gerson, moreover, appear as direct agents in the conduct of the visitation and not as advisors to the provincial councils. A transformation in the nature and duties of these officials may well have occurred between the time of the council and Gerson's years. Also worthy of investigation is the possible relationship between the ecclesiastical *reformatores* and the *enquêteurs-réformateurs* established by Louis IX (1226-1270) to protect the rights of his subjects. On the *enquêteurs-réformateurs* see John B. Henneman, "Enquêteurs-réformateurs and Fiscal Officers in Fourteenth-Century France," *Traditio*, 24 (1968), 309-349. Henneman also lists earlier studies on the same topic.

especially advised to find out if they have been guilty of any reserved sins or if they have incurred excommunication or other ecclesiastical censures which would require the attention of a prelate.[112]

The bishop and the *reformatores* should be aided in their visitation by theologians. Gerson desires that the theologians be members of the secular clergy since they command more respect than religious, especially mendicants. In addition to assisting the bishop, a theologian is expected to conclude the visitation in each area with a major sermon to the people. The sermon is to be geared to their level of understanding and should instruct them in the faith, admonish them to correct their vices, and, finally, lead them to a life of virtue. A jurist and a notary should also be part of the bishop's retinue. The notary is to record carefully those problems within the diocese whose resolution requires more time and attention than the schedule of the visitation allows.[113]

Getting down to specific details of the visitation, Gerson would have the bishops first inquire into matters of faith. They should investigate unorthodox beliefs among the people.[114] Gerson is especially suspicious of the Beguines and other small religious groups. He asks the bishops to check into the beliefs of some who profess to lead the eremitical life.[115] Bishops should also investigate reports of superstition and blasphemy. All complaints of the people, moreover, deserve investigation. Unjust excommunications, arrests, and taxation are to be rectified. Confessional facilities should be provided for those whose confessions involve cases of reserved sins, or sins which parishioners are normally and justifiably reluctant to reveal to their local clergy. Archdeacons are warned against using the visitation as an occasion of financial gain. The visitation, on the contrary, should lead to increased piety and spiritual edification of the faithful.[116]

The bishop, moreover, should visit hospitals, homes for lepers and indeed all places where the poor of Christ are lodged. He is to be especially solicitous about the treatment of the poor in such institutions. The financial resources of these institutions are to be so managed that all will benefit equitably; mismanagement of finances

---

[112] *Rememoratio agendorum durante subtractione*, G, 6, 110.
[113] *Rememoratio agendorum durante subtractione*, G, 6, 110-111.
[114] *Bonus pastor*, G, 5, 143.
[115] *Rememoratio agendorum durante subtractione*, G, 6, 111.
[116] *Bonus pastor*, G, 5, 143.

is to be quickly corrected. Gerson also urges the bishop to visit the homes of the mendicant orders, indeed, the homes of all religious. He is to admonish them for all immodesty in their style of living; the lives of religious are to be quiet and sober. They should remain faithful to the study of the Scriptures, to prayer and the divine office as well as to other religious forms of piety. The residences, moreover, of all ecclesiastics should be visited and their inhabitants urged to live honestly and chastely. They are to practice almsgiving, provide helpful counsel as well as perform works of charity. These activities constitute the very nature of their vocation as ecclesiastics.[117] Gerson also recommends that the bishop send, at different times during the year, written exhortations to the various religious communities in his diocese. He urges that the bishop write to priors, rectors and abbots of religious houses regularly in order to provide spiritual direction for superiors, professed religious, and novices.[118]

The considerable detail with which Gerson describes the conduct of episcopal visitations is sufficient proof of the importance of the visitation in any program of episcopal reform. The visitation provides the bishop with an excellent opportunity to determine whether he has been effectively utilizing the triple powers of his soul for the pastoral benefit of his people. By his investigation of the state of preaching and the education of the clergy and the young within his jurisdiction, he will know how effectively he has exercised his *vis rationalis* in promoting the growth of faith in his people. By his visitation, the bishop will be able to ascertain whether the personnel and activity of his curia have set a good example for the faithful. Has he so managed his own household as to inspire a sense of hope and trust in the people committed to his care? Only if he is free of avarice, hypocrisy, and material extravagance will the clergy and people be led to purge their lives of similar faults. If the bishop has so purged his life, then he has properly employed his *vis irascibilis* for the benefit of his people. Finally, through visitations the bishop will be able to investigate the sacramental life of his people. Has the religious life of his people been sacramentally oriented? If so, then he can be assured that he has used his *vis concupiscibilis* for the sanctification of his flock.

If the bishop's visitation reveals that he has successfully utilized the powers of his soul, then he can be sure that he has acted in

---

[117] *Scriptum est melius*, G, 2, 109-110.
[118] *Bonus pastor*, G, 5, 144.

accordance with the image of God within himself and renewed that same image in the souls of his people. Should the visitation lead to a less than positive conclusion regarding his pastoral activities then the bishop is obliged to reform and renew the trinitarian-like faculties of his soul in order that he might better secure the renewal and reformation of the image of God in his people. He is to so intensify the exercise of his *vis irascibilis, rationalis,* and *concupiscibilis* that he will bring about the purgation, illumination, and perfection of the image of God in those under his care. Through his renewed pastoral activity his people will grow in faith, hope and charity, thereby renewing the image of God within themselves and contributing towards the growth of the mystical body of Christ.

CHAPTER FIVE

CLERGY, LAITY, AND REFORM

Gerson's principles of church reform do not terminate with the episcopacy but extend to the parish clergy as well. Reform of the local churches involves, therefore, both diocese and parish. This extension of reform to the parish means, in effect, that the principles of hierarchy, hierarchical activity, and image will be operative on that level. The first section of this chapter will be concerned with the parish clergy as an integral part of the ecclesiastical order. Attention will also be given to the religious clergy, since many of Gerson's ideas on the parish clergy developed in conjunction with the numerous conflicts between these two groups, especially over the question of Christian perfection. In conjunction with the question of perfection, some brief investigation of the laity will be made. A more thorough investigation of the laity and reform will be undertaken in the chapter on personal reform. The interrelationship of hierarchical activity, the image of God, and reform will constitute the final portions of this chapter.

1. Parish Clergy

Basic to Gerson's understanding of the parish clergy is the fact that the parish clergy constitutes an essential and intrinsic part of the ecclesiastical hierarchy. The parish clergy, he maintains, is just as much a part of the ecclesiastical hierarchy as are pope, cardinals, archbishops, and bishops.[1] While asserting that the parish clergy is essential to the church's hierarchy, Gerson does not claim that it occupies as high a position or plays as important a role as the *praelati majores*. Members of the parish clergy are designated as *praelati minores*, and constitute a less important segment of the ecclesiastical hierarchy. This relatively lower position in the hierarchy is indicated by the fact that they are not called *sponsi Ecclesiae* in the same sense

---

[1] *Quomodo stabit regnum*, G, 7, 984. "S'ensuit que bien est aussi de l'ordonnance essentielle et estable de saincte esglise l'estat des cures, comme est celluy des prelas, cardinaulx, archevesques et evesques, voir que est celluy du pape, combien que ne soit mie si parfait."

as are bishops; they can, moreover, more readily resign their pastoral office than can bishops.[2] They are, furthermore, designated as *praelati secundi ordinis*. The dignity and honor accorded them, therefore, is of a lesser degree than the *praelati majores*.[3]

The parish clergy is an essential part of the church's hierarchy principally because Christ so instituted his church. The Scriptures are, as it were, the constitution of the church and in the Scriptures the parish clergy finds its justification. In his sermon of February 23, 1410 on the harmful effects of Alexander V's bull, *Regnans in excelsis*, which had been promulgated on October 12, 1409 in confirmation of the privileges of the mendicant orders, Gerson consoles the parish clergy with the fact that it stands in no need of a papal bull to vindicate its existence. The parish clergy had been established directly by Christ. If the parish clergy needs a bull to justify its existence then the Holy Scriptures must be considered as such.[4]

Gerson's arguments for the direct institution of the ecclesiastical hierarchy by Christ rest primarily upon four scriptural sources. The entire tenth chapter of St Matthew's Gospel narrates how Christ gathered the twelve apostles and commissioned them to go forth and preach the kingdom of God throughout Israel. Christ also described to the newly chosen apostles the nature of their work as well as the type of reception they can expect. The second scriptural source is the tenth chapter of St. Luke. St. Luke writes that in addition to the twelve apostles Christ appointed seventy two as his disciples. The disciples, too, were commissioned by him to go into every town and

---

[2] *De statibus ecclesiasticis*, P, 2, 534 A-B. "Status curatorum est de essentiali, ac intrinseca Ecclesiae hierarchia, sicut status praelatorum, quamvis inferior sit, et pro sua perfectione variabilior. Qua ratione curati simplices non aeque proprie dicuntur sponsi, sicut episcopi, liberiusque permittuntur cedere, vel renuntiare curis suis." The resignation of pastoral office to which Gerson refers centered around the question of whether a priest or bishop could resign his office to enter religious life. In general, medieval canonical and theological tradition made it much more difficult for the bishop to resign his office than the priest. The bishop was considered as bound to the pastoral care of his people by a solemn and perpetual vow from which only the pope could dispense. No such vow was considered as binding on the parish priest. The permission of his bishop sufficed. The priest, moreover, could ignore episcopal opposition if he felt that his actions were inspired by the Holy Spirit. Cf. St. Thomas, *Summa Theologiae*, 1, 2, q. 185, a. 4, q. 189, a. 7, Marietti, pp. 810-811, 855-856. Thomas also cites the pertinent canonical legislation.

[3] *De potestate ecclesiastica*, G, 6, 241. "Et dicuntur praelati secundi ordinis, dignitatis vel honoris, quales sunt curati...."

[4] *Quomodo stabit regnum*, G, 7, 984.

place to preach the news of his kingdom. Like the apostles, they are also given specific instructions as to how they are to conduct themselves in their work among the people. Both groups, moreover, received from Christ similar powers to enable them to carry out their mission within the newly-formed church. In this context the passages from Mt 16:19 and 18:16 are of extreme importance. Gerson regards Matthew 16:19 as conferring the power of the keys not only upon Peter but upon the apostles as well. In Mt 18:16, the disciples are the recipients of a similar power. They, too, have the authority to bind and to loose. Central to Gerson's thought, therefore, is the fact that Christ established the ecclesiastical hierarchy upon both apostles and disciples and to both he gave the power of binding and loosing.

According to Gerson the *praelati majores* are the successors of the twelve apostles and the *praelati minores* the descendants of the seventy-two disciples. He argues that this interpretation has the support of Scripture as well as the weight of ecclesiastical tradition and he enumerates Augustine, Jerome, Isidore, Bede, and Gratian as his authorities. Gerson also quotes Pope Damasus I (366-384) as saying that Christ established but two *ordines* among his early followers: the twelve apostles and the seventy-two disciples.[5] Gerson's explanation of the origin of the *praelati majores* and *minores* follows the interpretation traditionally adopted by teachers from the secular clergy at the University of Paris in their prolonged conflict with the mendicant orders. The alleged quotation from Pope Damasus is, in reality, a quotation from Pseudo-Damasus' *De chorepiscopis*, which had been incorporated in the canonical collection of Pseudo-Isidore.[6] Originally intended to disassociate *chorepiscopi* from the ranks of the ecclesiastical hierarchy, Damasus' statement was utilized in the thirteenth century by the secular clergy at the University of Paris to separate the mendicant orders from the ecclesiastical hierarchy and, therefore, from direct pastoral work with the laity.[7] The Pseudo-

---

[5] *De potestate ecclesiastica*, G, 6, 240-241.

[6] *Decretum*, 1, dist. 68, c. 5, ed. Friedberg, 1, 255. The Pseudo-Isidorian Decretals sought the reform of the Carolingian church and had as one of their immediate aims the protection of suffragan bishops and lower clergy from excessive control by metropolitans, provincial synods, and the secular powers. For bibliography see H. Fuhrmann, "False Decretals," *NCE*, 5, 821-824.

[7] *Chorepiscopi* appreared in the eastern church around the second or third centuries and in the West about the fifth century. By the Carolingian period they had considerably increased in numbers. In the West, they acted as auxiliaries to the bishops in the temporal and spiritual administration of their dioceses. The reform circles responsible for the Pseudo-Isidorian Decretals saw in the *chorepiscopi* a threat

Isidorian Decretals also contained other passages similar to that of Pseudo-Damasus which were attributed to Pseudo-Clement and Pseudo-Anacletus. Early Christian writers, moreover, such as Tertullian and Hippolytus saw adumbrations of the seventy-two disciples in Nm 11:16, where the Lord tells Moses to gather seventy elders to aid him in caring for his people. Gerson, however, prefers to see the Levites of the Old Testament as the direct predecessors of the disciples.[8]

The association of bishops and priests respectively with the apostles and disciples most probably goes back to St. Jerome († 420). Jerome's interpretation is found in a sermon attributed to St. Caesarius of Arles in 506 and was continued by Bede († 735), from whom it entered into the *Glossa Ordinaria*, thereby becoming an integral part of the medieval heritage. Given the aura of primitive authenticity by its inclusion in the Pseudo-Isidorian Decretals, this tradition was carried on during the Gregorian reform by Peter Damian († 1072) and found embodiment in the classic works of Peter Lombard and Gratian during the twelfth century. In the thirteenth century, Thomas Aquinas, Bonaventure, William Durandus, and Henry of Ghent saw bishops and priests as the successors of the apostles and disciples respectively. James of Viterbo, John of Paris, and Alvaro Pelayo continued the tradition into the fourteenth century.[9]

---

to episcopal power and sought their elimination. By the ninth and tenth centuries they were gradually replaced by archdeacons. Cf. Jacques Leclef, "Chorevêque," *DDC*, 3, 686-695.

[8] *De statibus ecclesiasticis*, P, 2, 534 A. "Status curatorum succedet statui septuaginta duorum discipulorum Christi quoad Legem novam et figuratus est in antiqua Lege per Levitas."

[9] The textual tradition that made bishops and priests successors of the apostles and disciples is treated in detail by Congar, "Aspects ecclésiologiques," pp. 59-63. Modern research has shown, however, that the categories of bishop and priest as understood by the medieval tradition do not pertain to the church as described in the New Testament or as manifested in the early years of the postapostolic period. Ministers in the New Testament are not designated as priests but as presbyters (πρεσβύτεροι) and bishops (ἐπίσκοποι). The New Testament, moreover, uses the latter terms interchangeably. Only in the postapostolic period does the bishop emerge as head of the presbyters. Clear evidence of a monarchical episcopacy comes only with Ignatius of Antioch in the early years of the second century. Even then the functions of bishop and presbyter are not clearly distinguished. The identification of the offices of bishop and presbyter with priesthood began towards the end of the second century as the notion of sacrifice became associated with the Eucharist. Since the New Testament, moreover, does not designate the apostles as presbyter-bishops or as ordaining such, it is difficult to see presbyter-bishops as successors of the apostles in the strict sense of the term. Apostles and presbyter-bishops existed simultaneously and exercised different roles within the communities. With the disappearance of the former, presbyter-bishops emerged as the

Since, according to Gerson, the parish clergy has been constituted by Christ as an integral part of the ecclesiastical hierarchy, certain consequences logically follow. First, no one will be able to charge that the parish clergy is of purely human origin and, therefore, not part of the ecclesiastical hierarchy established by Christ. This conclusion has direct consequences upon Gerson's attitude toward religious orders. They are not part of the essential hierarchy of the church and have not been directly instituted by Christ. Gerson frequently refers to the origins of the religious orders by such terms as *factitius* and *adventitius*.[10] A second consequence of the parish clergy's immediate institution by Christ is that the pope cannot abolish the parish clergy or refuse to recognize it as an essential part of the ecclesiastical hierarchy. The pope must accord the parish clergy due honor as part of the ecclesiastical order. Since bishops and priests are by divine law essential elements within the church their office and authority admits of no modification even at the hands of papal power. The bishops and parish clergy were directly instituted by Christ and are not the product of a papal decree.[11]

---

most important figures in the churches. On the development of ecclesiastical office in the early church see Hans von Campenhausen, *Ecclesiastical Authority and Spiritual Power in the Church of the First Three Centuries*, trans. J. A. Baker (London, 1969), as well as the works of Jean Colson, *L'évêque dans les communautés primitives* (Paris, 1951), *Les fonctions ecclésiales aux deux premiers siècles* (Bruges, 1956), *L'épiscopat catholique: Collégialité et primauté dans les trois premiers siècles de l'église* (Paris, 1963), and *Ministre de Jésus-Christ ou le sacerdoce de l'Evangile* (Paris, 1966). See also A. M. Farrer, "The Ministry in the New Testament," and Gregory Dix, "The Ministry in the Early Church," in *The Apostolic Ministry*, ed. by K. E. Kirk (London, 1946), pp. 113-182, 185-303, M. M. Bourke, "Reflections on Church Order in the New Testament," *CBQ*, 30 (1968), 493-511, and Raymond E. Brown, *Priest and Bishop* (New York, 1971).

[10] *De consiliis evangelicis et statu perfectionis*, P, 2, 681 A. "... sequitur quod status curatorum non est factitius, vel adventitius vel voluntarius. Patet, ex quo secundum praedicta est de primaria Christi institutione et ordinarius status."

[11] *Quomodo stabit regnum*, G, 7, 984. "S'ensuit que le pape ne pourroit destruire cest estat ou annuler, comme cet estat ne vient par son ordonnance positive mais par l'autorite de Dieu sans moyen." Cf. *De consiliis evangelicis et statu perfectionis*, P, 2, 681 A. The idea of a parish clergy as understood by Gerson and the medieval tradition has its roots not in the New Testament but in the developments of the fourth century. With the spread of Christianity to the country districts in the fourth century, individual priests were designated by the bishops to provide for the pastoral care of the people, first on a temporary basis and then permanently. As urban populations increased, priests were also assigned to distinct geographical areas within the city. Under the changing circumstances, priests were gradually given greater liturgical and jurisdictional powers. From all these developments there arose the parish, which encompassed a determined geographical unit and was under the permanent care of a determined priest. Close bonds with the bishop were always preserved and the parish

If the pope must recognize that the parish clergy is an essential part of the ecclesiastical hierarchy, so much more must the bishops. They must realize that the parish clergy receives its power not from the bishops but directly from Christ. To assert that the parish clergy receives its authority through episcopal delegation is, in effect, to reduce it to the status of a royal bailiff. Such royal officials have no power in their own right; all their authority is delegated from the king. For Gerson, the authority and jurisdiction of the parish clergy comes directly from Christ inasmuch as the parish clergy is the direct successor of the disciples.[12] The comparison of the parish clergy to a royal magistrate was commonplace in medieval ecclesiological discussions, and was utilized by theologians such as Thomas Aquinas, Godfrey of Fontaines and Henry of Ghent.[13]

Since the parish clergy has its ordinary jurisdiction directly from Christ through the disciples, it follows that parish priests cannot be removed from their office at the mere whim of the local bishops. Removal from office could only occur if the authority of the parish clergy were of a purely delegated nature such as that of royal magistrates. Permanence of office, therefore, follows from the fact of divine institution. Gerson argues, moreover, that his position is supported by canonical tradition. Canon law, he asserts, guarantees the curate continued possession of his parish, unless he is convicted of having committed some serious fault. Only under such circumstances can he be removed from office.[14]

The authority given directly by Christ to the parish clergy is the

---

priest was seen primarily as an associate of the bishop in the pastoral care of the laity. By the fourteenth century the parish curate performed many civic duties as well. He was present at the drawing up of all wills. He was custodian of public morality and had charge of public safety, health, and social welfare. At times, he was even concerned with the collection of taxes. For the historical development of the office of curate see B. Dolhagaray, "Curé," *DTC*, 3, pt. 2, 2429-2453, and F. Claeys-Bouuaert, "Cure," *DDC*, 4, 889-900 and "Curé," *DDC*, 4, 900-941. X. A. Baraniak, "Curé religieuse," *DDC*, 4, 941-961, discusses the historical events which led to the control of many parishes by the religious orders in the Middle Ages. The multifold duties of a curate in late medieval France are treated by Adam, *La vie paroissiale*, pp. 87-99.

[12] *De consiliis evangelicis et statu perfectionis*, P, 2, 680 D-681 A. "Sequitur ultra, quod curati parochiales non se habent ad episcopos, sicut balivi, vel praepositi ad regem vel principem. Patet, quoniam ipsi curati habent ordinariam jurisdictionem sive potestatem exercendi ea quae juris sunt in subditos, sicut et discipuli quibus succedunt. Praepositi autem et balivi non habent nisi subdelegatam jurisdictionem, non ordinariam."

[13] Congar, "Aspects ecclésiologiques," p. 68.

[14] *De consiliis evangelicis et statu perfectionis*, P, 2, 681 A.

power to provide for the spiritual welfare of the laity. The laity, therefore, must respect that authority and seek to have all its pastoral needs provided by the parish clergy. Mutual obligations, consequently, exist between the parish clergy and the laity. These obligations, moreover, are rooted in divine and natural law. If curates are obliged to show solicitude for their flock and give an account to the Lord for those entrusted to their care, then parishioners are equally obliged to place themselves fully under the care of their local pastors. To illustrate this point Gerson draws upon an example taken from the political sphere. Princes are obliged to protect, to defend and to rule their subjects. The people, in return, have the corresponding obligation to be loyal subjects of the princes and to pay the taxes necessary for their personal upkeep and the support of the realm.[15]

In the light of these conclusions Gerson insists that the religious life of the laity center around the parish and the parish clergy. All liturgical services and preaching are to take place primarily within the parish church. The parishioner, moreover, is to see his parish church as his mother and, as a loyal son, he must show her fitting honor. He is to find in the local curate his true spiritual father. In brief, the parish church is to be his gateway to God. For this reason, Gerson asserts, the church discourages strangers from moving from one parish to another and prevents them from being received into a new parish without the necessary letters required for such a change.[16]

Because it has been divinely established as an integral part of the ecclesiastical hierarchy, the parish clergy shares in the hierarchical activities of purgation, illumination and perfection. The parish clergy, moreover, receives the power to exercise these hierarchical activities directly from Christ and not through any delegation from pope or bishops. These activities are relatively similar to those exercised by other segments of the church's hierarchy. Correcting and admonishing the faithful as necessity demands is the primary function of purgation. The hierarchical activity of illumination operates through teaching and preaching, and the administration of the sacraments constitutes the activity of perfection. Through these

---

[15] *De consiliis evangelicis et statu perfectionis*, P, 2, 681 C.
[16] *Quomodo stabit regnum*, G, 7, 991. Gerson's idea of the parish church as the gateway to God is reminiscent of Gn 28:17 which serves as the entrance hymn for the Mass of the Dedication of a Church.

hierarchical activities the parish clergy fulfills its duty to provide for the *cura animarum*.[17]

With regard to preaching and teaching, Gerson does not expect the same quality of performance from the parish clergy as from bishops. The parish clergy is not obliged to give sermons of a highly intellectual nature as might a theologian. The parish clergy is to preach, however, in a manner proportionate to its level of education; its preaching should stress the basic message of the Gospels, especially in the area of belief, the commandments, and the seven deadly sins.[18] The parish clergy should realize, moreover, that it is preaching, for the most part, to ordinary working people who have little or no education. The Word of God, consequently, must be presented to them in a manner in which they can most effectively understand. Oftentimes it is better merely to read the commandments to them than engage in sermons that aim primarily at arousing religious curiosity. Did not St. Paul in 2 Tim 3:6-7 warn his disciple to avoid preachers who capture the fancies of weak women? Such preachers do very little to instill in the hearts of their listeners a knowledge of the truth. Gerson also warns against excessive preaching lest people become so inured to sermons that their effect is minimized. Just as men who overindulge in eating, lose all desire for food and as plants which are too frequently watered rot, so do parishioners become oversatiated with preaching.[19] The parish clergy may, if it so desires, invite outside preachers, presumably mendicants, to address the faithful, but such preachers should recognize that they preach only with the approval of the parish clergy.[20]

All sacramental activity on behalf of the faithful also falls primarily within the domain of the parish clergy. As in so much of Gerson's thought on the sacraments, the administration of the sacrament of penance holds a position of prime importance. Since the parish clergy is an intrinsic part of the church's hierarchy, not even the pope can deprive parish priests of their pastoral functions, especially in the area of penance. The mendicants, therefore, have no right to

---

[17] *De potestate ecclesiastica*, G, 6, 241. "... quibus ex statu et ordinario jure conveniunt tres actus hierarchici primarie, essentialiter et immediate a Christo, qui sunt purgare per correctionem, illuminare per doctrinam et praedicationem, perficere per sacramentorum ministrationem."

[18] *De statibus ecclesiasticis*, P, 2, 534 B.

[19] *Quomodo stabit regnum*, G, 7, 985.

[20] *De statibus ecclesiasticis*, P, 2, 534 C.

administer the sacrament of penance in parish churches without the explicit permission of the pastor. Gerson also argues that local pastors should have greater authority in the area of reserved sins, control over which was primarily exercised by the pope, bishops and mendicants. He objected that the mendicants frequently had greater power in confessional matters than did the local clergy.[21]

Gerson contends that the decree *Omnis utriusque sexus*, promulgated by the Fourth Lateran Council in 1215, strongly supports the privileged position of the parish clergy in the area of penance.[22] That decree provided that the faithful of both sexes, upon reaching the age of reason, were obliged to confess their sins yearly to their own priest and, upon fulfillment of the duly imposed penance, to receive the sacrament of Eucharist at least during Easter time. Should any member of the faithful desire to confess his sins to a priest other than his parish priest, he is first to obtain the necessary permission from his local pastor since, otherwise, all absolution would be invalid. Canonical tradition had long interpreted the phrase *proprius sacerdos* used in the decree as applying strictly to the parish clergy. The Second Lateran Council (1139), in its tenth canon, used the term, *proprius sacerdos*, in a similar context. The Fourth Lateran Council, in its thirty-second canon, described *sacerdos proprius* as *qui parochialem habet ecclesiam*.[23] As a result of the above tradition, Gerson concludes that it is spiritually safer to confess to one's parish priest. Since the parish priest is by divine law entrusted with the spiritual care of the faithful, he is also the duly authorized administrator of sacraments with regard to those under his jurisdiction.[24]

Gerson places strong emphasis upon the sacrament of penance in the *cura animarum* because it is a primary means by which the parish priest can come to know those committed to his care. He firmly believes that pastors should be extremely close to their parishioners and a principal way to achieve this spiritual intimacy is through the administration of the sacraments, especially penance. To express the need of the parish clergy to know its parishioners Gerson uses the adage: *Cognosce faciem pecoris tui*. The pastor should recognize and

---

[21] *Quomodo stabit regnum*, G, 7, 986.

[22] *Quomodo stabit regnum*, G, 7, 986. Cf. Alberigo, *Decreta*, p. 221.

[23] Alberigo, *Decreta*, pp. 167, 225-226. Cf. P. A. Kirsch, "Der sacerdos proprius in der abendländischen Kirche vor dem Jahre 1215," *AKK*, 84 (1904), 527-537.

[24] *Quomodo stabit regnum*, G, 7, 986. Cf. *De statibus ecclesiasticis*, P, 2, 535 A.

know the faces of his flock. This recognition takes place in the administration of all the sacraments, especially penance.[25]

Another aspect of the mutual obligations that exist between parish clergy and the laity is the former's right to tithes and other sources of financial income. Gerson is a strong defender of the parish clergy's right to receive tithes. This right was frequently challenged by mendicants who in sermons and in the confessional advised people not to pay their tithes to the parish clergy. Such mendicants were often motivated by a desire to secure income for their own monasteries. At other times they proposed the cessation of tithes as a reaction to the dissolute lives of individual curates. Gerson inveighs strongly against those mendicants, who maintain that ecclesiastics have a right only to necessary food and clothing, and that what remains after such expenses is the patrimony of the poor. Failure to observe these norms, they maintain, is tantamount to sacrilege. Gerson, however, denies that such norms apply to the parish clergy; they apply, rather, to members of religious orders, who have pronounced vows of poverty, or to ecclesiastics who have misused financial resources explicitly designated for the needs of the church and her poor.[26]

Gerson, moreover, argues against those who maintain that tithes and temporal possessions reduce the perfection of an ecclesiastic's life. To answer this charge, he resorts first to an *ad hominem* argument. If, he argues, tithes and temporal possessions render an ecclesiastic's life less perfect, then, members of religious orders should not seek offices held by either bishops or parish clergy since, according to the logic of the argument proposed, their lives would be less perfect because of the financial income and possessions normally affiliated with such offices. To profess a life of poverty, as the mendicants do, and, at the same time, to desire offices associated with financial and temporal possessions is a blatant contradiction.[27]

Gerson's position that the parish clergy has a right to tithes and possessions is based, however, on more than *ad hominem* arguments.

---

[25] *Quomodo stabit regnum*, G, 7, 990.

[26] *Quomodo stabit regnum*, G, 7, 991. As seen earlier, Gerson held that in the case of bishops and their curia what remained after their necessary expenses belonged to the patrimony of the poor. His more lenient attitude toward the parish clergy is partly explained by its impoverished condition. The controversy with the mendicants resulting from Alexander V's *Regnans in excelsis* in 1409 also exercised considerable influence upon Gerson's position.

[27] *Quomodo stabit regnum*, G, 7, 992.

He argues that since the parish clergy is by divine law an integral part of the ecclesiastical hierarchy, its right to financial income from tithes and other possessions is also of divine right. This conclusion is based on Lk 10:7, where Christ tells the disciples that they are to remain in the houses of those to whom they are spiritually ministering, eating and drinking what is provided for them, since the laborer is deserving of his wages. Gerson contends, moreover, that this principle of divine law is confirmed by natural and canon law. The parish clergy, therefore, is totally within its rights when it lays claim to tithes and other financial income. Parish priests can, moreover, draw up wills and freely distribute alms from their own resources.[28] The only restriction that Gerson would make upon the parish clergy is that it should not engage in simoniacal practices; it must avoid even the slightest suspicion of simony. He also warns the clergy that it should not refuse to minister to the spiritual needs of others in controversies over tithes and temporal possessions.[29]

Since the parish clergy is an integral part of the ecclesiastical hierarchy, Gerson reacts very strongly against those who would lessen its honor and prestige. No one is to attack or defame the parish clergy, even though it contains members who are not completely suitable for the *cura animarum*. The deficiencies and failures of a few should not lead to a condemnation or lessening of respect for all the parish clergy. If such were the case, then every level of ecclesiastical society would be subject to the same defamation, since the church contains many members who fail to live up to the high standards of their vocation.[30] Gerson argues that individuals who fall short of the ideals of their vocation should still receive honor and respect precisely because of their state within the church. He especially warns against sermons which would concentrate on the failures and weaknesses of the parish clergy; such sermons stir up the spirit of rebellion and seditiousness among the laity. On the contrary, every effort shoud be made to build up the laity's respect and honor for the parish clergy. Even though it contain sinners, the parish clergy should be respected because it is an intrinsic part of the church's hierarchical structure. The members of the parish clergy, therefore, deserve honor and respect because of their hierarchical state.[31]

---

[28] *Quomodo stabit regnum*, G, 7, 992.
[29] *De statibus ecclesiasticis*, P, 2, 535 B.
[30] *De statibus ecclesiasticis*, P, 2, 535 A.
[31] *Responsio ad errores de orationibus privatis fidelium*, P, 2, 655 B.

2. Religious Clergy

The hierarchical status of the parish clergy was the main issue stressed by Gerson in his sermon on Alexander V's *Regnans in excelsis*. In this sermon, given on February 23, 1410, he argued that the privileges granted the mendicants in the area of preaching and confessions so enhanced their influence in relationship to the *cura animarum* that they constituted a major threat against the hierarchical order of the church as established by Christ. Within the hierarchical structure of the church, the parish clergy is primarily responsible for the *cura animarum*. The privileges granted to the mendicant clergy by Alexander V, however, endangered the hierarchical position and activities of the parish clergy.

The conflict between the mendicant clergy and the parish clergy over their respective roles in the pastoral care of the faithful had been going on within the church since the thirteenth century.[32] The controversy, however, became intensified in 1409 when John Gorel, a Franciscan, defended a series of theses at the University of Paris which, in effect, maintained that the pastoral functions of preaching, hearing confessions, administering the sacraments as well as the right to receive tithes were not the private domain of the parish clergy. He further asserted that the parish clergy was not of divine institution. Gorel went so far as to claim for the mendicant clergy greater prerogatives in preaching and hearing confessions than those enjoyed by the parish clergy.[33] When the secular masters of the university reacted strongly against his assertions, the Franciscan freely withdrew his theses.[34] Gorel even conceded that the power to preach and to hear confessions was primarily the prerogative of the episcopacy and the parish clergy. Theologians of all four mendicant orders concurred with the ecclesiological principles espoused by Gorel in his recantation, which took place in the audience chamber of the bishop of Paris.[35] Gorel's submission, apparently, was not made with much sincerity, since he appealed his case to Alexander V, himself a Franciscan.

---

[32] For the chronology of the various phases of the conflict as well as the major literary aspects of the controversy, see Congar, "Aspects ecclésiologiques," pp. 44-52.

[33] Connolly, *John Gerson*, p. 108; Meyjes, *Jean Gerson*, pp. 306-308.

[34] For the reaction of the Parisian secular masters see the *Censura plurium in theologia professorum circa bullam a mendicantibus extortam*, P, 2, 442-446.

[35] *Quomodo stabit regnum*, G, 7, 984.

From this appeal issued Alexander's *Regnans in excelsis* of October 12, 1409, which condemned the position of the secular masters at the University of Paris and reaffirmed the right of the mendicants to preach, hear confessions, and accept tithes. The university, in reaction to Alexander's bull, immediately prohibited the mendicants from exercising their new privileges. Both the Dominicans and Carmelites agreed not to take advantage of these privileges, but the Franciscans and Augustinians resisted. The university then retaliated by obtaining a royal ban against the use of the parish pulpits by the members of these orders. Sermons were preached throughout Paris to explain the stand of the university. The sermon preached by the university's chancellor certainly ranked among the more important sermons on this occasion.[36]

Gerson's sermon of February 23, 1410 was built upon the notion of hierarchical order and contains many of his ideas on hierarchy and order analyzed in our first chapter. He clearly saw the concessions made to the mendicants by Alexander V as disturbing the *ordo ecclesiasticus*. The *praelati* have been principally instituted by Christ to lead the faithful to God and for this purpose have been entrusted with the hierarchical functions of purgation, illumination and perfection. As a result of the privileges granted to the mendicants the pope, in effect, has introduced disorder within the ranks of the ecclesiastical hierarchy. Only by maintaining and reasserting its hierarchical structure will the church be able to perform its work of leading the faithful to God. For this reason, ecclesiastical prelates, especially the bishop of Paris, as well as the entire university, have reacted in consternation at the promulgation of the papal bull which threatens to bring such harm to the *ordo praelatorum*.[37]

Gerson is especially cautious to minimize Alexander V's role in the entire episode occasioned by the bull. Both he and the university had earlier supported Alexander at the Council of Pisa. Gerson, therefore, represents Alexander as having been unknowingly misled by the leaders of the four mendicant orders. The mendicants have besieged the papal office with their requests and have extorted such a declaration from the papacy. Gerson is sure that the papal

---

[36] Connolly, *John Gerson*, pp. 108-109; Feret, *La faculté de théologie*, 4, 29-35, and Victor Martin, *Les origines du Gallicanisme*, 2 (Paris, 1939), 164-165. The complete sources for the controversy are given by Delaruelle, *L'Église au temps du Grand Schisme*, 1, 160, n. 28.

[37] *Quomodo stabit regnum*, G, 7, 982-983.

concessions were obtained more through the pope's inadvertence than with his cooperation. He is confident that the pope, an outstanding theologian in his own right, would never have promulgated such a decree if he had taken the time necessary to examine all the points contained therein. He asserts, moreover, that many theologians were of the opinion that the pope acted rather unwillingly in the entire matter, since he was under considerable pressure from the mendicants. Gerson strongly affirms that neither he, the bishop of Paris, nor the university have any intention of saying anything prejudicial to the Holy Father's honor, for they are all extremely certain that once sufficiently instructed on the entire matter he will understand the justness of their complaints and reverse his decision.[38]

Gerson insists that in this controversy over the papal bull both he and all the secular masters are working in behalf of the pope's honor; they are attempting, moreover, to preserve his office and authority within the church. They are, in effect, striving to return that authority to its proper finality. Papal power, as all power within the church, exists for the edification and not the destruction of its members. Alexander V has unknowingly and unwillingly frustrated the power of his office and prevented it from attaining its proper goal. Under the influence of the mendicant orders, papal authority has been directed towards the destruction of the mystical body, for by threatening the established hierarchical order of the church it has in effect weakened the church's very structure.[39]

In addition to his charge that the mendicants threatened to disrupt the hierarchical order of the church through the assumption of hierarchical activities in the area of preaching and confessions, Gerson also criticizes the religious orders of his day because they claimed to represent a higher state of Christian perfection than the parish clergy. They have engendered in the minds of many the belief that the religious life is more closely associated with the state of perfection than is the life of the parish clergy. Religious orders have so appropriated the term *status perfectionis* that it has become associated exclusively with their mode of life. They have failed to realize that the *status perfectionis* includes both *status perfectionis acquirendae* and *status perfectionis exercendae*.[40] They concede that

---

[38] *Quomodo stabit regnum*, G, 7, 982-983.
[39] *Quomodo stabit regnum*, G, 7, 983.
[40] *Redde quod debes*, G, 5, 491. "Videatur igitur si sequitur: iste status est

praelati majores enjoy a higher degree of perfection than religious, but they neglect the fact that the parish clergy also shares in the *status perfectionis exercendae.*[41]

The parish clergy shares with the bishops in the *status perfectionis exercendae,* since it participates in the hierarchical activities of purgation, illumination, perfection.[42] Like the bishops, the members of the parish clergy participate in the hierarchical activities of purgation through the various processes of correction, illumination by means of preaching and teaching, and perfecting through the administration of the sacraments.[43] Their powers, however, are not as extensive as those of the bishops. For this reason they are called *praelati minores* or *praelati secundi ordinis.* They do not enjoy the wide corrective powers of the bishops in the area of excommunication and interdict. Their obligations in the area of preaching and teaching, moreover, are not as weighty since they are not expected to bring the same degree of wisdom and knowledge to their preaching as are the bishops. In addition, their knowledge of the Scriptures need not be as extensive as that of bishops. Gerson would have the parish clergy rest content with a general knowledge of the Scriptures as well as a basic understanding of the commandments and precepts of the church. He also recommends the use of already prepared sermons drawn from patristic sources. The parish clergy's share in the hierarchical activity of perfection is also restricted in that it can administer only five of the seven sacraments, confirmation and orders being restricted to the episcopacy. Though less extensive than that of the bishops, the

---

perfectionis acquirendae, ergo simpliciter est status perfectionis; et an hic adjectivum 'acquirendae' distrahat aut limitet vel restringat."

[41] *Redde quod debes,* G, 5, 491. "Et quidem de majoribus praelatis pauci hoc negant quin sint in statu majoris perfectionis. Sed attendendo rationem facile est inspicere non affectatis quod similis ratio militat pro curatis. . . ." In the thirteenth century, Aquinas, reflecting the views of the mendicant orders, denied that the parish clergy is identified with the state of perfection. Cf. *Summa Theologiae,* 2, 2, q. 184, a. 6, Marietti, pp. 801-802.

[42] *De statibus ecclesiasticis,* P, 2, 534 C. "Status curatorum est status perfectionis, non solum acquirendae, sed etiam exercendae, cum sibi competat tam obligatio, quam autoritas reducendi animas ad Deum, secundum hierarchicos actus, qui purgare, illuminare, perficere, nominantur."

[43] *De consiliis evangelicis et statu perfectionis,* P, 2, 679 D-680 A. "Ex istis infero, quia status curatorum in ordine proximus est statui episcoporum. Patet, quia eadem opera hierarchica eis incumbunt quae et episcopis, etsi non in tam excellenti gradu. Debent enim subditos purgare arguendo et increpando; illuminare docendo et praedicando; perficere, sacramenta ministrando."

hierarchical activity of the parish clergy remains a genuine exercise of the powers of purgation, illumination, and perfection.

Since the parish clergy shares with the bishops in the *status perfectionis exercendae*, the state of the parish clergy clearly transcends that of religious orders.[44] The parish clergy not only achieves its own personal perfection but also fosters the growth of perfection in the faithful. As a result, the parish clergy contributes primarily towards the common spiritual good of the church. Religious, however, since they are in the *status perfectionis acquirendae*, are occupied principally with their own spiritual welfare. Since there is no doubt in Gerson's mind that the common good is more divine and far transcends the private good, he easily concludes that the parish clergy is superior to that of religious.[45]

The fact that the parish clergy is in the *status perfectionis exercendae* and participates in hierarchical activity, is, as it were, a direct result of its being an integral and essential part of the ecclesiastical hierarchy. Members of religious orders can find no direct institution of their way of life in the early church as established by Christ. They, consequently, can make no claim to being an intrinsic and essential part of the ecclesiastical hierarchy nor to a participation in the hierarchical activities of purgation, illumination, and perfection. Gerson frequently refers to the religious life as *religio factitia*, thereby emphasizing that the religious life was not directly established by Christ.[46] Though approved by the church, the religious life is essentially a human institution, and is, in a sense, foreign to the church's original structure. In addition to the word *factitia*, Gerson also uses such adjectives as *adventia* and *voluntaria* to emphasize the fact that religious life came into existence after the church's primary institution by Christ.[47]

Gerson contends that the growth of religious life in the church was considerably accelerated in the years following the Constantinian Donation. Because of the Donation, the church became considerably occupied with temporal cares. The parish clergy, as a result of the church's concern with temporalities, found itself called upon to

---

[44] *De statibus ecclesiasticis*, P, 2, 534 C. "Status curatorum superior est in ordine hierarchico Ecclesiae ad statum simplicium religiosorum. . . ."

[45] *De consiliis evangelicis et statu perfectionis*, P, 2, 680 C-D. ". . . quoniam curati ordinati sunt ad bonum commune; religiosi vero vacant bono privato, et singulari et sacrae stationi; bonum vero commune divinius est, et melius bono privato."

[46] *Gratia vobis et pax*, G, 2, 234.

[47] *De consiliis evangelicis et statu perfectionis*, P, 2, 681 A.

perform many activities additional to its spiritual functions. This concern with temporal matters, moreover, worked to the neglect of its spiritual duties. The religious clergy, therefore, was instituted primarily as an aid to the parish clergy, especially in the area of preaching and confessions.[48]

The conception of the religious clergy as coadjutors of the parish clergy characterizes, for the most part, Gerson's basic attitude toward religious. Throughout the whole controversy over the bull, *Regnans in excelsis*, and, indeed, throughout his whole life, Gerson's attitude toward the religious clergy was essentially moderate. Although he opposed the granting of special privileges to the mendicant orders in the area of preaching and confessions, he did not advocate that mendicants be totally deprived of pastoral activity. He was concerned primarily with the manner in which those activities were performed, that is, whether they were exercised independently of the parish clergy or with its permission. As long as religious recognized the prerogatives of the parish clergy as an integral part of the ecclesiastical hierarchy and as long as they acknowledged that the *cura animarum* was principally the domain of the parish clergy, Gerson had no objection to their assisting in the pastoral care of the faithful. Once a mendicant had received permission of his religious superior as well as the approval of the local pastor, Gerson welcomed him as a close associate of the parish clergy.

Gerson finds his attitude towards the religious clergy confirmed, moreover, by the practice of the early church. He argues that the writings of the Fathers clearly illustrate that in the early years of their existence, religious were subject to the authority of the parish clergy. The parish clergy cared, moreover, for their spiritual needs, especially the administration of the sacraments. In later years, he contends, religious began to adopt a more nomadic way of life and it was in an attempt to curb these *girovagi* that more stable forms of religious life were constructed, primarily the institution of religious superiors who would coordinate their religious activities as well as subordinate them to one single authority.[49]

---

[48] *De statibus ecclesiasticis*, P, 2, 536 A. "Status privilegiatorum ad praedicandum et confessiones audiendum statutus est post primariam Ecclesiae institutionem, rationabiliter ordinatus ad sublevamen eorum qui hierarchicos in Ecclesia status habent, praesertim post talem et tantam in temporalibus dotationem, quae secum attulit multam occupationem."

[49] *De consiliis evangelicis et statu perfectionis*, P, 2, 680 C. Gerson is most likely

In his *De potestate ecclesiastica*, written in 1417 during the Council of Constance, Gerson argues that the pope, as the head of the ecclesiastical hierarchy, as well as other high members of the hierarchy, can, for a reasonable cause, decide to give the parish clergy spiritual coadjutors. These coadjutors would naturally be members of the mendicant orders who would share in the hierarchical activities of the parish clergy. Gerson warns, however, that such action is not to be undertaken unless there is sufficient reason or if there is any chance that it would lead to irreverence or lack of respect for the parish clergy on the part of their parishioners. Gerson, moreover, clearly affirms that mendicants are not to be employed wherever the parish clergy is sufficiently capable of providing for the pastoral needs of the laity. He asks the rhetorical question: Who would assign a tutor to an adult who is prudent and capable of carrying on his own work, especially if he is unwilling to have such assistance?[50] When, however, the parish clergy has need of mendicants it should accept them in a friendly and gracious manner as long as they have the necessary permission from their legitimate superiors and are men of upright character.[51]

Gerson, therefore, would have members of the parish clergy and the mendicant orders show deep fraternal charity toward one another with each respecting the rights and prerogatives of the other. The spirit that should prevail between the two groups should be that which St. Paul describes in Gal 6:2. Both parish clergy and mendicants should strive to bear one another's burdens and in so doing fulfill the law of Christ which is charity. They should rid themselves of all malice towards each other and all internecine

---

referring here to the early stages of eremitical monasticism in Egypt, Syria, and Palestine, and the later development of cenobitic monasticism under such leaders as Pachomius (✝ 346), Basil (✝ 379), and Benedict (✝ 546). Pachomian monasteries, since they did not allow monks to be ordained, did depend upon the clergy of the neighboring villages for their liturgical and sacramental needs. The monasteries of St. Basil and St. Benedict, however, had their own priests. Gerson is exaggerating, moreover, when he states that monks were subjected to the authority of the parish clergy. Only in 451 did the Council of Chalcedon, canon 4, decree that monks were to be subjected to the authority of the bishops of their city or region. Cf. Alberigo, *Decreta*, p. 65. Gerson's historical perspective is also restricted by attributing the rise of cenobitic monasticism solely to a desire to restrain the *girovagi*. For the early history of monasticism see, for instance, Patrice Cousin, *Précis d'histoire monastique* (Paris, 1956), pp. 27-222.

[50] *De potestate ecclesiastica*, G, 6, 215.
[51] *De statibus ecclesiasticis*, P, 2, 535 C.

fighting should cease. The two groups have expended a considerable portion of their energies in fraternal conflict and have given great scandal to the laity. Such an attitude is far from the spirit of St. Paul who said in 2 Cor 6:3 that he would avoid giving any offense to those with whom he was working in order that the ministry of God's Word would not be brought into discredit. Gerson, moreover sees the continual controversies between the mendicants and the parish clergy as pharisaical. Is it not more holy, he asks, that both mendicants and parish clergy dedicate all their efforts towards helping others grow in the perfection of God's love rather than engage in empty glorification of their respective state of perfection within the Church? God is abundant in his riches towards all; he is, moreover, the God of peace and not division.[52]

Despite this irenic attitude, it is clear that Gerson does not consider the religious orders of his day as a dynamic force in the reform of the church. Since the eleventh century, the religious orders were among the foremost agents for reform within the church but by the fourteenth and fifteenth centuries they lost this leadership. Most orders in this latter period were in a general state of decline and few new ones were founded. Reasons for this loss in prestige were numerous. The destruction of property during the Hundred Years War resulted in considerable financial impoverishment. Many religious houses, furthermore, were under lay control. Observance of the rule and the religious vows became extremely relaxed and the level of intellectual formation declined. Membership also decreased as a result of the Black Death and the failure to attract young recruits. The Great Schism, finally, weakened the unity of the orders, for it resulted in internal divisions according to the various papal allegiances. Gerson must have been aware, however, that there were many promising signs of reform in the religious orders of his time, but these seem to have made little impression upon him. Most reform movements, moreover, did not reach their full momentum until after his death. For Gerson, therefore, hope for ecclesiastical reform lay not with the religious orders but with the hierarchical structures of the church.[53]

---

[52] *De statibus ecclesiasticis*, P, 2, 537 C.

[53] For an excellent analysis of the state of the monastic and mendicant orders in the late middle ages as well as the initiatives for reform within these orders see Delaruelle, *L'Église au temps du Grand Schisme*, 2, 1031-1105.

3. LAITY

The exaggerated claims of the religious orders had left many with the notion that the laity was excluded from the quest for Christian perfection. Gerson maintained, however, that Christian perfection was not restricted to religious orders which professed the vows of poverty, chastity, and obedience, but was, indeed, open to all Christians at every level of the church's society. Gerson never defined Christian perfection in terms of poverty, chastity, and obedience; he always described it as intimate union with God which is achieved through divine grace and the theological virtues of faith, hope, and charity.

Gerson was of the opinion that universality of Christian perfection was characteristic of the *ecclesia primitiva* and was shared in by apostles, disciples, and all believers. The *ecclesia primitiva* was, indeed, the era of *perfectio Christiana*.[54] In the early church there were no religious orders, for the foundations of St. Basil and St. Augustine had not yet come into existence, and yet the ideal of Christian perfection flourished everywhere regardless of one's state within the church. There were certainly many married persons in the early church who had attained a high degree of Christian perfection. Nowhere in the Scriptures do we read that Christ considered the vows of poverty, chastity and obedience as essential to Christian perfection. The lives of the apostles and disciples, moreover, were not characterized by their adherence to the life of the vows.[55]

Given the universality of Christian perfection, what then are the distinguishing features of the monastic and mendicant forms of life? Gerson regards the different religious orders primarily as particular means for the attainment of a common goal. Throughout the church's history, men have always sought forms of life which would

---

[54] *De perfectione cordis*, P, 3, 438 A. "Nam in Ecclesia primitiva, quando erat perfectio Christiana...."

[55] *Super assertiones Fr. Matthaei Grabow*, P, 1, 468 A. This treatise was written at the Council of Constance in 1418 in response to the exaggerated claims of the Dominican Matthew Grabow who restricted the pursuit of Christian perfection to the monastic and mendicant orders with their vows of poverty, chastity and obedience. Grabow's attacks were directed primarily toward the Brethren of the Common Life. When he failed to receive the support of the bishop of Utrecht, Grabow took his case to the Council of Constance. The Brethren of the Common Life found staunch advocates in Gerson and Pierre d'Ailly. The case was not settled until after the close of the council when Martin V condemned Grabow's views in May, 1419. Grabow recanted on October 22, 1419. Despite his recantation, he remained in prison in Rome and most probably died there.

most effectively secure for them the goal of Christian perfection. With the passage of time, however, these means became identified with the end desired, with the result that many believed their mode of life to be the sole or principal means to attain Christian perfection. This is precisely what has happened in the case of the monastic and mendicant orders.

Gerson, therefore, would prefer that religious orders cease describing their way of life as a *status perfectionis*. Imperfect Christians are too frequently found within their ranks. If the orders hesitate to stop using the term *status perfectionis* then they should stress that they are in the *status perfectionis acquirendae*, that is, they are in the process of acquiring perfection, and are, therefore, not yet fully perfect. They should also make clear that their way of attaining Christian perfection is but one approach among many. For some, a life patterned according to a set religious rule might well present the best way to reach the goal of Christian perfection. For others, such a form of life can be a hindrance and an obstacle; it would be much better if they remained in the world, for they can there more effectively fulfill their desire for Christian perfection.[56]

Closely related to Gerson's concept of the universality of Christian perfection and the different means for its achievement, are his ideas on the evangelical counsels and the commandments. The evangelical counsels, preached by Christ and recorded in Mt 5:1-12 and Lk 6:2-49, express the new spirit that is to characterize God's kingdom and are frequently referred to as beatitudes, since commitment to their values results in Christian happiness. These counsels have traditionally been associated with the religious life. Since the religious life, in turn, has often been equated with the life of Christian perfection, it is not surprising that the practice of the beatitudes, Christian perfection and the religious life have become identified. Gerson rejects this line of reasoning. As with religious life so too with the evangelical counsels, they do not constitute Christian perfection but are a means toward its realization. They are, as it were, disposing instruments which facilitate union with God. Christian perfection, therefore, is not identified with the beatitudes. If one must speak about the evangelical counsels in terms of perfection, he should realize that they are to be considered as *perfectio secundum quid.*[57]

---

[56] *Super assertiones Fr. Matthaei Grabow*, P, 1, 468 B. Cf. *De perfectione cordis*, P, 3, 437 C.

[57] *De consiliis evangelicis et statu perfectionis*, P, 2, 677 A. "... quoniam consilia

The essence of Christian perfection, Gerson maintains, is found essentially in the commandments; the commandments are the root of Christian life and spirituality. The evangelical counsels as such do not enter into the essential constitution of Christian perfection.[58] Gerson does not deny that they aid in the acquisition of perfection, but he refuses to regard them as the quintessence of perfection. There are, he argues, many people in every state of life who have achieved a high degree of Christian perfection without committing themselves to a way of life built upon the evangelical counsels. Their success has been possible because they have based their lives upon the commandments. The essence of Christianity is to be found in the observance of the divine commandments and in the perfect exercise of the virtues prescribed therein.[59]

4. HIERARCHY, IMAGE, AND REFORM

Investigation must now be made into the manner in which Gerson's reform principles are operative on the level of the parish clergy and the laity. The parish clergy will be studied first as an agent for reform within the church and then as the object itself of reform. The laity will be treated briefly in the context of its relationship with the reforming activities of the parish clergy. A more detailed analysis of the reform of the laity must await the study of personal reform in the succeeding chapter.

Like that of the bishops, the hierarchical activity of the parish clergy is essentially reformative and has as its primary function the restoration of the image of God in the souls of the laity. The aim of hierarchical activity is to so purge, illumine, and perfect the faithful that the image of God within them is reformed and renewed.[60] From

---

proprie, et maxime respiciunt materiam instrumentalem disponentem ad facilius et brevius acquirendam essentialem vitae Christianae perfectionem; et ideo sunt perfectio secundum quid, et accidentaliter...." Cf. P, 2, 673 A.

[58] *De consiliis evangelicis et statu perfectionis*, P, 2, 677 B. "... praecepta vero divina magis de directo, et immediate respiciunt illa quae essentialiter pertinent ad vitam Christianam, et spiritalem sicut virtutes, et actus earum." A similar view was expressed by Aquinas, *Summa Theologiae*, 2, 2, q. 184, a. 3, Marietti, p. 798.

[59] *De consiliis evangelicis et statu perfectionis*, P, 2, 677 A. "... nunquam tamen dicendus est homo perfectus, nisi habeat illa quae veniunt, et concurrunt ad essentialem constitutionem et perfectionem vitae spiritalis, quae sunt observantia praeceptorum divinorum, et exercitium virtutum, de quibus omnibus dantur praecepta, et de perfectione earum."

[60] *Domine si in tempore hoc*, G, 5, 212. "... vestrum est officium ut ceteros purgetis, illuminetis, perficiatis, quatenus coelestem portent imaginem...."

the point of view of reform, therefore, the parish clergy emerges as an instrument of major significance, for it is only through the agency of the clergy that the reformative dynamism of the ecclesiastical hierarchy reaches the people. As the lowest level of the ecclesiastical hierarchy, the parish clergy is more in contact with the laity and, therefore, can best accomplish its reform.[61] The role of the parish clergy in church reform also illustrates one of the primary principles of hierarchical order, namely, that the lowest is always brought to the highest through the agency of intermediaries.[62] Accordingly, the laity as the lowest segment of ecclesiastical society must be brought to the Trinity, the supercelestial hierarchy, through the agency of an intermediate hierarchy which is the church. Since the parish clergy represents the lowest extension of the ecclesiastical hierarchy, it is, therefore, closest to the laity and most instrumental in its sanctification and reformation.

The reformative activity of the parish clergy is also related to the *status perfectionis exercendae*, which the parish clergy shares with the bishops. Since fostering perfection in the souls of the laity is essentially identical with the exercise of the hierarchical activities of purgation, illumination, and perfection, it is also associated with the reformative power of all hierarchical activity. Growth in Christian perfection must, therefore, be seen as essentially identical with the process of personal reform. Christian perfection, moreover, has been defined by Gerson as union with God through grace and the theological virtues of faith, hope and charity. The renewal of the triple *vires*, which constitute the image of God in man, is likewise achieved through the same means. The universal call of the laity to Christian perfection, therefore, is, in effect, a call to reform and renewal of the image of God.

Since the parish clergy is closely affiliated with the episcopacy and has been designated its assistant, it follows that the reformative activity of the parish clergy will proceed in a manner similar to that of the bishops. As seen in Gerson's address to the Synod of Rheims in 1408, the hierarchical activity of the bishop proceeds according to the triple *vires* of his soul. The *vires* constitute the image of God in the bishop and by acting according to that image he restores the same image in those under his pastoral care.[63] The parish clergy no

---

[61] *De consiliis evangelicis et statu perfectionis*, P, 2, 679 D-680 A.
[62] *Quomodo stabit regnum*, G, 7, 981.
[63] *Bonus pastor*, G, 5, 124.

less than the bishops, has been made to the image of God through the triple powers of the soul. As good shepherds, the members of the parish clergy are to lay down their lives for their flock, that is, their pastoral activities are to proceed according to the image of God within them.[64] They are, therefore, to exercise the triple powers of their soul on behalf of their parishioners. By acting according to the image of God, they will accomplish the reformation of that same image in their parishioners. Under the guidance of the parish clergy, then, especially in the area of preaching, teaching, good example, and the administration of the sacraments, the triple powers of the laity will be reformed and renewed.

To be an effective agent for reform, the parish priest must himself undergo reform. Like all members of the church, he is called upon to undergo a process of personal reform. The parish clergy, moreover, is a *status perfectionis acquirendae* as well as a *status perfectionis exercendae*. The parish priest must, therefore, strive to renew and to reform the image of God within himself, for upon the quality of that personal reform depends his effectiveness as a reformative agent within the church. As all other Christians, he too must strive with God's grace to remove the traces of sin which have discolored and distorted the image of God within him. The parish priest must, therefore, embark upon the *via poenitentiae* which leads to full conversion and reformation of the image of God. Unless the triple powers of his soul are functioning properly, he will be unable to employ them in the pastoral care of his parishioners. The more he renews and reforms the image of God within himself the more he becomes an effective agent for reform within the church.[65]

In addition to personal reform, the parish clergy must also undergo a reform proper to its state within the church. Foremost in this reform was the problem of clerical education. The majority of parish priests in Gerson's time attained, at best, only a rudimentary education. Those who were fortunate enough attended grammar schools for a few years. In rural areas, this opportunity frequently was not available and candidates for the priesthood were trained under an apprentice system whereby they studied under the direction of their local pastor and then petitioned the bishop for ordination whenever

---

[64] *De consiliis evangelicis et statu perfectionis*, P, 2, 680 A. "Tenentur et in casu sicut episcopi animas pro ovibus ponere."

[65] *Domine si in tempore hoc*, G, 5, 212.

they felt qualified to handle the ordinary duties of the priesthood. Their training was generally restricted to the study of Latin, liturgical chant, the rubrics of the Mass, the categories of sins, and the administration of the sacraments. Needless to say, such an education was hardly calculated to instil in its products a desire for study and continued self-education.[66]

To improve the quality of clerical education, Gerson had called upon the bishops to establish theological schools in all cathedral and collegiate churches. He urged bishops to seek out clerics with intellectual promise and send them to the University of Paris for their theological training. Gerson realized, however, that despite these measures many candidates for the priesthood were financially and intellectually incapable of obtaining either a university or cathedral school education. In such cases Gerson was of the opinion that with proper vigilance the normal education of the parish priest was sufficient. In fact, he clearly asserts that parish priests can effectively provide for the pastoral care of the laity if they are guided by the spirit of charity and live a life of moral integrity. Their state does not require any high degree of learning. On this basis, Gerson argues against the claim that parish priests should yield some of their pastoral activities to the mendicant clergy because the latter enjoys a higher degree of education. With an ordinary amount of study, the parish clergy can amass knowledge sufficient for its pastoral activities.[67]

Gerson does, however, call upon the bishops to be extremely conscientious in their examination of candidates for the priesthood. Too often political influence or financial remuneration have been the decisive factors in the approval of candidates for ordination. Before approving candidates, bishops must be sure that they possess the knowledge necessary for the adequate fulfillment of their pastoral duties, especially in the area of preaching. Parish priests, moreover, should be instructed in the techniques of preaching so necessary for success in their pastoral work. With regard to content, the parish clergy should emphasize in its sermons matters primarily concerned with the commandments, faith, and morals.[68] The stress on the commandments should not be seen in the context of merely

---

[66] Adam, *La vie paroissiale*, pp. 141-151. On clerical education see also F. W. Oediger, *Über die Bildung der Geistlichen in späten Mittelalter* (Leiden, 1953).

[67] *De statibus ecclesiasticis*, P, 2, 535 A-B.

[68] *Bonus pastor*, G, 5, 131.

imparting the rudiments of Christian faith but more in the sense encountered earlier, namely, that they contain the essentials of Christian perfection and, therefore, play an important role in personal reform.

The importance of preaching in Gerson's ideas on reform is seen in the fact that it is through preaching and teaching that the parish clergy primarily exercises its *vis rationalis* in the pastoral care of the laity. The more effectively the parish clergy exercises that power, the more effective will be its impact upon the reform of the laity. Through preaching and teaching, the *vis rationalis* in the souls of the laity is reformed and renewed. In a similar context, the hierarchical function of illumination is exercised through the activity of preaching and teaching. Whether the process be described as the exercise of the *vis rationalis* or the hierarchical function of *illuminare*, the result is the same, namely a renewal and growth in the theological virtue of faith, resulting ultimately in the reformation of the image of God within the laity.

A second area of reform is related to the *vis irascibilis* which is concerned with the courage, strength, and conviction needed in order to live a life comparable to the priestly calling. Guided by the theological virtue of hope, the *vis irascibilis* enables the priest to encounter the numerous obstacles and hindrances that occur in the exercise of his office. His style of life, moreover, is to be such that it manifests the strength of character and commitment that would inspire hope and confidence in the souls of the faithful, thereby renewing the *vis irascibilis* within them. In the case of bishops, Gerson argued that avarice, hypocrisy and material extravagance so characterized their lives that they frequently failed to give good example. Given its impoverished state, Gerson could hardly make the same charge against the parish clergy. The parish clergy was not in a position to amass wealth and possessions. In fact, if the reform of the parish clergy requires anything, it requires that the parish priest be given a salary sufficient to guarantee him a decent standard of living and to enable him to command a normal degree of respect from the laity. Gerson called upon the bishops to ease the burden of ecclesiastical taxation that fell so heavily upon the shoulders of the parish clergy.[69] These taxes included tithes, annates, subsidies as well as the support of papal legates and the duties of hospitality. He also

---

[69] *Bonus pastor*, G, 5, 135-136.

defended the parish clergy's rights to tithes and other sources of income.[70]

The one area where Gerson felt that the parish clergy might be guilty of avarice concerned financial remuneration for the administration of the sacraments. For this reason he frequently called upon the members of the parish clergy, if at all possible, to administer the sacraments without financial recompense. They are to give freely what they have freely received.[71] Gerson also realized that the clergy must live from the altar and that Christ himself said that the laborer is worthy of his pay. When financial remuneration must be exacted, Gerson demands, above all, that it be free from all suspicion of simony. In his treatise on simony, he discusses the variety of intentions which can motivate a clergyman in the administration of his spiritual office and illustrates those intentions which are permissible and those which clearly fall into the category of simony.[72]

Since the parish clergy should exemplify a life of high moral integrity, Gerson was duly concerned with the problem of concubinage.[73] He especially urged that all candidates for the priesthood be carefully examined with regard to continence, since so much disgrace has come to the church because of the dissolute life of its clergy. He advises bishops, however, to move cautiously in matters related to concubinage, since many clerics, if forced to give up their concubines, would turn to a more dissolute form of life. For this reason, Gerson's attitude toward concubinage in the parish clergy at times shows considerable leniency. Excommunications and suspensions on the part of the bishop will do little good if there is no reasonable chance of amelioration.

Gerson's leniency flows from his great concern for the laity, especially their need for Mass and the administration of the sacraments. Better that they be administered by a priest in

---

[70] *De statibus ecclesiasticis*, P, 2, 534 D.

[71] *Redde quod debes*, G, 5, 490.

[72] *Ad reformationem contra simoniam*, G, 6, 179-181.

[73] For the extent of concubinage among parish priests in France see Adam, *La vie paroissiale*, pp. 151-163. Adam maintains that reformers such as Gerson, Jean of Varennes and Pierre d'Ailly tend to overestimate the degree of concubinage prevalent among the clergy of their time. Although local synods and councils legislated against concubinage, no firm conclusions as to its extent can be deduced from their statements. Adam concludes finally that extant records of diocesan visitations indicate that the number of priests living in concubinage remained small.

concubinage than not administered at all. He urges parishioners to be patient with such priests, for if they are tolerated by their bishops the laity should show a similar degree of toleration. Otherwise even greater scandals and divisions can occur within the church. He realizes that many holy men in the church's history have taken a view opposite to his on this entire matter but he feels that the evil of concubinage has become so strongly rooted in the church that it is almost impossible to enforce the ancient ecclesiastical legislation in the area of celibacy with any degree of rigor.[74]

Surprisingly Gerson has very little to say about the serious problem of absenteeism among the parish clergy. Many clerics never developed the desire or the ability for pastoral work. A considerable number found parish life too restrictive and retired to the more pleasant surroundings of the larger cities. Curates who wanted to improve their theological education could absent themselves for as many as seven or eight years. Others abandoned their parishes without even seeking episcopal approval. Many clerics received churches as benefices and then never advanced to the priesthood. In all these cases recourse was had to a vicar who would care for the parish during the absence of the curate. As was to be expected, little concern was shown with regard to the qualifications of such persons for their pastoral duties. Frequently the primary norm in their selection was financial, for it was to the curate's benefit to get a substitute as cheaply as possible. Under such circumstances the spiritual care of the laity suffered considerably.[75] While he does not inveigh against the problem of absentee curates, Gerson would submit their vicars to strict episcopal vigilance and control in the implementation of their pastoral duties, especially during the time of visitation. During episcopal visitations the same norms for pastoral efficiency were to apply to both vicars and curates.[76]

The third major area of clerical reform envisioned by Gerson is related to the sacraments, primarily their proper administration. The bishop is to thoroughly examine the clergy with regard to the proper formulae required for the administration of the sacraments.[77] Gerson strongly stressed the sacrament of penance above the other sacraments because he saw this sacrament as a primary instrument for

---

[74] Rememoratio agendorum durante subtractione, G, 6, 112-113.
[75] Adam, La vie paroissiale, pp. 163-170.
[76] De visitatione praelatorum, P, 2, 558 B, 560 B.
[77] Redde quod debes, G, 5, 490.

reform. He reminds the bishops that they are to secure good confessors for their diocese. They should, moreover, take measures to reduce the number of reserved sins since such procedures hinder the laity from approaching the sacraments.[78] Gerson emphasizes that it is through the sacrament of penance that the parish clergy comes to a true spiritual understanding and recognition of the members of its flock.[79]

The sacramental activity of the parish clergy is directly related to Gerson's reform principles, for through the administration of the sacraments the parish clergy exercises its *vis concupiscibilis*. Sacramental activity is also identified with the hierarchical activity of perfection. The immediate result of all sacramental action, whether conceived as an exercise of the *vis concupiscibilis* or as the hierarchical activity of perfection, is an increase in charity and in this charity the *vis concupiscibilis* of the parishioners is renewed, thereby resulting in the reform of the image of God within them.

Our analysis of clerical and lay reform in Gerson has established that his program of reform flows from the notions of hierarchy, hierarchical activity and image, and is essentially identical with the quest for Christian perfection. The entire process of reform, moreover, whether clerical or lay, must also be seen within the context of the theological virtues. The reformative functions which the parish clergy exercises through the *vis rationalis, irascibilis* and *concupiscibilis* are such primarily because these powers of the soul are under the directing force of the virtues of faith, hope, and charity respectively. The renewal of these *vires*, whether in the clergy or the laity, consists primarily in the increase of the virtues of faith, hope, and charity in the soul. Preaching and teaching generates faith; the example of a virtuous life inspires hope and the exercise of the sacraments results in charity. The reformative activity of the parish clergy in the fullest sense of the term, therefore, originates in the theological virtues and terminates in the generation of those same virtues within the laity. Hierarchy, hierarchical activity, image, and Christian perfection, have as their inner finality the growth of the individual in faith, hope, and charity. This growth makes the individual more intimately and actively a part of the mystical body and contributes, in turn, towards its growth and edification.

---

[78] *Pontificali dignitati*, G, 2, 90.
[79] *Quomodo stabit regnum*, G, 7, 990.

CHAPTER SIX

PERSONAL REFORM

All ecclesiastical reform must, in the final analysis, terminate in personal reform if it is to be in any way effective. This personal orientation is intrinsic to Gerson's ideas on episcopal and clerical reform. Hierarchy and hierarchical activity result in the reformation and sanctification of the individual and thereby contribute toward the growth and edification of the entire mystical body. The purpose of the present chapter is to analyze the process of personal reform. Like episcopal and clerical reform, personal reform rests heavily upon the principle that man has been made to the image and likeness of God. The present chapter, therefore, will investigate the various interpretations of the image utilized by Gerson. Attention will also be given to the consequences of sin upon the image and the various ways in which Gerson conceived of the image under sin. Our study, finally, will turn to the process by which the reformation and renewal of the image of God is achieved in man.

1. MAN AND THE IMAGE

All understanding of personal reform in Gerson's writings has its starting point in the fact that man has been created in the image and likeness of God. The scriptural data on this point are clear, especially in the book of Genesis. In Gn 1:26 we have its most succinct formulation: "Let us make man in our image, after our likeness." The same theme is repeated in Gn 5:1: "When God created man, he made him in the likeness of God," and again in Gn 9:6: "...for God made man in his own image." Patristic and medieval thinkers developed their speculations on Christian anthropology upon this scriptural basis and Gerson was no exception to this tradition.[1]

---

[1] For the biblical tradition on the image see L. Köhler, "Die Grundstelle der 'Imago Dei' Lehre: Genesis 1:26," *TZ*, 4 (1948), 16-22, and K. L. Schmidt, "Homo imago Dei im alten und neuen Testament," *EJ*, 15 (1947), 149-195. For an historical survey of the terms "image and similitude" in the Platonic, Judaic, and patristic traditions see R. Javelet, *Image et Ressemblance au douzième siécle*, 1 (Paris, 1967), 1-66. The main portion of Javelet's work is a synthesis of the various interpretations of image and similitude in the writers of the twelfth century. Unfortunately no such work exists for

Like many medieval thinkers, Gerson adheres to no fixed interpretation of the image. Throughout his writings his interpretation varies and each interpretation adds nuances to his understanding. All his interpretations, however, have this point in common: they are primarily concerned with man's intellectual and volitional capacities. The spiritual faculties of man, therefore, are always foremost in Gerson's speculations on the image. The more material aspects of man's nature only occasionally form an essential part of his image theory. These aspects man frequently shares with lower creation; Gerson seeks most what distinguishes him from the realm of the material. Intellect and will, consequently, are man's distinguishing traits and constitute him an image and likeness of God. All lower creation is, in a certain sense, guided by reason, since God's reason and providence order lower creatures to their proper finality, but this reason is extrinsic to their nature. Man alone enjoys reason as an intrinsic and essential part of his being.[2]

Man's dignity as an image is to be found not merely in the possession of intellectual and volitional faculties but more in the fact that through the use of those faculties he is capable of knowing and loving God.[3] Human nature, indeed, has been made primarily to know and to love God. This knowledge and love, moreover, constitutes the glory and felicity of every human creature, and it is by these qualities that man excels all other creatures on earth. Many of man's other perfections are possessed by lower animate creation and at times to a higher degree than in man himself but no other creature has the power to attain to the knowledge and love of God. Gerson sees in this fact a clear argument for man's dignity and immortality. Man has been created to know the divinity, to praise it and to give it due honor, and it is precisely for this reason that he is said to be made in the image and likeness of God.[4]

Before describing in detail the various ways in which Gerson understands the image in man, it is most important to realize that Gerson sees all creation as the work of the Trinity. Every creature, no

---

authors from the thirteenth to the fifteenth centuries. The Augustinian tradition on the image is treated by John E. Sullivan, *The Image of God: The Doctrine of St. Augustine and its Influence* (Dubuque, 1963).

[2] *Dominus his opus habet*, G, 5, 221.

[3] *A Deo exivit*, G, 5, 14. "Tu nempe, rationalis spiritus, sicut capax et particeps Dei solus factus es per intelligentiam atque rationem, hinc ad imaginem Dei et similitudinem factus affimaris."

[4] *Videmus nunc per speculum*, G, 7, 1124.

matter how insignificant in the scale of existence, bears the traces of the Trinity. He extends this influence even to accidents and prime matter, although he does not say how this is possible.[5] The trinitarian traces in creation reflect the divine characteristics especially those proper to each member of the Trinity. Those characteristics are the divine *potentia, sapientia*, and *bonitas* or *benevolentia*. Creation, therefore, is the outward and external manifestation of the divine power, wisdom and goodness. While there was no obligation on God's part to create the world, once that creation was decreed, God could not fail to leave his imprint upon it.[6]

Potentia signifies the creative power of the Trinity and is appropriated of the Father as efficient cause. *Sapientia* designates the infinite wisdom of the Trinity and is commonly an appropriation of the Son as formal or exemplary cause. *Bonitas*, finally, expresses the divine goodness and is appropriated of the Holy Spirit in the order of final causality. The *potentia* of the Father is considered in the category of efficient causality since it is through the divine omnipotence that all things have come into being. The *sapientia* attributed to the Son is representative of exemplary causality, for it is the divine *sapientia* which is the exemplar upon which all things have been created. The *bonitas* of the Spirit is identified with final causality, since it was out of love and the desire to communicate its own goodness that the Trinity began the work of creation.[7]

Gerson's vision of creation as embodying the trinitarian characteristics of *potentia, sapientia*, and *bonitas* reflects the thought of Bonaventure († 1274) and Hugh of St. Victor († 1141). Both writers exercised great influence upon Gerson and he frequently recommended their works to his readers.[8] In his *Itinerarium mentis ad Deum*, Bonaventure describes the condition of all creatures according

---

[5] *Collectorium super Magnificat*, P, 4, 333 A-B. "Etenim consistit in re qualibet, quantumcunque modicum habeat entitatis, et in accidentibus, et in materia prima vestigium Trinitatis."

[6] *Factum est prelium*, G, 7, 623. "C'est ycy en gros et en somme comment et pourquoy les anges furent creés quer ce fut de la puere bonté et volenté de Dieu pour espandre sa bonté par dehors et affin que les creatures louassent leur Createur et que la bonté de Dieu, sa puissance et sa sapience fussent monstrees par dehors es creatures comme on cognoit l'art et la prudence d'un ouvrier par œuvre." Cf. *Memoriam fecit mirabilium*, G, 7, 700-701.

[7] *Apparuit gratia*, G, 5, 67. "Amplius vero divina natura... monstraret potentiam Dei efficientem, et sapientiam exemplantem, et bonitatem cuncta finientem...."

[8] *Annotatio doctorum aliquorum qui de contemplatione locuti sunt*, G, 3, 293-294, *Ignem veni mittere*, G, 2, 276-280, and *De libris legendis a monacho*, P, 2, 709 A-C.

to origin, magnitude, multitude, beauty, plenitude, operation, and order. These characteristics he regards as a sevenfold testimony to the divine *potentia, sapientia,* and *bonitas.*[9] Hugh of St. Victor considers the magnitude, beauty, and usefulness of all creation as reflecting the same trinitarian characteristics. He also attributes *potentia* to the Father, *sapientia* to the Son, and *bonitas* to the Holy Spirit.[10] A similar trinitarian tradition continued among other members of the Victorine school. Godfrey of St. Victor († 1194) argues from the magnitude, beauty, and goodness of the world to the trinitarian qualities of *potentia, sapientia,* and *bonitas.*[11] Richard of St. Victor († 1173) sees the same trinitarian attributions as rooted in Scripture. He maintains, however, that they can also be reasoned to by an analysis of creation.[12]

---

[9] *Itinerarium,* 1, 14, Quaracchi, 5, 299a.

[10] *De sacramentis,* 1, 3, 26-29, MPL, 176, 227 C-231 B; *De tribus diebus,* 1, *MPL,* 176, 811 C-D; 16, *MPL,* 176, 823 D; 27, *MPL,* 176, 838 B-C.

[11] *Microcosmus,* 1, 40, ed. P. Delhaye, *Le Microcosme de Godefroy de Saint Victor* (Lille, 1951), pp. 60-61.

[12] *De tribus appropriatis personis, MPL,* 196, 993 C-D. The Victorine use of *potentia, sapientia,* and *bonitas* reflects the influence of Abelard († 1142). Cf. Abelard's *Expositio in Hexaemeron, MPL,* 178, 760 C, *Introductio ad Theologiam,* 13, *MPL,* 178, 999 C, and *Theologia Christiana,* 1, 2, *MPL,* 178, 1125 C-D. See also D. E. Luscombe, *The School of Peter Abelard* (Cambridge, 1969), pp. 115-121. The position that the triad of *potentia, sapientia,* and *bonitas* originated with Abelard is maintained by J. Hofmeier, *Die Trinitätslehre des Hugo von St. Victor* (Munich, 1963), pp. 225-227, and Damien van den Eynde, *Essai sur la succession et la date des écrits de Hugues de Saint-Victor* (Rome, 1960), pp. 68-69. A similar triadic formula was employed by writers from the school of Chartres such as Gilbert de la Porrée († 1154), William of Conches († 1155), and John of Salisbury († 1180). Alan of Lille († 1202) followed in the same tradition. Cf. Javelet, *Image et ressemblance,* 1, 199-200; 2, 161-164. For the school of Chartres, see especially J. M. Parent, *La doctrine de la création dans l'école de Chartres* (Paris, 1938), pp. 67-76. R. W. Southern, however, has recently challenged the commonly accepted affiliation of Gilbert de la Porrée, William of Conches, and John of Salisbury with the school of Chartres. See "Humanism and the School of Chartres," in *Medieval Humanism and Other Studies* (New York, 1970), pp. 66-73. Like the Victorines, the masters of Chartres were influenced by Abelard, especially William of Conches. John of Salisbury, moreover, reveals that the writers of Chartres were also indebted to Plato's *Timaeus.* They interpreted the three causes at work in the formation and ordering of the universe, i.e. Demiurge, Idea, and Good, in a trinitarian context. These causes, efficient, formal, and final, reflected the *potentia, sapientia,* and *bonitas* of the Trinity. Cf. *Policraticus,* 7, 5, ed. C. Webb, 2 (Oxford, 1909), 108. See also William of Conches, *Glossae super Platonem,* ed. E. Jeauneau (Paris, 1965), p. 68. Abelard himself acknoweldges his indebtedness to Plato. Cf. *In ep. ad Rom.,* 1, *MPL,* 178, 804 A-B. In the final analysis, however, both the masters of St. Victor and of Chartres would regard their triadic formula as essentially rooted in the Scriptures. What they sought to achieve primarily was a harmonization of the Gospel and the Hellenic tradition. See M.-D. Chenu, *La théologie au douzième siècle* (Paris, 1957), p. 139.

Since the Trinity leaves its trace upon creation, Gerson also argues that man can arrive at some knowledge of the Trinity from a study of creation. He finds justification for his position in Rom 1:20: "Ever since the creation of the world his invisible nature, namely, his eternal power and deity, has been clearly perceived in the things that have been made." Thus through the magnitude of the world, man is able to recognize the *potentia* of God. Through its beauty he is able to attain to some notion of the divine *sapientia* and in its order and goodness he can recognize the divine *bonitas*.[13]

Although all creation mirrors the Trinity in bearing the traces of *potentia, sapientia*, and *bonitas*, Gerson realizes that certain creatures reflect those trinitarian characteristics more perfectly than others. Upon this fact, he establishes the distinction between a *vestigium* and an *imago* of the Trinity. Reflections of the Trinity can be found in all created things and in this sense they are *vestigia Trinitatis*. Man, however, more perfectly mirrors the Trinity and, consequently, is designated an *imago*. The distinction between *vestigium* and *imago* is rooted in the fact that although all creation reflects the divine nature, man alone is capable of participating in that nature.[14] That participation consists primarily in his capacity to know and to love God.[15]

Since he is an *imago* and not a *vestigium*, man reveals more

---

[13] *Si terrena dixi vobis*, G, 7, 1044. "...nam per visibilia mundi invisibilia cognoscuntur, etc.; par la grandeur des choses crees je congnois la puissance de Dieu; par la beaute je congnois sagesse et par l'ordonnance et bonte je congnois sa liberalite. Si congnois comme par une trace et odeur; ung mirouer umbrage la benoite trinite, en tant que puissance est actribue au Pere, sagesse au Filz, bonte et liberalite au Saint Esperit."

[14] *Simile est regnum*, G, 2, 254. "Una pretiosa margarita cujus nomen est ens purum usquequaque perfectum relucet et invenitur in omnibus creaturis tanquam in vestigiis signatibus potentiam, sapientiam, et bonitatem ipsius. Sed praecipue refulget in creaturis rationalibus tamquam in imaginibus quae sapientiae sunt divinae nedum representativae sed participes et capaces. Unde recta patet imaginis atque vestigii distinctio." The distinction between *vestigium* and *imago* is reminiscent of Augustine. Cf. *De Trinitate*, 6, 10, 12, *CCSL*, 50, pp. 242-243, and Étienne Gilson, *The Christian Philosophy of St. Augustine* (New York, 1960), pp. 210- 224. Bonaventure continues the Augustinian tradition of interrelating trinity, creation, vestige and image. For him, as for Augustine, whatever has been created by God bears the trinitarian *vestigia*. Man alone is an *imago*. Cf. *Itinerarium*, 1, 2; 3, 1, Quaracchi, 5, 297, 303 and Gilson, *The Philosophy of St. Bonaventure* (New York, 1938), pp. 204-237. St. Thomas retains the same basis for the distinction between *imago* and *vestigium* in his *Summa Theologiae*, 1, q. 93, a. 4, Marietti, 453-454.

[15] *Factum est prelium*, G, 7, 623. "Touteffoiz creature espirituele et raisonnable fut creée plus espicialement et haultement pour cognoistre et amer Dieu comme ymage plus parfaicte."

perfectly the nature of the Trinity. He can arrive at some understanding of the Trinity through the process of self-knowledge. In one of his sermons, Gerson considers the hypothetical case of a person seeking a deeper knowledge of the Trinity. He refers the person not to learned books or teachers but to his own interior self. Such knowledge is to be found only within oneself. Only by understanding the intellectual and volitional faculties and activities of his soul, will a person gradually come to a better comprehension of the Trinity in whose image he has been made.[16] Self-knowledge, consequently, emerges as a primary means for discerning the trinitarian image in man. Through self-knowledge man can arrive at some analogical knowledge of the persons of the Trinity. Self-knowledge, therefore, is so important for Gerson that its absence in a person is inexcusable. There is no disgrace in having to admit that one knows little about certain fields of knowledge, but to admit that one does not know himself is shameful.[17]

Gerson argues that long before Christianity the pagan world was convinced of the value of self-knowledge and accepted the principle of *gnothi seauton* as an oracle of Apollo. Juvenal wrote that this principle ought to be imprinted on everyone's memory and inscribed upon their hearts. Persius too used the same principle when he warned his readers not to seek self-knowledge by going outside themselves.[18] In the Old Testament, the Canticle of Canticles proclaims that the person who lacks self-knowledge is no better then a brute animal. Gerson interprets the phrase "*si ignoras te*" of Ct 1:7 to indicate a person who lacks self-knowledge. Such a person is, in reality, an animal and deserves nothing better than to follow in the tracks of the flock.[19]

By understanding himself, then, man can come to some knowledge of the Trinity. He can reason that since he has been made from nothing, the God who created him must be all-powerful. Thus he can establish *potentia* as one of the major characteristics of God. Such a creator must also be all-wise, even though man cannot

---

[16] *In nomine Patris*, 6, 7, 676.

[17] *Dedit illi scientiam sanctorum*, G, 7, 586.

[18] *Vade in domum tuam*, G, 5, 584. Cf. Juvenal, *Satires*, 11: 27-28, and Persius, 4:52, ed. S.G. Owen, *Saturae* (Oxford, 1882).

[19] *Canticordum du pélerin*, G, 7, 116-117. "Et tu scez que n'est reins tant necessaire a creature raisonable, comme est c'est oracle divin: Cognois toy. E celo venit notiselisos grece, latine cognosce tepsum; aultrement l'omme n'est que une beste. Si ignoras te, o pulcherrima mulierum egredere et abi post capras aut vestigia gregum."

comprehend the depth of that wisdom; thus God is also the highest *sapientia*. Finally, man can conclude that his creator must be characterized by extreme liberality and benevolence, thereby verifying the note of *bonitas*. Through such an analysis, Gerson maintains, man can argue to a trinitarian concept of God in terms of *potentia, sapientia*, and *bonitas*.[20]

While Gerson always conceives of the image in man in a trinitarian context, the manner in which he understands the triadic structure of the image will vary. Since all creation manifests the divine power, wisdom and goodness, it is not surprising to find that he describes the image of the Trinity in terms of *potentia, sapientia*, and *benevolentia*.[21] Man as an image of the Trinity, consequently, shares in a finite manner in these trinitarian characteristics. He reflects the power of the Father when he shows fortitude, constancy, and perseverence. He demonstrates these virtues by placing his hope in no other power but that of the Father. Man's faith reflects the wisdom of the Son and by his charity and benevolence he manifests the goodness of the Holy Spirit.[22] By participation in the divine *potentia, sapientia*, and *benevolentia*, therefore, man is an image of the Trinity. In this participation lies his beauty as an image of God.[23] Because he is an image of the Trinity, the man of deep faith, moreover, should have no difficulty in recognizing that the God according to whose image he has been made is one in essence and three in persons.[24]

Gerson, moreover, associates the trinitarian characteristics of *potentia, sapientia*, and *benevolentia* with the various powers and faculties of the soul. As seen in the study of episcopal reform, he identifies the trinitarian image in man with the triple *vires*.[25]   The

---

[20] *Videmus nunc per speculum*, G, 7, 1134.

[21] *Videmus nunc per speculum*, G, 7, 1132-1133. "... tu es la tres belle ymaige laquelle Dieu le souverain Maitre a voulu faire pour monstrer son art par dehors, sa puissance, sa saigesse et sa benevolence...."

[22] *In nomine Patris*, G, 7, 678. "Si disons pour nostre instruction morale que chascune ame crestienne doit porter ce nom et son ymage en soy et en son cuer telement qu'elle soit forte et sage et bonne; forte par esperance, en soy conformant a la puissance et a l'excellence du Pere; saige par foy et par creance, en soy conformant a la verite et saigesse du Filz; bonne par charite et benivolence, en soy conformant a la bonté du Saint Esperit."

[23] *La mendicité spirituelle*, G, 7, 280.

[24] *Videmus nunc per speculum*, G, 7, 1133.

[25] *Bonus pastor*, G, 5, 125 "Fiat igitur ab utroque pastore quod proponit Dominus: det animam suam pro ovibus suis; utique animam quae imago est beatae Trinitatis secundum triplicem vim praenominatam." Cf. *De theologia mystica*, G, 3, 288.

vires on both the natural and spiritual level reflect the characteristics of the Trinity. In its search for truth, the *vis rationalis* is a reflection of the *sapientia* of the Son. The fortitude of the *vis irascibilis* is but an image of the *potentia* of the Father and the desire of the *vis concupiscibilis* for the good mirrors the *benevolentia* of the Holy Spirit. The same trinitarian parallels exist on the spiritual level once the soul is infused with sanctifying grace. Infused with the virtue of faith, the *vis rationalis* is conformed to the *sapientia* of the Son. The *vis irascibilis* under the guidance of hope experiences the *potentia* of the Father and the *vis concupiscibilis* under the influence of charity participates in the *benevolentia* of the Holy Spirit.[26]

Gerson frequently compares the triple *vires* under the influence of the theological virtues with the properties of fire, which he describes as *fulgor, vigor,* and *ardor*. The *vis rationalis* illumined by faith is consequently designated as the *fulgor animae*; the *vis irascibilis* strengthened and confirmed by hope becomes the *vigor animae*. The *vis concupiscibilis* enkindled by charity is described as the *ardor animae*. *Vigor, fulgor* and *ardor*, in turn, are conceived as reflections of the Trinity. *Vigor* reflects the *potentia* of the Father, *fulgor* the luminescence of the Son's *sapientia*, and *ardor* the fire of the Spirit's *charitas*.[27]

Gerson regards John the Baptist as a man who reflects the image of the Trinity in his life through the three *vires*. His *vis concupiscibilis* was enflamed by charity, his *vis rationalis* enlightened and instructed by wisdom, and his *vis irascibilis* strengthened by the power of hope. Throughout his life, he was strongly driven forward by the love of God; the wisdom of God guided and instructed him and the divine power continually strengthened him.[28] Gerson also interprets various passages in Scripture in terms of the triple *vires*. One such passage is from Acts 17:28, where Paul speaks to the Athenians about God and quotes the poet Epimenides: "In him we

---

[26] *Apparuit gratia*, G, 5, 69. "Sit in nobis fides vera et viva secundum vim rationalem ex recognitione immensae sapientiae; sit spes certa secundum vim irascibilem ex professione ejus summae potentiae; sit caritas fervida ex consideratione summae benevolentiae et gratiae quae apparuit nobis hodie in circumcisionis humilitate."

[27] *Suscepimus Deus misericordiam*, G, 5, 541. "... triplex ignis proprietas, fulgor scilicet, vigor et ardor; fides fulget in vi rationali, spes roborat in irascibili, caritas ardet in concupiscibili, quoad tria appropriata Patris et Filii et Spiritus Sancti; in Patrem vigorem, in Filio fulgorem, in Spiritu Sancto ardorem concipimus."

[28] *Sicut scriptum est*, G, 3, 29. "Fuit enim vis ejus concupiscibilis inflammata per caritatem, vis rationalis illustrata et edocta per sapientiam, vis irascibilis per potentiam et virtutes roborata."

live and move and have our being." We live in God through faith, for the just man lives by faith; this adherence to God by faith is radically situated in the *vis rationalis*. We move in God through hope, for hope enables us to desire those things which are above and this hope resides in the *vis irascibilis*. Finally, we have our being in God through charity and this charity is radicated in the *vis concupiscibilis*.[29]

Gerson does not hesitate to use ways other than the triple *vires* to describe the image of the Trinity in man. He frequently identifies this image with the threefold faculties of memory, intellect, and will.[30] This identification of the *imago* in man with *memoria, intellectus*, and *voluntas* reveals a strong Augustinian influence. Although there are clear indications from Gerson's writings that he was familiar with the *De Trinitate*, there is also the possibility of indirect Augustinian influence through Bonaventure with whose writings Gerson was well acquainted. Augustine describes the triad of memory, intellect, and will in several different manners. The first is that of *mens, notitia,* and *amor*. The second involves *memoria sui, intelligentia,* and *voluntas,* and the third, *memoria Dei, intelligentia,* and *amor*.[31] Gerson uses the first triad of *mens, notitia,* and *amor* only rarely.[32] Of the remaining triads, he primarily employs the second, *memoria sui, intelligentia,* and *voluntas*. The activities of man's memory, intellect and will which Gerson conceives as reflecting the trinitarian activities generally have the self rather than

---

[29] *Postulare dignata est*, G, 2, 64. ".... in quo vivimus per fidem formatam, nam justus ex fide vivit et hoc in vi rationali; movemur per spem desiderantem quae sursum sunt, in irascibili; sumus per caritatem radicatam in concupiscibili."

[30] *Collectorium super Magnificat*, P, 4, 261 C. "Quibus ita notatis de pulchritudine generaliter, facilis est applicatio ad pulchritudinem animae rationalis spiritualis, quae imago est benedictissimae Trinitatis, in qua potentiae tres principales animae, scilicet memoria, intelligentia, et voluntas, sunt tanquam lineamenta, qualia sunt indelibiliter impressa, nec tolluntur etiam a damnatis." Cf. *Pax hominibus*, G, 7, 767.

[31] Gilson, *The Christian Philosophy of St. Augustine*, p. 219. The first triad can be found in *De Trinitate*, 9:2, 2-5, 8, *CCSL*, 50, pp. 294-301; the second in *De Trinitate*, 10:11, 17-12, 19, *CCSL*, 50, pp. 329-332; the third in *De Trinitate* 14:8, 11-12, 16, *CCSL*, 50A, pp. 435-444. For a more detailed analysis of the Augustinian triads see Michael Schmaus, *Die psychologische Trinitätslehre des heiligen Augustinus* (Münster, 1927) pp. 235-281, 310-399 and Sullivan, *The Image of God*, pp. 115-162. For Bonaventure's interpretation of the image in terms of *memoria, intellectus,* and *voluntas* see *Itinerarium*, 3, 1-6, Quaracchi, 5, 303a—305b; *Quaestiones disputatae de mysterio Trinitatis*, q. 1, a. 1, 4, Quaracchi, 5, 45b; *Soliloquies*, 1, 2, Quaracchi, 5, 30 a-b.

[32] *Super cantica canticorum*, P, 4, 28 A. "... dum conditus est ad imaginem et similitudinem Dei, quae consistit in mente, notitia et amore."

God as their object.[33] Gerson, moreover, finds the trinitarian image in man not simply in the fact that man possesses *memoria, intellectus,* and *voluntas.* There must be an aspect of oneness as well as threeness, otherwise, the triune aspect of the image would not be sufficiently illustrated. He finds the notion of unity expressed in the soul in which memory, intellect, and will inhere.[34]

The trinitarian nature of the image according to memory, intellect, and will is further reflected in the activities of those faculties. Gerson sees an analogy between the operation of these faculties and the trinitarian activities of generation and spiration. This analogy can be discovered by a process of self-reflection and analysis. Gerson understands memory here in the basic Augustinian sense of the mind's self-knowledge. When the memory is freed of sense images and concentrates upon itself, it is capable of achieving self-knowledge which is expressed in the intellect through the *verbum.* The activity, therefore, of *memoria* and *intelligentia* is a reflection of the Son's generation by the Father, with memory corresponding to the Father and intelligence to the Son. Just as, moreover, the mutual love of the Father and Son is responsible for the generation of the Spirit, so too there arises in the soul a love of self in the *verbum.* The activity of the *voluntas* thus corresponds to the procession of the Holy Spirit from the Father and Son.[35] Gerson bemoans the fact that many people are so preoccupied with the external world that they are unable to perceive this internal activity of their faculties, which, if fully understood, would allow them to recognize the image of the Trinity within themselves. Because of their preoccupations, such people are oblivious of the true role of their memory; ignorance clouds their understanding, and carnal and terrestrial affections bind their will.[36]

As in the case of the triple *vires, memoria, intellectus,* and *voluntas* are also considered by Gerson as a reflection of the trinitarian characteristics of *potentia, sapientia,* and *bonitas,* which are attributed to the Father, Son, and Holy Spirit respectively. He regards the soul's

---

[33] For Gerson's occasional use of the triad *memoria Dei, intelligentia,* and *amor* see *Collectorium super Magnificat,* P, 4, 266 D.

[34] *De nobilitate,* P, 3, 210 A. "... quae creatura est ad imaginem et similitudinem beatissimae trinitatis, secundum tres potentias in una essentia, memoriam, intelligentiam et voluntatem...."

[35] *Videmus nunc per speculum,* G, 7, 1133. Cf. *Si terrena dixi vobis,* G, 7, 1047.

[36] *In nomine Patris,* G, 7, 676.

capacities of memory, intellect, and will as finite expressions of the divine power, truth, and goodness. Occasionally, Gerson exchanges the terms *potentia* and *unitas* but both are considered as appropriations of the Father.[37] By associating the faculties of memory, intellect, and will with the triad of *potentia, sapientia*, and *bonitas*, Gerson shows how closely he follows Bonaventure and the Victorines who, like many medieval thinkers, fused Platonic and Augustinian thought in the formulation of their teaching on the image.[38]

Although Gerson generally describes the image of God in man according to the triple *vires* or the triple faculties of memory, intellect, and will, he occasionally uses other triadic formulae. He employs, though rarely, the Augustinian triad of *mens, notitia, amor*.[39] At times he modifies the triad of *memoria, intellectus*, and *voluntas* into that of *sensualitas, intellectus*, and *voluntas*. At other times, he will use the triadic formula of *posse, scire*, and *velle*.[40] This triad describes not so much the faculties of the soul as their activities. These activities are, moreover, identified with the triple *vires*, with *posse* corresponding to the *vis irascibilis, scire* to the *vis rationalis*, and *velle* to the *vis concupiscibilis*[41]. Regardless of the manner in which Gerson describes the image of the Trinity, he always regards it as a reflection of the trinitarian characteristics of *potentia, sapientia*, and *benevolentia*.[42]

From the above descriptions of the trinitarian image in man, it is clear that Gerson does not draw any distinction between *imago* and *similitudo*. He uses both terms interchangeably as does the author of the first chapter of Genesis. Many patristic and medieval authors

---

[37] *Anagogicum de verbo et hymno gloriae*, P, 4, 546 C-D. Cf. *Canticordum du pélerin*, G, 7, 136.

[38] Cf. Bonaventure, *Itinerarium*, 3, 5-6, Quaracchi, 5, 305 a-b., Hugh of St. Victor, *De sacramentis*, 1, 3, 21, *MPL*, 176, 225 D, and 1, 3, 26-27, *MPL*, 176, 227 C-230 B, and Richard of St. Victor, *De Trinitate*, 3, 16, *MPL*, 196, 925 D-926 A, and 6, 15, *MPL*, 196, 979 B-980 B.

[39] *Super cantica canticorum*, P, 4, 28 A.

[40] *Sicut scriptum est*, G, 3, 29. "Hic est supremus ternarius hierarchicus: bene velle, scire, et posse; haec Trinitatis supercoelestis imago: potentia, sapientia et bonitas seu voluntas."

[41] *Consideranti mihi*, G, 5, 145. "... conformiter ad tria appropriata in divinis quae sunt potentia, scientia et bonitas, et tria quae in omni operatione concurrere necesse est, quae sunt posse, scire, velle; juxta tres vires animae irascibilem, rationalem et concupiscibilem."

[42] *Omne regnum in se divisum*, G, 7, 754. Cf. *Anagogicum de verbo et hymno gloriae*, P, 4, 546 C-D and *Canticordum du pélerin*, G, 7, 136.

when writing on the image and likeness of God in man drew a distinction between the two terms. They frequently associated the *imago* with man's original endowments given in creation. *Similitudo* was reserved to describe the more perfect actualization of the image through grace. Gerson, however, follows in the tradition of those who treated *imago* and *similitudo* as essentially identical.[43]

Gerson, moreover, allies himself with those patristic and medieval authors who laid great stress on the permanence of the image.[44] For Gerson, man from the very moment of his creation is an image of God; the image, therefore, is a *donum naturae*. Man can disfigure or discolor the image within himself through sin but he can never destroy it.[45] This permanence is emphasized by Gerson in the fact that the demons of hell are incapable of destroying the image of God within their souls. Regardless of their eternal estrangement from God, they still possess the faculties of memory, intellect, and will. The light of those faculties remains inextinguishable, even in the darkness of hell. To illustrate his point, Gerson compares the souls of the demons to the light of the sun. Even if the earth and the planets were to cease existing, the sun would continue to radiate and illumine. The sun will always remain a source of light unto itself. The faculties of memory, intellect, and will, therefore, continue to function and to

---

[43] Irenaeus, Clement of Alexandria, Origen, Gregory of Nyssa, and John Chrysostom distinguished between image and similitude. Augustine, Bernard of Clairvaux, Thomas Aquinas, and Bonaventure all continued in the same tradition. Among those who failed to draw any distinction between image and similitude can be listed Athanasius, Gregory of Nazianzus, Basil, Hippolytus, Theodore of Mopsuestia, Theodoret of Cyrus and Cyril of Alexandria. The identification of both terms was continued in the western tradition by Hilary of Poitiers and Ambrose. In the twelfth century, image and similitude were at times distinguished and at other times considered as synonymous, even by the same author. Such is the case with Peter the Venerable, Abelard, Peter Lombard, and Hugh of St. Victor. For the patristic tradition regarding the distinction between image and similitude see Walter J. Burghardt, *The Image of God in Man According to Cyril of Alexandria* (Woodstock, 1957), pp. 1- 11. On the relationship of image and similitude in twelfth-century thought see Javelet, *Image et ressemblance*, 1, 213-214. Aquinas' teaching on the distinction between image and similitude can be found in his *Summa Theologiae*, 1, q. 93, a. 9, Marietti, p. 461. For Bonaventure's position cf. *2 Sent.*, d. 16, a. 2, q. 3, Quaracchi, 2, 405a-406b.

[44] The patristic and medieval tradition on the permanent nature of the image is exemplified by Origen, Cyril of Alexandria, Gregory of Nyssa, Augustine, Hugh of St. Victor, Bernard of Clairvaux, and Bonaventure. Irenaeus and Didymus of Alexandria appear to have maintained that the image was lost through sin. Cf. Burghardt, *The Image of God*, pp. 153-159. Burghardt rightly stresses the conflicting testimony regarding the permanence of the image even within the same patristic authors. On the medieval tradition see Javelet, *Image et ressemblance*, 1, 285-297.

[45] *Pax hominibus bonae voluntatis*, G, 7, 767.

shed their light even though they are estranged from God.[46] Gerson does not hesitate to call the devil himself an *imago Dei* and he roots that image directly in the devil's natural powers.[47]

The image of God, moreover, remains intact in the souls of all the condemned. As images of God, their memory, intellect, and will have been created and given to them to aid them in attaining a knowledge and love of God. These natural faculties cannot be taken from them even though they have been damned for eternity. Gerson's reasoning rests primarily on the fact that these faculties are a part of their natural being and cannot be deprived them regardless of their state or condition. As humans they will always remain images of God and will, therefore, always possess something of the splendor characteristic of any creature created in God's image. Regardless of the fact that man has abused and perverted his faculties of memory, intellect, and will, those faculties still retain their intrinsic nobility.[48]

Although the image is natural to man and retains its brilliance whether condemned to estrangement from God in eternity or temporarily disfigured by sin, grace does add to it a definite dimension. Without doing any violence to man's natural faculties, grace enhances the quality of the image. Grace works in harmonious accord with man's faculties of memory, intellect and will and brings them to their highest degree of realization. Grace so increases the beauty and elegance of the image that the soul is rendered most pleasing and acceptable to God, so much so that if it were to depart from the body it would immediately be received by God into the glory of heaven.[49] Gerson compares the soul made in the image of God to a portrait. Grace does not change that portrait but adds a new variety of colors. These colors, moreover, do not distort the portrait but rather result in a more faithful representation. Through the application of these colors, the portrait becomes a more realistic and more beautiful reflection of its model. In the case of man, the more beautiful the image becomes through grace, the more faithfully does it represent the Trinity upon which it was patterned and created.[50]

---

[46] *Collectorium super Magnificat*, P, 4, 333 B. "Nec potest aboleri triplex haec potentia, mente ipsa stante. Unde nec in daemonibus lux harum potentiarum, seu virium, seu aptitudo naturalium extinguitur, quin in se lux existat, prout esset sol in luce sua, etiamsi nihil extra se actualiter illustraret."

[47] *Dedit illi gloriam regni*, G, 5, 182.

[48] *Anagogicum de verbo et hymno gloriae*, P, 4, 546 D.

[49] *Anagogicum de verbo et hymno gloriae*, P, 4, 546 D-547 A.

[50] *Collectorium super Magnificat*, P, 4, 261 B-C. Comparison of the image of God

Grace also has a restorative value for the image. This restoration is achieved when the soul's faculties are freed from obstacles that prevent their proper operation; once freed these faculties can concentrate on their primary object which is God. Grace, therefore, restores memory, intellect, and will to their proper finality. Grace achieves this by enabling the memory to free itself from external distractions. As a result of this freedom, memory can concentrate on the self and therein recognize God as its author. Grace restores the intellect by liberating it from the excessive domination of sense images. Since the intellect must work in conjunction with the sense faculties, it will never be completely free of sense images, but grace does help it to achieve the subjugation of sense impressions to the more intellectual aspects of its own activity, thereby allowing greater knowledge of self and of God. The will is also freed by grace from all carnal desires and is, thereby, able to attain a true love of God. The result of this activity is that the image of the Trinity is able to shine forth more beautifully in the triple faculties of man's soul.[51]

The relationship of the soul to the triune God as image to exemplar in no way entails any participation in the essence of the Trinity. As an image of God, the soul's memory might be majestic, its intellect clear, and its will free; the soul, moreover, might be immortal and its true life primarily spiritual, but all this is not to say that the soul as such is or becomes part of God. While stressing that the soul is made to the image of God, Gerson is always careful to emphasize that this does not in any way imply participation in or identification with the divine essence. He assiduously avoids any statements which would imply any confusion between the boundaries of the human and the divine.[52]

His insistence on this point is strongly reminiscent of his controversy with John of Schoonhoven († 1431), head of the Canons

---

in man to a painting was a commonplace in patristic thought. Gregory of Nyssa in his *De opificio hominis*, 5, MPG, 44, 137 A compares the creation of man as an image to the action of a painter transferring human forms to a picture by means of appropriate colors. The more skillful the painter is in the utilization of colors, the more perfect an image does his painting become. Dionysius in his *De ecclesiastica hierarchia*, 4, 3, MPG, 3, 473 C utilizes a similar comparison and asserts that the more undivided the painter's attention to the archetype, the more faithful will be its reproduction in the painting. Cf. Gerhart Ladner, "The Concept of the Image in the Greek Fathers and the Byzantine Iconoclastic Controversy," *Dumbarton Oaks Papers*, 7 (1953), pp. 3, 10-13.

[51] *Videmus nunc per speculum*, G, 7, 1137. "...affin qu'en cest trinite reluise purement la Trinité divine."

[52] *Videmus nunc per speculum*, G, 7, 1126.

Regular of Groenendael, over the *De ornatu spiritualium nuptiarum* of John Ruysbroeck (✝ 1381). In that controversy, Gerson claimed that Ruysbroeck's manner of describing the mystical union between God and the soul bordered on the heretical, since the language used by him, if taken literally, implied a union of identity, that is, the soul in mystical union would be absorbed into the divine essence. Gerson labeled all such speculation as Manichaean. Even though the soul is an image of God, it always remains finite no matter how perfectly it reflects the trinitarian nature. This finiteness is especially manifested in man's mutability, for he changes from thought to thought, affection to affection, and decision to decision. Though he enjoys the distinction of being an image of God, man still remains limited and contingent.[53]

2. REGNUM PERSONALE ET DIVINALE

Gerson's concepts of *regnum personale* and *regnum divinale* constitute another aspect of his thought on personal reform and are closely related to his ideas on the image of God in man. Gerson's conception of the soul as a *regnum* is of importance not only because of its relationship to his teaching on the image but also because it introduces, on the personal level, the notions of *ordo, lex,* and *pax,* which play such an important role in his understanding of church reform. Gerson maintains that God grants to every rational creature membership in three kingdoms or societies. The first kingdom he designates variously as *regnum naturale et intrinsecum* or *regnum monasticum et personale.* The second is the *regnum civile* or *politicum* and the third the *regnum divinale* or *evangelicum.*[54]

A *regnum* is for Gerson an ordered society. A society, moreover, is ordered insofar as it commands and obeys according to the principles of the divine law.[55] This law he describes as the divine wisdom, the divine will, or the divine judgment of right reason insofar as it applies to the use of created things. The divine law is participated in by all

---

[53] For a brief resume of the controversy see Connolly, *John Gerson,* pp. 241-248. The definitive work on this famous controversy is Combes, *Essai sur la critique de Ruysbroeck par Gerson,* 3 vols. (Paris, 1945-1949).

[54] *Dedit illi gloriam regni,* G, 5, 183. The conception of the soul as a *regnum* is found primarily in Gerson's early writings, i.e. from the last decade of the fourteenth to the first few years of the fifteenth century.

[55] *Dedit illi gloriam regni,* G, 5, 184. "Regnum in sua generalitate est societas ordinata in imperando et obediendo secundum legem aeternam. . . ."

creatures in varying degrees but most especially by rational creatures. As is frequently the case, Gerson refuses to be caught up in the subtle controversy over whether divine law is predicated primarily of the divine intellect or the divine will. He feels that this discussion has been sufficiently developed by St. Thomas and can be solved relatively well provided one is cautious in his use of terminology and does not get caught up in the fantasies and creations of his own mind.[56]

The first *regnum*, the *regnum intrinsecum* or *personale*, is a society only in an accommodated sense because what it primarily describes is the order and relationship that should exist between man's intellectual, volitional and sensitive faculties. Order is established among those faculties by the dictates of right reason with which man is naturally endowed. Right reason, therefore, is the agent of justice within man which grants each faculty its proper hierarchical rank.[57] In this hierarchy of human faculties, the function of reason is to provide counsel as to possible courses of action by working in harmonious conjunction with the intellectual virtues of wisdom and prudence. Will is to be the lord and master of the *regnum*, although in its activity it must be open to and accept the counsel provided by reason. Will, moreover, is to operate in accordance with the moral virtues. The functions of man's sensitive faculties, finally, are to be subordinated to reason and will, becoming, as it were, their *ancillae*.[58]

The second *regnum* is the *regnum civile et politicum* and is described by Gerson as a society ordered under one head and functioning in accordance with positive and civil law. Such law can be divinely inspired for the promotion of a citizen's spiritual welfare or it can be the product of mere human endeavor aimed at the citizen's purely temporal well-being. The second *regnum* is not as pertinent to the topic of individual renewal as the first and third *regna*, since it is primarily concerned with man's political life. The third and final *regnum*, the *regnum divinale et evangelicum*, is described as the ordering of the soul's faculties to God under the influence of charity which comes with grace. This is the kingdom of which Christ speaks in Mt 6:33: "But seek first his kingdom and his

---

[56] *Dedit illi gloriam regni*, G, 5, 184. Cf. *Summa Theologiae*, 1, 2, q. 90, a. 1; q. 93, a. 1, Marietti, pp. 410-411, 420-421.

[57] *Dedit illi gloriam regni*, G, 5, 184-185.

[58] *Omne regnum in se divisum*, G, 7, 753-754.

righteousness. . . ." This *regnum* and its *justitia* are equated by Gerson to the rule of charity.[59]

From what has been said thus far about the *regnum personale* and the *regnum divinale*, it follows that there is a very close relationship between the two *regna* and Gerson's notion of the image. Gerson, indeed, uses the terms *regnum* and *imago* interchangeably. He describes the *regnum* according to the same faculties utilized for the image, namely, reason, will, and the senses. The activities of these faculties are described in terms of *posse, scire,* and *velle* which correspond respectively to the operation of the sensitive, intellectual, and volitional faculties of the soul. *Scire* represents man's intellectual powers which guide the will in its activity of choosing or *velle. Posse* refers to the power of man's sensitive faculties in executing the dictates of man's intellect and will. These faculties, moreover, reflect the *potentia, sapienta,* and *bonitas* of the Trinity in whose image the soul has been created.[60] While he speaks of the *regnum divinale* as the soul's faculties operating under the influence of charity, the other theological virtues of faith and hope are naturally implied since grace always involves the infusion of the three theological virtues. Thus the *regnum divinale* is essentially similar to the image in man operating under the influence of the theological virtues.

Rather than speak of the finality of each *regnum*, Gerson uses the term glory. The end or glory of each of the three *regna* is *pax.* Following the traditional Augustinian description, he defines peace as the tranquility which comes from order. Order is, in turn, described as the arrangement of like and unlike things whereby each is disposed according to its proper place.[61] This disposition of things according to their proper place is identical with the virtue of justice. In the combination of justice, order, and peace, Gerson finds verified two important scriptural principles. The first is from Is 32:17: "*Opus justitiae est pax.*" Justice, by disposing all things according to their proper place, gives rise to order and from the tranquility of order

---

[59] *Dedit illi gloriam regni*, G, 5, 185.

[60] *Omne regnum divisum in se*, G, 7, 754. "Et par ce estoit ce royaume en pais et tranquilite sans division; et estoit samblable au souverain royaume de la haulte dignite et de la haulte trinite comment l'example ressamble a son examplaire et l'image a la chose qu'elle represente. Car en ce royaume estoit pouoir, savoir et valoir. Ce que raison savoit, voulente vouloit, et sensualite pouoit et executoit. Ainsi y estoit puissance sans labeur, quant ad ce qui est adproprie au Pere; cognoissance sans erreur, quant ad ce qui est adproprie au Filz; et voulente franche sans langueur quant ad ce qui est approprie au Saint Esperit."

[61] *Dedit illi gloriam regni*, G, 5, 185. Cf. *De Civitate Dei* 19:13, *CCSL*, 48, p. 679.

there results peace. The second important scriptural passage is contained in Ps 84:11: "*Justitia et pax osculatae sunt.*" Since justice and peace are necessarily described in terms of each other and are so intimately related, it can be said with Scripture that justice and peace have embraced and kissed.[62]

The peace which is produced in the *regnum personale* is the intrinsic tranquility which comes from the harmonious ordering and functioning of all man's faculties. When his intellectual, volitional, and sensitive faculties preserve their proper hierarchical order, and function harmoniously in the issuance of commands or in the obedience thereto, then man is interiorly at peace and his faculties enjoy the tranquility of order. In the soul of such an individual, justice and peace can truly be said to have embraced. This peace within the individual exists only as long as he is free from sin. Sin represents injustice; it introduces disorder and results in the cessation of all true internal peace. On an analogous level, the *regnum civile et politicum* also enjoys its peace which consists in the ordered and harmonious activity of its citizens in both issuing and obeying commands.[63] The peace of the third kingdom, the *regnum divinale* or *evangelicum*, comes from the enjoyment of God's intimacy. This peace results from recognizing that all things are his creatures and are essentially ordered towards him. On the level of grace, such peace is the result of God's charity and is preserved as long as charity remains in the soul. Since man, while on earth, is never fully confirmed in grace and preserves the option of turning away from God, he is always capable of losing that peace. Only with the full confirmation of man in grace which comes with heaven, will man be permanently established in charity and enjoy perpetual peace.[64]

While not playing as important a role in Gerson's thought on personal reform as the *imago*, the notions of *regnum personale* and *regnum divinale* do serve to deepen our knowledge and understanding of the image. They provide the added dimensions of *justitia, ordo* and *pax*. The *regnum personale* allows us to see man's intellectual and volitional faculties not merely as reflecting trinitarian activities but also as manifesting their relationship to one another on the natural level. The *regnum divinale* corresponds more closely with the supernatural aspects of the image and shows the order and peace

---

[62] *De directione cordis*, P, 3, 468 C.
[63] *Dedit illi gloriam regni*, G, 5, 185.
[64] *Dedit illi gloriam regni*, G, 5, 185.

that reigns in man's faculties when they are properly related to their creator through charity.

3. Sin and the Image

Man's condition at the time of his creation in Adam was one of order and peace. His reason counselled and guided him without error; his will followed the dictates of reason and executed its commands without any hesitation or reluctance. His sensitive faculties obeyed the decisions of his intellect and will without any indication of rebellion. What reason knew, the will chose and the sensitive faculties executed.[65] In short, man was in a state of tranquility and peace. In this state man fully reflected the Trinity in whose image he had been created. In their ability to execute the decisions of man's intellect and will, man's sense faculties mirrored the *potentia* of the Father. The *sapientia* of the Son was reflected in the intellect's capacity to attain knowledge without error. The *bonitas* generally attributed to the Holy Spirit is found in the alacrity with which the will acted under the counsel of reason.[66]

The peace and harmony existing within his sensitive, intellectual, and volitional faculties were part of man's original inheritance and were intensified and strengthened by the grace of original justice. The sin of Adam, however, shattered that peace and harmony. Man was suddenly transformed from an image of the Trinity to an image of the devil. Reason which had been created as a counsellor for the will became blind and mute; no longer was its voice heard guiding the will to proper courses of action. The will also shared in the spirit of rebellion; no longer would it listen to the dictates of reason. Its former power as lord and master of the other faculties was destroyed; it had now become subservient to the forces of sensuality. The powers of man's sensitive faculties were also disoriented. Intended to serve the intellect and will, these faculties blinded the intellect and replaced the will as the dominant power within the soul. The image of God in man thus became considerably less recognizable and the pain of division was felt in the kingdom of man's soul.[67]

---

[65] *Omne regnum divisum in se*, G, 7, 753-754. "Tel fut ce royaume en sa premiere institucion en nostre premier pere Adam. Quant raison conseilloit sans erreur, voulente franche creoit et escoutoit et commandoit sans contrester, et sensualite obeissoit sans murmure."

[66] *Omne regnum divisum in se*, G, 7, 754.

[67] *Omne regnum divisum in se*, G, 7, 754. Cf. *Convertimini*, G, 7, 575.

Gerson frequently uses Scripture to describe the state of man after the fall. His favorite passage is Ps 48:13: "*Et homo, cum in honore esset, non intellexit: comparatus est iumentis insipientibus, et similis factus est illis.*" After the incursion of sin, man became like the mute beasts. The honor of which the Psalmist speaks is that which was man's in his first state of innocence. Then he perfectly reflected the Trinity in whose image he was created, since all his faculties functioned harmoniously and peacefully. Man, however, did not truly comprehend the honor in which God had created him; he failed to understand that he was made in God's image. As a result, he has fallen into a state of ignorance and impotence. Therefore, he has been justly compared to foolish and senseless beasts and has truly become like them.[68]

The image of God in man, whether described as man's natural faculties of memory, intellect, and will, or sense, reason, and will, remains essentially intact, although, as has been seen, those faculties are considerably hampered in their operations by the effect of sin. The qualities of the image which came with grace and which brought the image to a greater degree of beauty and perfection have disappeared. Despite the Fall and its consequences, however, man still remains an image of God, an image of the Trinity. The loss of grace and the consequent disorientation in man's natural faculties occur not only at the time of the Fall but also whenever man sins. At each instance, however, the natural image imprinted on man's faculties remains and serves as the basis for the creature's return to God and renewal in grace. Because of sin, however, the image is frequently spoken of as deformed, dirty, or defiled.[69]

Gerson describes man's state after the Fall in different ways. At times he compares it to an exile where man has been placed after the sin committed by Adam. Man has been ejected from his homeland. He is poor, sick, imprisoned, wounded, and without clothing. His home is no longer one of enjoyment but a place of sorrow, tribulation, desolation, and anguish. He has gone from riches to poverty, nobility to vileness, and from life to death.

Closely associated with the notion of exile is that of pilgrimage. Since the sin of Adam, all men are exiles from their true homeland;

---

[68] *Poenitemini . . . Je vouldroie bien savoir,* G, 7, 797.

[69] *Pax hominibus bonae voluntatis,* G, 7, 767. "Chascun est fait a l'image de Dieu, ja soi ce qu'aucuns la facent laide et orde par leurs pechies." Cf. *Collectorium super Magnificat,* P, 4, 261 C.

they are pilgrims.[70] Heb 13:14 reminds man of his condition as a pilgrim: "For here we have no lasting city, but we seek the city which is to come."[71] That city is the city of heaven. Gerson argues that the Our Father is sufficient to remind man that his life on earth is a pilgrimage. By the very fact that the prayer contains the phrase: "Our Father who art in heaven," man should be aware that his status on earth is that of a pilgrim. If his father is in heaven then it follows that he is in a strange country; he is far from his paternal heritage, far from his homeland.[72] St. Paul emphasized this point in Phil 3:20 when he said that our homeland is in heaven.[73] Gerson asserts, moreover, that all the patriarchs, prophets, and kings of the Old Testament considered themselves as pilgrims. Moses was so conscious of man's pilgrim status on earth that he named his first son Gershom, which is synonymous with the word pilgrim. Gerson is here referring to Ex 2:22 where Moses, while in exile in the land of Midian, named his son Gershom which he interpreted by the phrase: "I have been a sojourner in a foreign land." The first son of Levi also bore the name Gershom. King David reiterated the same idea in Ps 38:13 when he said to the Lord: "For I am thy passing guest, a sojourner, like all my fathers."[74]

Gerson also describes man after the sin of Adam as living in a desert, a wasteland, which is practically uninhabitable, impassible and without water. In short, this earth has become a dark and profound abyss of misery.[75] He refers to man as living in a *regio egestatis*, a

---

[70] *Obsecro vos*, G, 7, 748-749. The idea of man as a *peregrinus* was one of the most widely used themes in early Christian and medieval thought. For an analysis of this theme in the scriptural, patristic, and medieval traditions see Ladner, "Homo Viator," pp. 235-257. In addition to its extensive bibliography, Ladner's article also studies themes closely allied to the idea of *peregrinus*, namely those of *alienatio* and *ordo*. For an analysis of the importance of *peregrinatio* in the late medieval church see Delaruelle, *L'Église au temps du Grand Schisme*, 2, 796-810. Delaruelle shows that the *peregrinus* was one of the most characteristic personalities of the late middle ages. The *peregrinus*, moreover, constituted a special *ordo* in the church and enjoyed the privilege of wearing a distinctive garb. Special liturgical offices and plays were also built around the notion of man as a pilgrim. Gerson's own *Testamentum peregrini*, G, 7, 142-143, exemplifies the medieval tradition.

[71] *Testamentum peregrini*, G, 7, 142. Other scriptural sources on the idea of man as a pilgrim include 2 Pet 2:11 and Heb. 11:13.

[72] *Obsecro vos*, G, 7, 749.

[73] On the notion of homeland, see the article on *conversatio* in *DSAM*, 2, 2206-2212 and *TWNT*, 6, 525-528, 533-535 under the words πολίτευμα and πολιτεύομαι.

[74] *Obsecro vos*, G, 7, 749-750.

[75] *Tradidit Jesum Judas*, G, 5, 550.

barren land.[76] St. Augustine used this phrase in his *Confessions* when at the end of the second book he described the state of his soul during his adolescent years: "I went away from Thee, my God, in my youth I strayed too far from Thy sustaining power, and I became to myself a barren land." [77] Gerson extends the use of the term to all men living in the state of sin. The term has its roots in the parable of the prodigal son in Lk 15:14. After the prodigal son had spent all his money, a famine arose in the country where he was living and he began to be in want: "*Et, postquam omnia consummasset, facta est fames valida in regione illa, et ipse coepit egere.*"

Another favorite Augustinian description used by Gerson to depict the state of man in sin is that of *regio dissimilitudinis*. Created to the image and likeness of God, the soul has so disfigured itself through sin that it no longer fully reflects its creator. While not fully destroyed, the image has become unclear, confused and distorted. Because of sin, the soul has been justifiably exiled and wanders now in the land of unlikeness. No longer true to itself, the soul has virtually become a region of dissimilitude.[78] The phrase "*regio dissimilitudinis*" occurs in the seventh book of the *Confessions* where, at the end of the long journey that has culminated in his intellectual conversion, Augustine, through the light of divine grace, sees himself as he truly is. At that moment he shook with fear and love and then looking at himself he realized how much he had become unlike God and his true self. He realized that he was far from God "*in regione dissimilitudinis.*" [79] Gilson contends that Augustine's concept of the *regio* is primarily metaphysical and represents basically the Platonic region of becoming, situated between the realm of pure nonbeing and the immutable being of God.[80] For Gerson, as for many of his medieval predecessors, the *regio dissimilitudinis* is primarily the region of sin and spiritual deformity.[81]

---

[76] *A Deo exivit*, G, 5, 17.

[77] Augustine, *Confessions*, 2:10, trans. by F. J. Sheed (New York, 1942), p. 31. Latin text in *CSEL*, 33, p. 43. The notion of the wasteland must also have been familiar to Gerson through the romances of the Arthurian cycle. For the theme of the wasteland in medieval vernacular literature see Ladner, "Homo Viator," pp. 246-249.

[78] *Omnia dedit ei Pater*, G, 5, 417. Cf. also *Canticordum du pélerin*, G, 7, 18.

[79] Augustine, *Confessions*, 7:10, *CSEL*, 33, p. 157.

[80] Étienne Gilson, *The Mystical Theology of St. Bernard*, trans A.H.C. Downes (London, 1955), pp. 224-225, n. 43.

[81] For a further study of the term *regio dissimilitudinis* see A. E. Taylor, "Regio dissimilitudinis," *AHDL*, 9 (1934), 305-306; Etienne Gilson, "Regio dissimilitudinis de

The soul whose likeness to the image of God has been tarnished and is consequently wandering in the *regio dissimilitudinis* is described by Gerson as "*curva*" or "*incurvata*." Originally created as *recta* or upright the soul through sin has descended to and prefers what is temporal, earthly, perishable, and pleasing to its animal nature. The soul which is *recta* has preserved or recovered its image and likeness to God and is characterized by a love of heavenly values and the desire for the divine and the eternal.[82] Gerson finds the notion of *anima curva* in Ps 37:4-7 where the Psalmist expresses the weight of sin that he feels within himself. Because of sin there is no soundness in his flesh, no health in his bones; his iniquities have become an overwhelming burden. His soul is foul and festered; he is utterly bowed down and prostrate: "*miser factus sum et curvatus ad terram*." [83]

To express the full sense of *anima curva*, Gerson uses passages from Scripture where man in sin is frequently compared to the beasts. His favorite passage is Ps 48:13. By sinning man disregards the dignity in which he has been created and has become like the stupid ox. The Psalmist uses the example of beasts because of their proclivity towards the terrestrial wherein lies the similarity with man in sin. According to Gerson, man too has become like the beasts through sin. He compares the life of sinful man to that of cattle and swine whose interest is exclusively focused upon earthly things. The faces of swine are always turned downward toward the mire and their stomachs are always close to the earth.[84] The Psalmist expresses similar thoughts when he uses such statements as "our soul is bowed down to the dust," and "my soul cleaves to the dust," and again, "I sink in deep mire where there is no foothold." [85] Gerson also finds

---

Platon à saint Bernard de Clairvaux," MS, 9 (1947), 108-130; F. Chatillon, "Regio Dissimilitudinis," *Mélanges E. Podechard* (Lyons, 1945), pp. 85-102; J. C. Didier, "*Pour la fiche regio dissimilitudinis*," MSR, 7 (1951), 205-210; Gervais Dumeige, "Dissemblance," DSAM, 3, 1330-1346. See also the articles of P. Courcelle, "Tradition néo-platonicienne et traditions chrétiennes de la 'région de dissemblance,'" "Répertoire des textes relatifs à 'la région de dissemblance' jusqu' au xive siècle," AHDL, 32 (1957), 5-23, 24-34, and "Témoins nouveaux de la 'région de dissemblance,'" BEC, 118 (1960), 20-36. Javelet surveys the use of *regio dissimilitudinis* in twelfth-century authors in his *Image et ressemblance*, 1, 266-285 and 2, 239-243.

[82] For an analysis of the biblical sources of the patristic and medieval doctrines on the terms *curva* and *recta* see Arimaspus, "Pour la fiche anima curva," RMAL, 1 (1945), 177-178, 421-422. See also Pierre Michaud-Quantin, "Pour la fiche anima curva," RMAL, 5, (1949), 135-136.

[83] *Poenitemini...Repentez vous*, G, 7, 883-884.

[84] *A Deo exivit*, G, 5, 15.   [85] Pss 43:25; 118:25; 68:2.

the notion of *anima curva* verified in classical authors. The satires of
Persius employ the phrase *anima curva* and Gerson believes that
Persius understands the term in basically the same sense as that used
by the Psalmist. He finds his clearest proof in Satire 2:61 where
Persius says: *"O curvas in terra animas et coelestium inanes."* [86]

Sin, then, has had an extremely detrimental effect upon the image
of God in man. Sin has tarnished, dulled and discolored that image
to a point where it is hardly recognizable. Sin, furthermore, has
resulted in man's exile from his homeland; his life has become one
long pilgrimage. Unlike his God, in whose image he was originally
created, he wanders in the region of dissimilitude and has become a
barren land. Deprived of grace, he is no longer upright but bowed
down to the earth in the likeness of the beasts.

4. CONVERSION AND REPENTANCE

Sin may disfigure the image in man but it cannot completely
destroy it. Man's natural faculties remain essentially intact and when
aided again by grace they can be restored to their proper spiritual
orientation. Man can regain his dignity as an image of God; he can
return from the *regio dissimilitudinis* and the *regio egistatis*. He can
cease to be *incurvata* and become *recta* in the full biblical sense of
the term. Man is capable of experiencing a change of heart and mind;
in brief, man is capable of conversion.

The notion of conversion plays an integral role in Gerson's
understanding of personal reform. He finds this notion rooted in the
Old Testament, especially the prophets Hosea and Joel. In Hos 14:1-
2, the prophet calls upon Israel to return to the Lord. Too long has
Israel strayed from the true paths of the Lord by its sin. Israel is to
return to the Lord in a spirit of penitence and say to him: "Take away
all iniquity and accept that which is good." Jl 2:12-13 represents the
Lord as summoning Israel to return to him with all its heart. The
return or conversion of Israel is to be externally manifested in fasting,
weeping and mourning. The prophet reminds the Israelites that these
signs are to be more than just external; they are to be indications of
an internal change of heart, for the Lord asks the Israelites to rend
their hearts and not their garments. [87]

Closely associated with the experience of conversion is that of

---

[86] *A Deo exivit*, G, 5, 15.
[87] *Convertimini ad me*, G, 7, 574-575.

repentance.[88] Gerson's concept of repentance has already been investigated in the context of his program of theological reform and is essentially the same in the area of personal reform except that in the latter case he stresses more its sacramental aspects. In addition to contrition, Gerson always adds the need for an integral confession in which nothing is hidden through shame, hypocrisy or fear. Finally there is the element of satisfaction imposed by the judgment of the confessor. Only when the three conditions of contrition, confession, and satisfaction are verified can there be true and complete *poenitentia*. Then only can the soul be said to have become fully converted.[89]

The sacramental emphasis in Gerson's understanding of *poenitentia* is witnessed especially in his attitude towards the Flagellants.[90] He criticizes them specifically for their tendency to rely primarily upon individual penitential practices. He insists upon the

---

[88] Throughout Scripture conversion and repentance were intimately related. The Hebraic root *šûb* generally described conversion in the sense of "going back again," or "returning." Conversion, consequently, involved a radical reorientation of one's whole personality towards God. Penance was naturally implied in conversion but was designated by no special term in Hebrew. In the Septuagint the Hebraic *šûb* was always rendered by ἀποστρέφω or ἐπιστρέφω. The idea of regret was generally expressed by μετανοέω but since that word denoted a change of mind or feeling, it also came to convey the idea of religious and ethical conversion. In the Jewish Hellenistic tradition μετανοέω was commonly used for and preferred to ἐπιστρέφω and this use continued into the New Testament. The Vulgate translated μετανοέω as *poenitentia*, a term which emphasized more sorrow and regret than radical reorientation toward God. This tendency is visible in Gerson's understanding of *poenitentia*. Cf. G. Bertram, "ἐπιστρέφω," *TWNT*, 7, 722-729, J. Behm and E. Würthwein," μετανοέω," *TWNT*, 4, 972-1004, and J. Giblet, "Pénitence," *DB*, 7, 627-687.

[89] *Contra curiositatem studentium*, G, 3, 228.

[90] Although individual flagellation was practiced in the early and medieval church, especially within monastic circles, organized processions of flagellants did not appear until the thirteenth century. The first manifestation of such processions was in Perugia in 1260 when the city was suffering under the miseries of war and plague and became caught up in the eschatological expectations occasioned by the writings of Joachim of Flora. The movement spread throughout Italy and northern Europe but declined rapidly when it received considerable opposition from ecclesiastical and civil officials. In the middle of the fourteenth century it gained new vigor with the ravages of the Black Death. At this period, however, the movement became strongly anticlerical and in 1349 incurred the condemnation of Clement VI. At the Council of Constance, Gerson attacked the Flagellants in his *Contra sectum se flagellantium* and criticized St. Vincent Ferrer for not sufficiently opposing their activities. The council, however, did not see fit to add any further condemnations beyond that of Clement VI. The sect of the Flagellants should not be confused with the penitential fraternities known as *disciplinati*, who remained orthodox and operated under ecclesiastical supervision and approval. Cf. Paul Bailly, "Flagellants," *DSAM*, 5, 392-408, and Émile Bertaud, "Discipline," *DSAM*, 3, 1302-1311.

point that the sacraments of the New Law are the main channels of divine grace and that their effectiveness is not dependent upon the internal dispositions of the priest but upon their own intrinsic power. Gerson firmly asserts that whatever militates against the reception of the sacraments, especially the sacrament of confession, must be assiduously rejected. He argues that the Flagellants neglect sacramental confession. In their enthusiasm, they have become so taken up by the penitential practice of flagellation that they have downgraded the effectiveness of sacramental *poenitentia*. Many claim that flagellation is a more effective means for the remission of sin than confession. Some would even go so far as to prefer flagellation to martyrdom, saying that the Flagellants' suffering is self-inflicted while that of martyrs is imposed through the agency of others. Gerson is totally unsympathetic to such arguments. He continually insists that the sacraments are indispensable for the attainment of any true degree of *poenitentia*.[91]

Gerson's attitude in the case of the Flagellants must not be interpreted as a rejection of penitential practices outside the sacramental realm. He heartily approves, for example, of the church's custom of fasting and abstinence. After the removal of personal sins through sacramental confession, penitential practices can play an important role in the individual's reconciliation with God. Such practices can strengthen and intensify the radical conversion achieved through the sacraments. The fast and abstinence observed during the Lenten period serve to conquer and repress the radical force of sin whose power of attraction remains strong even after confession. Fast and abstinence also elevate the soul to a greater love and confidence in heavenly values. Finally, these penitential practices strengthen and intensify the theological virtues in man.

Gerson's reaction, therefore, against the Flagellants is not against penitential practices in themselves. These he approves and finds of great value as long as they are subordinated to the sacramental dimension of *poenitentia*. The sacramental remains foremost; next come those penitential activities that have the full sanction and approbation of the church, such as fasting and abstinence and all such practices which the church commands of its members. What he reacts to is excessively self-imposed or self-justifying forms of *poenitentia*.[92] In addition to the practices of fasting and abstinence,

---

[91] *Contra sectam se flagellantium*, P, 2, 660 C-D.
[92] *Convertimini ad me*, G, 7, 583-584.

Gerson recognizes other factors which help to foster the penitential spirit. Human experiences such as inspiration, adversity, and prosperity can incite the soul to *poenitentia*. The emotions also help to intensify the spirit of repentance. The cardinal and theological virtues as well as the gifts of the Holy Spirit further deepen the penitential experience. Prayer too can make its contribution, especially the seven petitions of the Our Father. The petition for forgiveness of sins, if sincerely expressed, can be most conducive to repentance. But even when discussing the nonsacramental aspects of *poenitentia*, Gerson is quick to stress the sacramental. While there are many practices and various incentives which promote and maintain the penitential spirit, the sacraments remain the primary context within which *poenitentia* is achieved and expressed. *Poenitentia* is renewed and intensified through the sacraments and not through the sacrament of penance alone but through all the seven sacraments.[93]

When properly understood and utilized, *poenitentia* can have a strong restorative effect upon the soul. By his sinful acts man has become a slave to sin and guilty of *lèse-majesté* towards his sovereign Lord. He has been exiled upon earth and enclosed within the dark prison of the flesh. Man's spiritual restoration can only be achieved through *poenitentia*, which is the gateway to full reconciliation with God and to freedom from sin.[94] Through *poenitentia* man will be able to return from exile; he will draw closer to the goal of his pilgrimage and eventually arrive at his natural homeland which is heaven.[95]

Poenitentia is also a primary means for restoring peace to the soul because it reestablishes the proper hierarchy and harmony among man's natural faculties. On the spiritual level, grace results in the proper orientation of man's faculties to God. The peace achieved through *poenitentia*, moreover, revivifies the soul and results in what Gerson calls *naissance gracieuse*.[96] According to Gerson, man

---

[93] *Contra curiositatem studentium*, G, 3, 237. "Poenitentia... per sacramenta renovatur."

[94] *Contra curiositatem studentium*, G, 3, 225. "Est itaque rationalis homo post peccatum velut servus nequam, reus criminis laesae majestatis projectus in exilium hujus vallis miseriae, detrusus quoque in carcerem tenebrosum carnis corruptae faetulentiae; ubi in tenebris sedens lumen caeli non videt, nisi reconcilietur prius per poenitentiam, quam esse recte dicimus ostiariam liberantem nos a vinculis peccatorum...."

[95] *Pour ce que toute humaine creature*, G, 7, 317.

[96] *Poenitemini ... Repentez vous car penitence donne*, G, 7, 948. "Donnez

experiences three moments of birth which he describes as *douloureuse, gracieuse*, and *glorieuse*. The first refers to natural birth and is common to all men both good and evil. The second and third are spiritual forms of birth and refer to man's birth by grace and by glory at the end of his life. For Gerson there is a causal relationship between *naissance gracieuse* and *poenitentia*. The first birth of grace in man's soul in baptism as well as all subsequent renewal in grace requires *poenitentia*. Through *poenitentia* comes grace and the theological virtues of faith, hope and charity.[97]

5. REFORMATION OF THE IMAGE

The renewal of man through *poenitentia* constitutes his reformation as an image of God. The process of reform begins with baptism, which is the initial experience of *poenitentia*. In baptism the soul which has been created in God's image is regenerated, purified of the stains of original sin and restored to its full beauty.[98] This is a genuine rebirth and Gerson uses the verb *renascor* to describe it.[99] He compares it, moreover, to man's physical birth, for in the grace of baptism man has been conceived anew but now into the life of the Spirit. The grace of baptism, therefore, restores and reforms the image. Trough the reforming grace of baptism, the natural image of God in man is purified and made more beautiful. Comparing the image to a picture, Gerson sees baptismal grace as adding more distinct lines and colors to those already contained in the picture. The image, therefore, becomes a truer and more faithful

doncques, sire, paix par vostre intercession; donnez paix en nostre temps moyennant bonne penitence vraie et entiere, car c'est celle qui appaise Dieu, qui rent foy, esperance, charite et touz les biens lesquelz peche nous oste et emble; c'est elle qui l'ame morte par peche vivifie et ressuscite par naissance gracieuse pour avoir finablement la glorieuse, quam nobis concedat ille qui est benedictus in saecula saeculorum."

[97] *Poenitemini . . . Repentez vous car penitence donne*, G, 7, 937. "En ceste nativite gracieuse sont donnez et infuseez toutez vertuz, en especial les trois theologiquez, foy, esperance et charite pour garder l'ame. . . . Pour tant dit Nostre Seigneur les paroles proposeez: poenitemini, repentez vous, car penitence donne gracieuse naissance."

[98] *Tota pulchra es*, G, 7, 1069. "O ame devote créée de Dieu a son ymaige et de son precieux sang amoureusement rachetee, considere et te remambre que jadiz puisque tu estoyes layde et diffiguree par pechié originel il pleust a ton Dieu toy regenerer, abelir et purifier par le sacrement de baptesme et comme nouvellement te concevoir par grace en tant que lors quant il te veist telle il te daingna appeller sa mie et toute belle te nomma. . . ."

[99] *Jacob autem genuit Joseph*, G, 5, 362. "Nos denique singuli Deo renascamur felici nativitate, hic per gratiam et in futuro per gloriam quae est natale sanctorum. . . ."

representation of its creator.[100] The process of reformation that occurs in baptism takes place each time the soul is cleansed of serious sin through the sacrament of penance. Venial sin, while not destroying the spiritual dimensions of the image, does nevertheless tend to tarnish and discolor it. In this case, restoration of the image can be effected either through sacramental penance or penitential practices.

Since the soul has been created not merely according to the image of God but, more specifically, according to the image of the Trinity, its reformation will naturally take place according to the trinitarian dimensions of the image.[101] In his *Mendicité spirituelle*, Gerson succinctly described the reformation of the image according to the trinitarian characteristics of *potentia*, *sapientia*, and *benevolentia*. Through God's presence in the soul by grace, vices are uprooted and supplanted by virtues which reflect the *potentia* of the Father. The *sapientia* of the Son is witnessed in the fact that the soul is clearly able to understand its faults, its sins, and its general fragility in the light of truth. The result of the foregoing activity is that the soul rediscovers its beauty and sees itself as a reflection of the *bonitas* of the Holy Spirit. This moment of transformation is compared by Gerson to the time of day when the rising sun dispels the darkness of night. Then all creation appears renewed and restored to the fullness of its power. The color of created things appears brightest and everything seems at the peak of its beauty. Thus it is when the light of justice is born again in man's soul.[102]

Gerson also employs the dramatic technique of a soliloquy to express the trinitarian nature of conversion and reformation.[103] In the soliloquy, man acknowledges that he has been made to the image and likeness of the Trinity and, therefore, reflects the trinitarian *potentia*, *sapientia*, and *bonitas*. He realizes, moreover, that because of this image-like relationship, he should place his hope and trust in no other *potentia* than that of God nor should he desire any *sapientia* outside of God. By thus modeling his activity upon the divine *potentia* and *sapientia*, he will preserve his own interior *bonitas*.

---

[100] *Anagogicum de verbo et hymno gloriae*, P, 4, 546 D-547 A. "Verbum gloriae secundum mysteriam fidei nostrae tradit hominem reformatum esse in Baptismo per gratiam, infusionemque virtutum habitualium, et est haec reformatio veluti quaedam superinductio colorem deiformium ad lineamenta naturalis imaginis, et similitudinis."

[101] *Emitte spiritum tuum*, G, 5, 257-258. "Reformetur dehinc anima ad imaginem et similitudinem benedictissimae Trinitatis. . . ."

[102] *La mendicité spirituelle*, G, 7, 276-277.

[103] *La mendicité spirituelle*, G, 7, 279-280.

Man, however, recognizes that he does not always imitate the divine exemplar. Too frequently he has allowed the divine image within himself to become ugly, dirty, and discolored. Such is always the case whenever he allows himself to be dragged into the mire of sin or preoccupied with worldly cares and pleasures. As the soliliquy continues, man realizes that when he is in such a dejected state there is really only one course of action open to him and that is to return to God in whose image he has been made. Once he turns to God, God will turn to his creature since it bears his image. He will cleanse the image of the stain of sin that has so tarnished and distorted it; he will illumine the soul and dispel the dark shadows of sin. As a result of this divine activity, the image will again become beautiful and pleasing.

What God demands of man in this process of conversion is that he adhere to him as his sole source of power. He is to recognize God, moreover, as the source of his light and knowledge. Finally he is to be attracted to God as the origin of all sweetness, love, and pleasure. This triple conversion is, in effect, a conversion to God's *potentia, sapientia,* and *benevolentia* and is possible only because man bears within himself the trinitarian image. He places his hope in the divine *potentia;* he rests his faith in the divine *sapientia,* and his charity upon the commands of the divine *voluntas.* By so turning to God, he becomes anew the *imago Dei,* the *imago beatae Trinitatis.* Thus in the words of Ps 102:5 he can say to his God that his "youth is renewed like the eagle's." [104]

Gerson also describes the trinitarian nature of personal reform in terms of memory, intellect, and will. This reform begins at the moment of baptism. Baptismal reform proceeds according to man's memory, intellect, and will. The soul of a newly-baptized child enjoys God's presence although not with the full consciousness and freedom characteristic of an adult, since the child has not yet reached the age of reason nor does it merit or act virtuously according to the accepted understanding of those activities. Yet because of the infusion of the theological virtues which come with the grace of baptism, the child is said to be united with God which means, in effect, that the trinitarian image of memory, intellect, and will within him has been reformed. [105]

---

[104] *La mendicité spirituelle,* G, 7, 268. Cf. *Emitte spiritum tuum,* G, 5, 257 and Ps 102:5.

[105] *Collectorium super Magnificat,* P, 4, 334 B. "Ratio est, quia imago suae mentis

In the case of adults, the reformation of man's triple faculties takes place first in his memory which no longer wanders outside itself but is preoccupied with its own presence and the transcendent presence of God. The intellect, furthermore, becomes enlightened by its control over sense images and fantasies. Because man is a composite of matter and spirit, the intellect is never completely free of sense images; it can only strive to control its sense imagination. This control is attained when man's intellect has been reformed by grace. Through the reformative power of grace, the will also is freed from the domination of carnal desires. In the final analysis, the reform of man's memory, intellect, and will means that he reflects more clearly the divine Trinity in whose image he has been created.[106]

The reformative dynamism of grace and the theological virtues proceeds, moreover, according to the hierarchical activities of purgation, illumination, and perfection. The virtue of hope is essentially purgative. Directed towards the memory, hope purifies, elevates, and strengthens that faculty. Faith is basically illuminative and has as its purpose the conversion of the intellect to the divine light. Charity, finally, is perfective; it orientates and intensifies the will's love of God, thereby uniting man more closely to him.[107] The soul, therefore, in which grace and the theological virtues are operative is essentially in the process of reformation and the trinitarian image of memory, intellect, and will is continually being renewed in the likeness of its divine exemplar. Grace and the theological virtues have a similar transforming effect upon the *vis rationalis, irascibilis*, and *concupiscibilis*. Regardless of the manner in which it is described, reform always takes place in a hierarchical context. The renewal of the triple *vires* in the individual soul is achieved through the hierarchical activities of purgation, illumination, and perfection exercised by bishops and clergy. The reformation of memory, intellect, and will occurs, moreover, in a similar context. The penitential spirit so essential for the conversion of the image is primarily described in terms of the sacraments, especially penance. Gerson objects to the Flagellants principally because their penitential activities neglected the sacramental and engendered an independence of the church's hierarchy. When he

---

ad sui reformata est honorem principii, secundum memoriam, intelligentiam et voluntatem."
   [106] *Videmus nunc per speculum*, G, 7, 1137.
   [107] *Collectorium super Magnificat*, P, 4, 342 B-D.

discusses penitential practices he gives careful priority to those practices which have clear ecclesiastical approval.

Mystical theology which is the fullest realization of personal reform must also be seen in close relationship with hierarchical activity. Gerson's views on the nature of mystical theology, at least until 1425, reveal a remarkable coherence with the finality of hierarchical order.[108] Mystical theology, indeed, can only be fully understood in the context of the finality of the entire hierarchical order. Both mystical theology and hierarchical order terminate in love, union, and peace. Mystical theology, for Gerson, involves primarily the affective powers of the soul and is essentially realized in a love of God which is ecstatic, unitive, and peaceful.[109] The union that results from love is regarded by Gerson principally as a union of wills. The immediate consequence of this union is peace, for in mystical union the soul becomes fully satiated and is at rest. The soul attains its highest good which is God and rests in the tranquility which that possession brings.[110] The importance attributed to the Spirit in all hierarchical activity also finds a parallel in his mysticism, for at the time of the Council of Constance Gerson's mysticism became more Spirit-centered.[111] As a result of the close relationship between mysticism and hierarchical order, mystical prayer represents primarily an intensification of the whole thrust of hierarchical activity, a privileged moment in the ordinary working of the hierarchical order.

In brief, then, personal reform in Gerson is not simply the result of individual endeavor but takes place within the context of the church's hierarchical structure. The result is not only personal reform and renewal but also the edification of the church as Christ's mystical body.

---

[108] André Combes maintains that in this year Gerson underwent a personal conversion as to the nature of mystical experience. Mystical theology for him consequently was no longer primarily an act of love or the operation of man's affective faculty of *synderesis* but more a complete cessation of all human activity in the presence of the divine initiative which comes through grace and unites the soul to God. Cf. *La théologie mystique*, 2, 465-568.

[109] *De theologia mystica*, G, 3, 282-284. For variant definitions of mystical theology which, nevertheless, all center upon love as the determining characteristic of mystical union see *De theologia mystica*, G, 3, 274.

[110] *De theologia mystica*, G, 3, 288-289.

[111] Combes, *La théologie mystique*, 2, 221, 224-227.

CONCLUSION

Our research has clearly demonstrated that the basic principles of church reform in Gerson's thinking are hierarchical. The church, *hierarchical* according to Gerson, is essentially a hierarchy and has its archetype in the angelic orders. The hierarchical organization of the church, moreover, is not accidental but reflects the direct intention of Christ, its founder. Gerson concludes, furthermore, that the ecclesiastical hierarchy is perfectly complete from the very moment of its origin. Since the church has been and will be conserved integrally throughout history, it cannot suffer any deficiency in its hierarchical structure. The ecclesiastical hierarchy, finally, is essentially dynamic; its activity takes the form of purgation, illumination, and perfection. These activities, in turn, are reformative and have for their immediate purpose the promotion of charity, unity, and peace within and among the members of the church. The ultimate effect of hierarchical activity is the growth and edification of the church as Christ's mystical body. The causal relationship between hierarchy, reform, and the mystical body constitutes, therefore, the most essential aspect of Gerson's ideas on church reform.

The church of Gerson's time, however, hardly resembled its celestial archetype and much less exhibited the qualities of charity, unity, and peace that should result from the proper functioning of its hierarchy. All signs, moreover, pointed not to the edification but to the destruction of the mystical body. Racked with heresy, moral degradation, and schism, the church reflected more the realm of chaos and disorder. Gerson, nevertheless, sought the resources for reform primarily within the church's hierarchical structure. The church, indeed, possessed in its hierarchical order the power of self-reform which Gerson designated as the *semen vivificum et reformativum*.

This *semen* is, in reality, the Holy Spirit. Recourse to the reformative power of the Spirit, however, does not lead Gerson to any excessively spiritualistic interpretation of the church; the Spirit in Gerson is always linked to the ecclesiastical hierarchy and has as its primary purpose the preservation of that hierarchy. Deprived of its proper head, the church has, through the activity of the Spirit, the resources necessary for the restoration of its hierarchical integrity.

The Holy Spirit is especially operative whenever the church is gathered in council, since the council represents the totality of the hierarchical order. In council, the ecclesiastical hierarchy, under the guidance of the Spirit, has the power to achieve its own reformation by selecting a new head. Through this reformative activity, moreover, charity, unity, and peace are restored to the ecclesiastical hierarchy. Once its hierarchical integrity has been renewed, the church can, more effectively, provide for the growth and edification of its members.

Law

The notion of law also emerged as an essential element in Gerson's teaching on reform. His interest in law, however, lay principally in its relationship to hierarchy. Law governs and maintains the proper functioning of hierarchical order. As divinely instituted, the ecclesiastical hierarchy is primarily governed by divine law. Positive ecclesiastical legislation, though necessary and helpful to the maintenance of hierarchical order, must, in the final analysis, remain subservient to divine law. As long as proper order is preserved among the various laws which govern the church, its hierarchy will function effectively.

The church of Gerson's day, however, was a confusion of laws. He saw this confusion as originating in the period of the Constantinian Donation and reaching its peak of intensity with the Great Schism. Legal confusion has frustrated the reformative dynamism of the hierarchical order and, as a result, the ecclesiastical hierarchy could not be restored to its integrity. As long as legal confusion reigned within the church, the hierarchy would remain deprived of its head. Only through a general council could the ecclesiastical hierarchy be assembled and under the reformative guidance of the Spirit provide for the proper election of a new head. Positive church law, however, having assumed the authority of divine law, presented innumerable obstacles to the convocation of a general council. To achieve this convocation Gerson called for a conversion to the principles of divine law. He demanded, moreover, that *epikeia* be applied to the existing maze of positive ecclesiastical laws so that they might again be subordinated to divine law and redirected towards their proper finality. Divine law, then, working in conjunction with positive ecclesiastical law, provides for the harmonious functioning of the hierarchical order in a general council. Once gathered in council, the reformative power of that order becomes operative and restores unity to the church through the election of a new pope.

The role of the theologian is intimately related to the notions of hierarchical order and law. This relationship rests upon the fact that the theologian is primarily the guardian and interpreter of divine law. To him belongs the power of distinguishing the elements of divine law from the maze of positive laws which had produced legal disorder within the church. The interpretative power which the theologian enjoys does not mean that he can treat the law as his private domain. His function is not only to discern the principles of divine law and to redirect positive ecclesiastical law to its proper finality but also to place both positive and divine law at the service of the hierarchical order. The theologian's role, therefore, is not one of opposition to the ecclesiastical hierarchy but one of harmonious cooperation. Through his mastery of divine law, which is the life of the ecclesiastical hierarchy, the theologian insures the proper functioning of the hierarchical order. Only in virtue of divine law, moreover, does that order exercise its reformative power. The theologian, therefore, is always to be conceived as being for and at the service of the ecclesiastical hierarchy.

Gerson's call for theological reform must also be seen in the context of service to the church's hierarchy. He was of the opinion that as a result of *curiositas* and *singularitas*, the theologian had misdirected his activity. As he saw it, the theologian had abandoned the tradition of the older masters and had set forth upon a sea of useless speculation, thereby transcending the proper limitations of theological investigation. The primary font and limit of all theological endeavor should be the Scriptures. In the Scriptures, moreover, was to be found the clearest enunciation of the principles of divine law so essential to the proper functioning of the ecclesiastical hierarchy. Gerson's call for theological reform entailed, therefore, a penitential return to the Scriptures. Penitence alone can initiate the theologian in the riches of the Gospel. Only through a penitential spirit can the theologian fully comprehend the principles of divine law contained in the Scriptures. The theological knowledge attained through the spirit of penitence is to be placed by the theologian at the service of the church's hierarchical order. By so acting, he contributes toward the proper maintenance, operation, and reformation of that order.

At the Council of Constance, Gerson was concerned with reform primarily in so far as it related to the restoration of the ecclesiastical hierarchy, which had suffered considerable harm as a result of the schism. His main energies were directed toward the resolution of the schism and the restoration of the church to its full hierarchical integrity. As a result of this preoccupation as well as his concern with the problem of tyrannicide, Gerson gave relatively little attention to other areas of reform espoused by the council. He continually supported the council's attempt to secure needed reform in the area of belief and morals but nowhere with the detail and force he expended in areas related to the settlement of the schism. Gerson did not serve on any of the several reform commissions that were established by the council nor do his writings reveal any detailed program of reform in belief and morals proposed to the council. All this is not to say that Gerson was unconcerned with reform in the area of belief and morals; he was passionately committed to such reform but he sought its effective realization more through the local churches than through the universal council. Gerson, moreover, says surprisingly little about the role of the papacy in the reform of the church. His experiences with the papacy in the past had led him to become distrustful of that institution as a major instrument of reform. The full scope of Gerson's program for the reform of faith and morals, therefore, is revealed not so much in his thoughts on conciliar reform as in his concept of diocesan and parochial renewal.

Our research has shown the position of prominence occupied by the episcopacy in the area of doctrinal and moral reform. This research, moreover, reinforces our basic thesis that Gerson's thinking on reform is essentially hierarchical, since on the diocesan level the bishop emerges as the major agent for reform. While Gerson may construct his program of episcopal reform upon an image theory, that theory is, in reality, nothing but a another manner of explaining the hierarchical activities of purgation, illumination, and perfection. The same may be said for Gerson's interpretation of episcopal activity in terms of promoting Christian perfection.

The work of reform inaugurated by the episcopacy is extended, moreover, to the parish through the agency of the clergy. Gerson is continually at pains to show that the parish clergy is an integral part of the hierarchical order and as such participates in its reforming activity. Our analysis has shown that hierarchical activity, whether exercised by the episcopacy or parish clergy, is essentially re-formative. While the bishop may set the general guidelines for reform within his diocese and may himself play an important role in reform, it is primarily through the parish clergy that the full reformative dynamism of the hierarchical order is brought to bear upon the individual Christian.

The process of individual reform, according to Gerson, has been principally constructed on the idea of the image. The image of God, distorted by sin, is restored to its former beauty through penitence and conversion. This process, moreover, is essentially reformative and takes place within a decidedly hierarchical context. Personal reform in Gerson is never simply a matter between God and the individual. Grace and the theological virtues which are the dynamic force behind all personal renewal are mediated to the individual through the hierarchical structures of the church. This mediation is achieved primarily through the sacraments which have been entrusted to the hierarchy. Thus it is only in cooperation with the hierarchy that true personal reform can be effectively achieved. The call to perfection, which Gerson extends to all Christians, is essentially an invitation to this manner of personal reform. Mystical prayer, finally, which represents the pinnacle of Christian perfection must also be seen within a hierarchical context.

What is especially characteristic of Gerson's thought on reform is its triadic and, for the most part, trinitarian orientation. The celestial archetype of the church consists of the angelic triads. According to that archetype, the church is represented as triadically structured in pope, prelates, and laity. The reformative activities proper to the hierarchical order of the church are explained through the ternary formula of purgation, illumination, and perfection. These activities, moreover, proceed according to the triple *vires* of the soul operating under the dynamism of the theological virtues of faith, hope, and charity. The *vires*, together with their corresponding activities and virtues, reflect the trinitarian characteristics of the Father, Son and Holy Spirit. The same trinitarian-like structures and activities associated with the hierarchy and operative in council, bishop, and priest are realized in the individual members of the laity. Whether conceived according to the triple *vires* or the triad of memory, intellect, and will, the souls of the laity reflect the trinitarian image of God which is restored through hierarchical activity and the theological virtues. Through a triadic process of reform, therefore, the church moves ever closer to its trinitarian origins.

Gerson's concept of reform can also be described as conservative, in the sense that reform proceeds according to the laws and nature of the church, at least as Gerson understood them. Reform, consequently, is the reassertion of authentic church structures combined with a deep moral and pastoral renewal of both hierarchy and laity. Gerson's thought, therefore, like that of many of the conciliarists of his day, was far removed from the radical and laicizing ideas proposed by such thinkers as Marsilius of Padua and William of Ockham. The strong hierarchical orientation of Gerson's ecclesiology shows how alien much of Marsilius' and Ockham's thought was to him. Gerson never reduced the papacy to a human institution but always recognized its divine foundation by Christ. He granted the papacy, moreover, the plenitude of jurisdictional power and only in certain circumstances did he advocate curtailing the use of that power. Furthermore, his conciliar solution to the schism was not proposed as the normal procedure in ecclesiastical affairs but was geared primarily to meet the extraordinary needs presented by the schism. Gerson readily granted that in normal circumstances a council must always be convoked by the papacy and its proceedings must have papal approval. True, he showed little confidence in the pope as a leader of reform within the church but events throughout the schism substantiated the correctness of his view. His attitude, moreover, was principally engendered by the personalities of the various popes and not by the very nature of their office.

Gerson endeavoured, moreover, to renew the role played by both university and theologian within the church and above all he sought the revitalization of the episcopal and priestly dignity by making bishops and priests central to his program of reform. He sought to strengthen their part in reform even at the expense of the monastic and mendicant orders and, in this respect, his ideas represent a departure from the traditional role played by those orders in church reform throughout the centuries. His views in this regard may well have come from the realization that such orders were no longer viable instruments of reform. Gerson stressed more the potentialities for reform that were contained in the traditional ecclesiastical structures.

Given the circumstances of the times and the condition of the ecclesiastical hierarchy, the question may well be asked whether Gerson's program of reform was sufficiently realistic. How realistic was it to expect that the council and the ecclesiastical hierarchy could assume leadership in the reform and renewal of the church? Even before his death in 1429, Gerson must have realized that the Council of Constance had failed to provide for the necessary reform of the church. How many bishops, even in his own native France, embodied the episcopal ideals presented by Gerson? Given its impoverishment, ignorance, and nature of recruitment, could the parish clergy ever exercise the leadership in reform which Gerson expected of it? There is, therefore, in Gerson's program of reform a decidedly idealistic strain. Though many of his expectations for reform were unrealistic, those expectations were nonetheless valid, for they embodied the genuine aspirations and ideals of Christianity. Intrinsically very little criticism can be made of Gerson's goals for church reform; what was lacking was the men and circumstances in which those ideals could be concretely realized. Gerson, however, never succumbed to the temptation of pessimism with regard to the cause of church reform; he worked optimistically for its accomplishment until his last days.

Another characteristic of Gerson's thought on reform which deserves mention is its irenicism. With the exception of his attacks against Petit and Hus, Gerson rarely gives the impression of an angry or hypercritical reformer. He personally embodied the spirit of charity, unity, and peace that he made so essential to his ideas on reform. There are no personal or vitriolic attacks against the papacy. Rather than castigating John XXIII for his flight from Constance, Gerson preferred to utilize his energies in a more positive manner by encouraging the bishops to remain in council and proceed with the settlement of the schism. He does not censure bishops for their failure to show leadership in the reform of the church but holds up the evangelical image of the bishop as pastor of souls and seeks to inspire the bishops to actualize that image within themselves.

He is sympathetic and most understanding of the plight of the parish clergy, especially its poverty and lack of education; yet, he continually strives to make the clergy realize the inner dignity of its vocation and the great potentialities of its office for the reform of the church. While he did not conceive of the religious orders as major agents in ecclesiastical reform, he, nevertheless, always retained a most cordial relationship with them throughout his life. He was fully aware of the confused state of theology and canon law yet he used his office as chancellor not to castigate but to bring those disciplines to a truer understanding of their nature and function. Finally he sought to make all Christians realize that the fullness of Christian perfection was their rightful heritage within the church.

This irenicism produced in Gerson a sincere openness of mind. Although he recognized the privileged position of the primitive church, his ideas on reform can never be reduced to a return to the church's halcyon days. He realized that the passage of time continually created new problems within the church which required new solutions. Furthermore, he regards the Holy Spirit as operative in and through changing circumstances. Although, in his view, the Donation of Constantine gave impetus to the development of canon law, Gerson does not criticize this evolution within the church's legal structure. Changing conditions within the church required new legal structures. He never called for a return to a church governed exclusively by divine law as was, in his opinion, the primitive church; he was not, therefore, opposed to canon law as such or to canonists. What he objected to was their confusion of the principles of divine, natural, and positive law within the body of canon law.

He realized well that the schism had presented the church with circumstances which it had never encountered earlier and that, therefore, new approaches would have to be taken if unity were to be restored. The principle of *epikeia* was to be utilized as the church faced the new challenges to its existence. His vision of the bishop as *lex viva* and the embodiment of *epikeia* proceeded from the same attitude toward change within the church. The church's law could never comprehend the variety of circumstances occurring within a diocese. For this reason the bishop must always be present among his people. Through visitations he is able to see at first hand whether church legislation was really applicable in the concrete and changing situations of human life and to correct any injustices that might occur through an overly strict interpretation of the law.

Gerson's openness of mind extended even to the point of admitting that the hierarchical structures of the church could be modified through the instrumentality of the Holy Spirit. If circumstances necessitated, the Holy Spirit could restructure the church's hierarchical order. Gerson did not envision such a change during his own times but the mere consideration of the possibility shows the spirit of openness that permeated his ideas. This spirit does not contradict the conservatism of his reform principles but reveals the genuineness of that conservatism which could adhere faithfully to traditional principles and yet remain ever sensitive to the evolving needs of the church.

SELECT BIBLIOGRAPHY

PRIMARY SOURCES

Abelard. *Expositio in Hexaemeron, MPL,* 178. Paris, 1855.
— —. *Introductio ad Theologiam, MPL,* 178. Paris, 1855.
— —. *Theologia Christiana, MPL,* 178. Paris, 1855.
Alberigo, Joseph et al., eds. *Conciliorum oecumenicorum decreta.* Rome, 1962.
Aquinas, Thomas. *Summa Theologiae.* 4 vols. Rome, 1952-53.
Aristotle. *Ars rhetorica,* ed. W. D. Ross. Oxford, 1959.
— —. *De anima,* ed. P. Siwek. Rome, 1965.
— —. *Ethica Nicomachea,* ed. I. Bywater. Oxford, 1895.
— —. *Metaphysica,* ed. W. Jaeger. Oxford, 1957.
— —. *Physica,* ed. W. D. Ross. Oxford, 1950.
— —. *Politica,* ed. W. D. Ross. Oxford, 1957.
Augustine. *Confessiones, CSEL,* 33. Vienna, 1896.
— —. *De civitate Dei, CCSL,* 47-48. Turnhout, 1955.
— —. *De Genesi ad litteram, CSEL,* 28, pt. 1. Vienna, 1894.
— —. *De libero arbitrio, CCSL,* 29. Turnhout, 1970.
— —. *De Trinitate, CCSL,* 50-50A. Turnhout, 1968.
— —. *De vera religione, CCSL,* 32. Turnhout, 1962.
Bernard of Clairvaux. *De moribus et officio episcoporum, MPL,* 182. Paris, 1862.
Bonaventure. *Opera omnia.* 10 vols. Quaracchi, 1882-1902.
Denifle, H., and Chatelain, E. *Chartularium Universitatis Parisiensis.* 4 vols. Paris, 1889-1897.
Dionysius Areopagita. *Opera omnia, MPG,* 3. Paris, 1857.
— —. *Dionysiaca,* ed. P. Chevallier. 2 vols Paris, 1937.
— —. *Oeuvres complètes,* trans. M. De Gandillac. Paris, 1943.
Finke, Heinrich, ed. *Acta Concilii Constanciensis.* 4 vols. Münster, 1896-1928.
Friedberg, Aemelius, ed. *Corpus Juris Canonici.* 2 vols. Leipzig, 1879-1881.
Gerson, Jean. *Oeuvres complètes,* ed. P. Glorieux. 7 vols. Paris, 1960-1968.
— —. *Opera omnia,* ed. L. E. du Pin. 5 vols. Antwerp, 1706.
— —. *De mystica theologia,* ed. A. Combes. Lugano, 1959.
Godfrey of St. Victor. *Microcosmus,* ed. P. Delhaye. Lille, 1951.
Gregory the Great. *Homiliae in Evangelia, MPL,* 76. Paris, 1865.
— —. *Moralia in Job, MPL,* 75. Paris, 1862.
— —. *Regula pastoralis, MPL,* 77. Paris, 1862.
Hugh of St. Victor. *De sacramentis, MPL,* 176. Paris, 1854.
— —. *De tribus diebus, MPL,* 176. Paris, 1854.
— —. *Expositio in hierarchiam coelestem, MPL,* 175. Paris, 1854.
John of Salisbury. *Policraticus,* ed. C. Webb. 2 vols. Oxford, 1909.
Juvenal. *Saturae,* ed. S. G. Owen. Oxford, 1882.
Mourin, Louis. *Édition critique et étude de six sermons français inédits de Jean Gerson.* Paris, 1946.
Ockham, William. *Dialogus,* ed. M. Goldast, *Monarchia,* 2, 398-957. Frankfurt, 1614.
Persius. *Saturae,* ed. S. G. Owen. Oxford, 1882.
Plato. *Res publica,* ed. J. Burnet. Oxford, 1902.
Richard of St. Victor. *De tribus appropriatis personis, MPL,* 196. Paris, 1855.
— —. *De Trinitate, MPL,* 196. Paris, 1855.
Seneca. *Dialogorum libri XII,* ed. Emil Hermes. Leipzig, 1923.

— —. *Ad Lucilium epistolae morales*, ed. Otto Hense. Leipzig, 1915.

Von der Hardt, H., ed. *Magnum Oecumenicum Constantiense Concilium*. 6 vols. Frankfurt and Leipzig, 1697-1700.

William of Conches. *Glossae super Platonem*, ed. E. Jeauneau. Paris, 1965.

SECONDARY SOURCES

Adam, P. *La vie paroissiale en France au xivᵉ siècle*. Paris, 1964.

Antoine, Thomas. *Jean de Gerson et l'éducation des dauphins de France*. Paris, 1930.

Baudry, L. *Guillaume d'Occam. Sa vie, ses oeuvres, ses idées sociales et politiques*. Paris, 1949.

Bess, Bernhard. *Johannes Gerson und die kirchenpolitischen Parteien Frankreichs vor dem Konzil zu Pisa*. Marburg, 1890.

— —. *Studien zur Geschichte des Konstanzer Konzils*. Vol. 1: *Frankreichs Kirchenpolitik und der Prozess des Jean Petit über die Lehre vom Tyrannenmord bis zur Reise König Sigismunds*. Marburg, 1891.

Bliemetzrieder, F. *Das Generalkonzil im grossen abendländischen Schisma*. Paderborn, 1904.

— —. *Literarische Polemik zu Beginn des grossen abendländischen Schisma*. Paderborn, 1904.

Bougerol, J. G. "Saint Bonaventure et la hiérarchie dionysienne," *AHDL*, 36 (1969), 131-167.

Buisson, Ludwig. *Potestas und Caritas. Die päpstliche Gewalt im Spätmittelalter*. Cologne, 1958.

Burghardt, Walter J. *The Image of God in Man According to Cyril of Alexandria*. Woodstock, 1957.

Chenu, M.-D. *La théologie au douzième siècle*. Paris, 1957.

Combes, André. *Essai sur la critique de Ruysbroeck par Gerson*. 3 vols. Paris, 1945-1949.

— —. *Jean de Montreuil et le chancelier Gerson. Contribution à l'histoire des rapports de l'humanisme et de la théologie en France au début du xvᵉ siècle*. Paris, 1942.

— —. *Jean Gerson, commentateur dionysien. Pour l'histoire des courants doctrinaux à Université de Paris à la fin du xivᵉ siècle*. Paris, 1940.

— —. *La théologie mystique de Gerson*. 2 vols. Paris, 1963-1965.

Congar, Y. M.-J. "Aspects ecclésiologiques de la querelle entre mendiants et séculiers dans la seconde moitié du xiiiᵉ siècle et le début du xivᵉ siècle," *AHDL*, 28 (1961), 35-151.

— —. "Incidence ecclésiologique d'un thème de dévotion mariale," *MSR*, 7 (1950), 277-292.

— —. *L'ecclésiologie du haut moyen âge*. Paris, 1968.

— —. *Vraie et fausse réforme dans l'Église*. 2nd ed. Paris, 1968.

Connolly, J. L. *John Gerson. Reformer and Mystic*. Louvain, 1928.

Coville, A. *Jean Petit. La question du tyrannicide au commencement du xvᵉ siècle*. Paris, 1932.

De la Brosse, Olivier. *Le pape et le concile. La comparaison de leur pourvoirs à la veille de la réforme*. Paris, 1965.

De Lagarde, George. *La naissance de l'esprit laïque au déclin du moyen âge*. 5 vols. Paris, 1956-1970.

Delaruelle, E. et al. *L'Église au temps du Grand Schisme et de la crise conciliaire*. 2 vols. Paris, 1962-1964.

De Lubac, Henri. *Corpus Mysticum*. Paris, 1949.

— —. *Exégèse médiévale*. 2 vols. (4 parts). Paris, 1959-1962.

Denifle, H. *Die Entstehung der Universitäten des Mittelalters bis 1400*. Berlin, 1885.

De Vooght, Paul. "Gerson et le conciliarisme," *RHE*, 63 (1968), 857-867.
— —. "L'ecclésiologie des adversaires de Huss au Concile de Constance, *ETL*, 35 (1959), 5-24.
— —. *Les pouvoirs du concile et l'authorité du pape au Concile de Constance*. Paris, 1965.
— —. *Les sources de la doctrine chrétienne d'après les théologiens du xive siècle et du début du xve*. Paris, 1954.
D'Irsay, Stephen. *Histoire des universités françaises et étrangères des origines à nos jours*. 2 vols. Paris, 1933.
Douie, D. *The Conflict between the Seculars and the Mendicants at the University of Paris in the Thirteenth Century*. London, 1954.
Dress, Walter. *Die Theologie Gersons. Eine Untersuchung zur Verbindung von Nominalismus und Mystik im Spätmittelalter*. Gütersloh, 1931.
Feret, P. *La faculté de théologie de Paris au moyen âge et ses docteurs les plus célèbres*. 4 vols. Paris, 1894-1897.
Figgis, John N. *Studies of Political Thought from Gerson to Grotius, 1414-1625*. Cambridge, 1907.
Fink, K. A. "Papsttum und Kirchenreform nach dem Grossen Schisma," *TTQ*, 126 (1946), 110-122.
Franzen, A. "The Council of Constance: Present State of the Problem," *Concilium*, 7 (1965), 29-68.
Franzen, A. and Mueller, W., eds. *Das Konzil von Konstanz. Beiträge zur seiner Geschichte und Theologie*. Freiburg, 1964.
Gilson, Étienne. *History of Christian Philosophy in the Middle Ages*. New York, 1955.
— —. *Jean Duns Scot. Introduction à ses positions fondamentales*. Paris, 1952.
— —. *The Christian Philosophy of Saint Augustine*. New York, 1960.
— —. *The Philosophy of St. Bonaventure*. New York, 1938.
Glorieux, P. "Autour de la liste des oeuvres de Gerson," *RTAM*, 22 (1955), 95-109.
— —. "Gerson et les Chartreux," *RTAM*, 28 (1961), 115-153.
— —. "L'activité littéraire de Gerson à Lyon. Correspondance inédite avec la Grande Chartreuse," *RTAM*, 18 (1951), 238-307.
— —. "L'année universitaire 1392-93 à la Sorbonne à travers les notes d'un étudiant," *RSR*, 19 (1939), 429-482.
— —. "La vie et les œuvres de Gerson. Essai chronologique," *AHDL*, 18 (1950-51), 149-192.
— —. "Le chancelier Gerson et la réforme de l'enseignement," in *Mélanges offerts à Étienne Gilson*, pp. 285-298. Paris, 1959.
— —. "L'enseignement universitaire de Gerson," *RTAM*, 23 (1956), 88-113.
— —. "Les 'Lectiones duae super Marcum' de Gerson," *RTAM*, 27 (1960), 344-356.
Guelluy, R. *Philosophie et théologie chez Guillaume d'Ockham*. Paris, 1947.
Hahn, F. "Zur Hermeneutik Gersons," *ZTK*, 5 (1954), 95-109.
Haller, Johannes. *Papsttum und Kirchenreform*. Berlin, 1903.
Hefele, C., and Leclercq, J. *Histoire des Conciles*. 16 vols. Paris, 1907-1921.
Hofmeier, J. *Die Trinitätslehre des Hugo von St. Victor*. Munich, 1963.
Javelet, Robert. *Image et ressemblance au douzième siècle*. 2 vols. Paris, 1967.
Kantorowicz, Ernst. *The King's Two Bodies. A Study in Medieval Political Theology*. Princeton, 1957.
Kuttner, Stephan. *Kanonistische Schuldlehre von Gratian bis auf die Dekretalen Gregors IX*. Città del Vaticano, 1935.
Ladner, Gerhart B. "Die mittelalterliche Reform-Idee und ihr Verhältnis zur Idee der Renaissance," *MIÖG*, 60 (1952), 31-59.
— —. "Erneuerung," *RAC*, 6, 240-275.

— —. "Homo Viator: Medieval Ideas on Alienation and Order," *Speculum*, 42 (1967), 233-259.

— —. "Reformatio," *Ecumenical Dialogue at Harvard*, ed. S. Miller and G. E. Wright, 172-190. Cambridge, Mass., 1964.

— —. "Religious Renewal and Ethnic-Social Pressures as Forms of Life in Christian History," *Theology of Renewal*, ed. L. K. Shook, 2, 328-357. New York, 1968.

— —. "The Concept of the Image in the Greek Fathers and the Byzantine Iconoclastic Controversy," *Dumbarton Oaks Papers*, 7 (1953), 3-34.

— —. *The Idea of Reform. Its Impact on Christian Thought and Action in the Age of the Fathers*. Cambridge, Mass., 1959.

— —. "Two Gregorian Letters. On the Sources and Nature of Gregory's Reform Ideology," *Studi Gregoriani*, 5 (1956), 221-242.

— —. "Vegetation Symbolism and the Concept of Renaissance," *De artibus opuscula XL: Essays in Honor of Erwin Panofsky*, ed.Millard Meiss, 1, 303-322. New York, 1961.

Langlois, E. "Le traité de Gerson contre le Roman de la Rose," *Romania*, 45 (1918), 23-48.

Lavisse, E., ed. *Histoire de la France*. Vol. 4, pts. 1-2. Paris, 1902-1904.

Leff, Gordon. *Heresy in the Later Middle Ages*. 2 vols. Manchester, 1967.

— —. *Paris and Oxford in the Thirteenth and Fourteenth Centuries*. New York, 1968.

Leidl, August. *Die Einheit der Kirchen auf den spätmittelalterlichen Konzilien*. Paderborn, 1966.

Lewis, P. S. *Later Medieval France*. London, 1968.

Loomis, L. R. *The Council of Constance*. New York, 1961.

Luscombe, D. E. *The School of Peter Abelard*. Cambridge, 1969.

Martin, V. *Les origines du Gallicanisme*. 2 vols. Paris, 1939.

Meyjes, G. H. M. Posthumus. *Jean Gerson. Zijn Kerkpolitiek en Ecclesiologie*. The Hague, 1963.

Morrall, John B. *Gerson and the Great Schism*. Manchester, 1960.

Mourin, Louis. *Jean Gerson, prédicateur français*. Bruges, 1952.

Oakley, Francis. "Figgis, Constance, and the Divines of Paris," *AHR*, 75 (1969), 368-386.

— —. *The Political Thought of Pierre d'Ailly*. New Haven, 1964.

Oberman, Heiko A. "From Occam to Luther," *Concilium*, 17 (1966), 122-132; 27 (1967), 135-144.

— —. *The Harvest of Medieval Theology*. Cambridge, Mass., 1963.

O'Malley, John W. *Giles of Viterbo on Church and Reform*. Leiden, 1968.

— —. "Historical Thought and the Reform Crisis of the Early Sixteenth Century," *TS*, 28 (1967), 531-548.

Ozment, Steven E. *Homo Spiritualis. A Comparative Study of the Anthropology of Johannes Tauler, Jean Gerson and Martin Luther (1509-1516) in the Context of their Theological Thought*. Leiden, 1969.

— —. "The University and the Church. Patterns of Reform in John Gerson," *MH*, New Series, 1 (1970), 111-126.

Parent, J. M. *La doctrine de la création dans l'école de Chartres*. Paris, 1938.

Pascoe, Louis B. "The Council of Trent and Bible Study: Humanism and Scripture," *CHR*, 42 (1966), 18-38.

Post, Gaines. *Studies in Medieval Legal Thought*. Princeton, 1964.

Rashdall, H. *The Universities of Europe in the Middle Ages*, ed. F. M. Powicke and A. B. Emden. 3 vols. Oxford, 1936.

Rief, Josef. *Der Ordobegriff des jungen Augustinus*. Paderborn, 1962.

Roques, René. "La notion de hiérarchie selon le Ps.-Denys," *AHDL*, 17 (1949), 183-222; 18 (1950-51), 5-44.

— —. *L'univers dionysien*. Paris, 1954.

Roques, René et al. "Denys l'Aréopagite," *DSAM*, 3, 244-429.

Salembier, L. "Gerson," *DTC*, 6, 1313-1330.

Schaeffer, C. *Die Staatslehre des Johann Gerson*. Cologne, 1935.

Schmaus, M. *Die psychologische Trinitätslehre des hl. Augustinus*. Münster, 1927.

Schmiel, David. *Via Propria and Via Mystica in the Theology of Jean Charlier de Gerson*. St. Louis, 1969.

Schneider, J. "Die Verpflichtung des menschlichen Gesetzes nach Johannes Gerson," *ZKT*, 75 (1953), 1-54.

Schwab, J. B. *Johannes Gerson, Professor der Theologie und Kanzler der Universität*. Würzburg, 1858.

Seidlmayer, M. *Die Anfänge des grossen abendländlichen Schismas*. Münster, 1940.

Stelzenberger, J. *Die Mystik des Johannes Gerson*. Breslau, 1928.

Sullivan, John E. *The Image of God. The Doctrine of St. Augustine and its Influence*. Dubuque, 1963.

Tierney, Brian. *Foundations of the Conciliar Theory*. Cambridge, 1955.

— —. "Hermeneutics and History: The Problem of *Haec Sancta*," *Essays in Medieval History Presented to Bertie Wilkinson*, ed. T. A. Sandquist and M. R. Powicke, 354-370.

— —. "Ockham, the Conciliar Theory and the Canonists," *JHI*, 15 (1954), 40-70.

— —. "Pope and Council," *MS*, 19 (1957), 197-218.

Ullmann, W. *The Growth of Papal Government in the Middle Ages*. 3rd ed. London, 1970.

— —. *The Origins of the Great Schism*. London, 1948.

Valois, Noël. *La France et le Grand Schisme d'Occident*. 4 vols. Paris, 1896-1902.

Van Hove, A. *Commentarium Lovaniense in Codicem Iuris Canonici*. Vol. 1, Tome 1: *Prolegomena*. 2nd ed. Malines, 1945; Tome 2: *De legibus ecclesiasticis*. Malines, 1930.

Vansteenberghe, E. "Gerson à Bruges," *RHE*, 31 (1935), 5-52.

— —. "Un programme d'action épiscopale au début du xve siècle," *RSR*, 19 (1939), 24-47.

Vaughn, Richard. *John the Fearless. The Growth of Burgundian Power*. New York, 1966.

Vereecke, L. "Droit et morale chez Jean Gerson," *RHDFE*, 32 (1954), 413-427.

Vignaux, Paul. *Nominalisme au xive siècle*. Montreal, 1948.

Ward, Charles F. *The Epistles on the Roman of the Rose and Other Documents in the Debate*. Chicago, 1911.

Wayman, Dorothy G. "The Chancellor and Jeanne d'Arc, February-July,1429," *FS*, 17 (1957), 273-305.

Wilks, Michael. *The Problem of Sovereignty in the Later Middle Ages*. Cambridge, 1963.

Wylie, J. H. *The Council of Constance to the Death of John Huss*. London, 1900.

INDEX OF PERSONS

INDEX OF SUBJECTS